Taking Down
Our Harps

Taking Down Our Harps

Black Catholics in the United States

Diana L. Hayes and **Cyprian Davis, O.S.B.**
editors

ORBIS BOOKS

Maryknoll, New York 10545

Chapter 4, "And When We Speak: To be Black, Catholic, and Womanist" by Diana L. Hayes, is a condensed and revised version of Chapters 7 and 8 of Diana L. Hayes, *And Still We Rise: An Introduction to Black Liberation Theology* (Mahwah, N.J.: Paulist Press, 1996).

Chapter 8, "Black Spirituality" by Jamie T. Phelps, O.P., was originally published in *Spiritual Traditions for the Contemporary Church*, ed. Robin Maas and Gabriel O'Donnell, O.P. (Nashville: Abingdon Press, 1990).

Chapter 11, "*Varietates Legitimae* and an African-American Liturgical Tradition" by D. Reginald Whitt, O.P., was originally published in *Worship* 71 (1997).

Queries regarding rights and permissions should be addressed to: Orbis Books, P. O. Box 308, Maryknoll, New York 10545-0308.

Published by Orbis Books, Maryknoll, NY 10545-0308
Copy editing and typesetting by Joan Weber Laflamme
Manufactured in the United States of America

Library of Congress Cataloging-in-Publication Data

Taking down our harps   :   black Catholics in the United States   /
Diana L. Hayes and Cyprian Davis, editors.
    p.   cm.
  Includes bibliographical references.
  ISBN 1-57075-174-9   (pbk.)
  1. Afro-American Catholics.   I. Hayes, Diana L.   II. Davis,
Cyprian.
  BX1407.N4   H398   1998
  282'.73'08996073—ddc21

                    98-37447

In Memory of

Joseph Nearon, S.S.S.
Thea Bowman, F.S.P.A.
Bede Abrams, O.F.M. Conv.
Dolores Harrell, S.N. de N.

Scholars and Theologians
Who sang a new song.

By the rivers of Babylon—
   there we sat down and there we wept
   when we remembered Zion.
On the willows there
   we hung our harps.
For there our captors
   asked us for songs,
and our tormentors asked for mirth, saying,
   "Sing us one of the songs of Zion!"

How could we sing the Lord's song
   in a foreign land?
                              —Psalm 137, *NRSV*

Contents

PART III
ETHICAL IMPLICATIONS

PART IV
PASTORAL AND LITURGICAL IMPLICATIONS

Preface

Taking Down Our Harps

Black Catholics in the United States

DIANA L. HAYES

Black Catholics in the United States today are a people who have come of age. As their Black bishops noted in their historic pastoral letter, "What We Have Seen and Heard"[1]:

> Within the history of every Christian community there comes the time when it reaches adulthood. This maturity brings with it the duty, the privilege and the joy to share with others the rich experience of the "Word of Life.". . . We, the descendants of Africans brought to these shores, are now called to share our faith and to demonstrate our witness to our risen Lord.

This coming of age can be seen in a number of ways, as will be seen within this text, including the Black Catholic Congress movement, a national gathering of Black Catholics from every level of the church coming together to discuss issues critical to them as people of African descent who are also Roman Catholic. The Congress movement rests upon historic foundations, laid between the years 1889 and 1895, when lay Black Catholics (Negro laymen) held five consecutive national meetings to address issues still relevant today. These issues include racism, evangelization of Blacks, greater inclusion of Blacks in the religious life of the church, and greater representation of Blacks in the church's institutional structure, from lay brothers and sisters to the bishops of the church.

The congresses did not continue into the twentieth century as Black Catholics, instead, concentrated their efforts at the parish level. However, with the Second Vatican Council and the movement for civil rights among Black Americans, significant changes began to take place in the lives of Black Catholics.

Today, much has changed, yet much remains the same. In the century between the Fifth Congress, held in 1895, and the Sixth, held in 1987, in Washington, D.C., the numbers of African American Catholics who participate at every level of the church as bishops and priests, religious brothers and sisters, theologians, deacons, catechists, directors of religious education, liturgists, youth ministers, pastoral associates, and active laity have grown; a growth fueled by persistence, struggle, and faith.[2]

As stated, many of the issues confronting Black Catholics today remain the same as in the last century, despite the increasing numbers of persons of African descent in the church, both locally and globally.[3] However, the focus is quite different. Rather than seeking what would seem today to be merely token acceptance and assimilation into the church, which was the predominant pattern prior to the 1960s, today they are developing their own unique and holistic Catholicism and calling upon the church to inculturate itself more fully into their culture. The Seventh Black Congress (New Orleans, 1992) and Eighth Black Congress (Baltimore, 1997) continued to build on the work of earlier congresses with an emphasis on rebuilding family and community.

This work is an effort to present and develop many of the issues Black Catholics have confronted and continue to confront on national, regional, and local levels. The theologians, ethicists, historians, liturgists, and religious educators whose writings make up this work have been involved in the dialogues that have been taking place and thus have been actively engaged in the development of an emerging Black Catholic theology. They teach and/or are engaged in roles that put them in contact with all aspects of the church from the laity to the episcopacy and, therefore, in dialogue with the actualities of the Black Catholic world. However, they are not the only participants but are representative of the many who are engaged in this critical effort.

In developing this work they are attempting to present, in keeping with our African understanding of community, a shared perspective of where Black Catholics have journeyed from, where they are today and, hopefully, where they are going. They recognize that they and their church are on a pilgrim journey and see that journey as one shared, not only with their fellow Black Catholics, but with the greater Black community, national and global, as well as with their fellow Roman Catholics throughout the world.

Taking Down Our Harps consists of an introduction by co-editor Diana L. Hayes and four major sections that present the historical context, aspects of Black Catholic theology, ethical implications, and pastoral and liturgical implications of Black Catholic theology. The four sections are reflective of the integration of these perspectives into the totality of Black Catholic religious thought in the United States today and the holistic way in which it is expressed. A conclusion by co-editor Cyprian Davis ends the work.

- Introduction—"We've Come This Far by Faith: Black Catholics and Their Church" provides a brief historical overview of the emergence of Black Catholic theology. It is set in the context of African American Catholics' affirmation of the authenticity of their faith and their cultural heritage.

- Historical Context—"God of Our Weary Years: Black Catholics in American Catholic History" by Cyprian Davis provides an in-depth look at the significant roles that Black Catholics played in American Catholic history through the nineteenth century, including their persistent efforts toward ordination and the religious life.

- Aspects of Black Catholic Theology—This section seeks to set forth the parameters of a Black Catholic theology. The first article, by Diana L. Hayes, explores a Black Catholic understanding of faith through scripture in "Through the Eyes of Faith: The Seventh Principle of the *Nguzo Saba* and the Beatitudes of Matthew," showing how that faith has enabled us both to persevere within the church and to assert our unique presence as a challenge to the church. Jamie T. Phelps next develops both the christological and ecclesiological perspectives of African American Catholics in "Inculturating Jesus: A Search for Dynamic Images for the Mission of the Church among African Americans." Beginning "from below" by focusing on Black Catholic humanity and the humanity of Jesus, Dr. Phelps seeks to explore the meaning of Jesus Christ for African Americans today in a nation and church that have been both sources of renewal and oppression. In "And When We Speak: To Be Black, Catholic, and Womanist," Diana L. Hayes articulates the historical origins of womanist theology as a critique of Black and feminist theologies and discusses the developing theology of Black Catholic womanists, presenting a challenging interpretation of Mary, the Mother of God. Finally, M. Shawn Copeland presents the methodological context of Black Catholic theology in "Method in Emerging Black Catholic Theology." In her presentation, Dr. Copeland first analyzes the method of correlation from the perspective of Black Catholic theologians, laying out both the difficulties with that method and their response. She then reviews the elements of critique, retrieval, and social analysis in the construction of a Black Catholic theology and raises questions for its future.

- Ethical Implications—This section addresses the ethical concerns of a Black Catholic theology as it interacts with issues affecting the Black community. Bryan N. Massingale's article, "The Case for Catholic Support: Catholic Social Ethics and Environmental Justice," applies Catholic social teachings to his analysis of environmental racism and its disproportionate impact on persons of color and the poor. He then calls for greater involvement by the church and its members in the struggle for environmental justice. Toinette Eugene, in "Between 'Lord, Have Mercy!' and 'Thank You, Jesus!': Liturgical Renewal and African American Catholic Assemblies," examines the role of social justice in relation to the reform of the sacred liturgy in keeping with the context (the lived experience) of African American Catholics.

- Pastoral and Liturgical Implications—This section explores how Black Catholic theology can and does serve as a challenge to the ministry and liturgical life of all Catholics in the United States. It begins with Jamie T. Phelps's exposition of "Black Spirituality," which reveals the continued influence of our African heritage upon the spiritual life of Black Catholics today. There is a common spirit, she notes, within all persons of African descent that "sees all of life in the context of the encounter with the divine," a spirit "rooted in a distinctive and ancient world view." Her essay is followed by Giles Conwill's "Black Catechesis: Catching the Flame and Passing It On," which discusses the often painful history of catechesis for Black Catholics in the United States. With that as foundation, he looks critically at the catechetical process from within a Black world view, discussing the necessity for and parameters of a Black catechesis. Clarence

Rufus J. Rivers contrasts Euro-American and African American perceptions and receptions of worship as they affect the development and understanding of liturgy in "The Oral African Tradition Versus the Ocular Western Tradition: The Spirit in Worship." And, last in this section, "*Varietates Legitimae* and an African-American Liturgical Tradition" by D. Reginald Whitt analyzes the meaning of the recent instruction on the Roman liturgy and inculturation, *Varietates Legitimae,* for Black Catholics in the United States and their efforts to inculturate the Catholic faith. He shows that the instruction, rather than denying the possibility of new rites, actually shows how they might arise due to liturgical inculturation.

- Conclusion—"Speaking the Truth: Black Catholics in the United States" by Cyprian Davis reveals the progress of Black Catholic efforts to speak the truth of their continued and persistent presence in the Catholic church. It refutes the assertion that to be Black and Catholic is unauthentic, and it affirms the growth and development of a Black Catholic theology that is fully representative of the voices and experiences of Black Catholics.

NOTES

[1] Cincinnati, Ohio: St. Anthony Messenger Press, 1984.

[2] At this time there are thirteen active Black bishops, three hundred active priests and brothers, four hundred permanent deacons, three hundred women religious, six systematic theologians, and growing numbers active in various ministries within the church.

[3] At this time there are approximately 2.3 million Black Catholics in the United States, making up one of the largest Black religious groups in this country.

Introduction

We've Come This Far by Faith

Black Catholics and Their Church

DIANA L. HAYES

The Black Catholic Bishops of the United States issued their first and, to date, only pastoral letter, "What We Have Seen and Heard," in 1984.[1] They did so in recognition of their belief that "the Black Catholic community in the American Church has now come of age." This coming of age, they noted, "brings with it the duty, the privilege and the joy to share with others the rich experience of the 'Word of Life.'"[2]

Today, we are witnesses to further signs of that coming of age. African American Catholics[3] are claiming our rightful place in the Roman Catholic Church, nationally and globally. Basing our claim for recognition and inclusion on our history in the American church that predates the Mayflower, our persistent faith gives living expression to the "Word of Life" that we have received and that we fully embrace:

> You are no longer strangers and sojourners, but you are fellow citizens with the saints and members of the household of God, built upon the foundation of the apostles and prophets, Christ

This article is partially based on the *Lineamenta:* "Strangers and Sojourners No More: To Be Truly Black and Authentically Catholic," *Origins* 20:30 (January 3, 1991), which was the study document for the VIIth National Black Catholic Congress held in New Orleans, Louisiana, in July 1992.

1

Jesus himself being the cornerstone, in whom the whole structure is joined together and grows into a holy temple in the Lord; in whom you also are built into it for a dwelling place of God in the Spirit (Eph 2:19-22).

Strangers and sojourners no longer, African American Catholics will no longer be required, in the words of the Psalmist, to "sing the LORD's song in a foreign land" (Ps 137, *NRSV*). Instead, we are taking down our harps and converting that "foreign land" into a homeland, one rich with the woven tapestries of our voices, lifted in praise and song; of our spirituality expressed in deep and heartfelt prayer and preaching; and of our cultural heritage—a colorful mixture of peoples of Africa, the Caribbean, the West Indies, South America, and North America.

Evidence of this newfound land can be seen throughout the United States today in dioceses large and small, rural, urban and suburban; all blessed and invigorated by the presence and spirit of Black Catholics who are busy about the work of Jesus Christ. We are seeking, in Jesus' name, to "preach good news to the poor, . . . to proclaim release to the captives, and recovering of sight to the blind, to set at liberty those who are oppressed, to proclaim the acceptable year of the Lord" (Lk 4:18-19). For in their holistic world view all of life is necessarily interconnected; the sacred and the secular, the workplace and the church, are all imbued with the spirit of God and thus are the responsibility of people of faith.

A NEW BIRTH

In many ways the voices of these new and yet-so-old Catholics can be understood as calling forth a new witness. We see ourselves as "a chosen race, a royal priesthood, a holy nation, God's own people" who work to "declare the wonderful deeds of him who called [us] out of darkness into his marvelous light." Throughout our existence in the United States we were seen as "no people," but today African American Catholics affirm that we "are God's people"; once little mercy was given us "but now [we] have received mercy" from God on high (1 Pt 2:9-10).

As part of that witness we recognize the necessity of exposing the inaccurate education received by all, of whatever race, who dwell in this land regarding the contributions of our Black and Catholic foremothers and forefathers to the present status of the United States. The truth of our history, both in this and other adopted lands and in our motherland as well, must be recovered, for that history reveals the proud and distinctive heritage that is ours, one which predates the Greek and Roman empires as well as Christopher Columbus. Black Catholics must also tell our story within our church, a story which has as part of its richness a cherished role in the life of the church dating back to Africa. For it was our African foremothers and forefathers who received the teachings of Christ from the church's earliest beginnings; they who nurtured and sheltered those teachings, preserving them from the depredations of those still pagan; they who received, revitalized, and rechristianized those teachings, too often distorted at the hands of their would-be masters, in the new lands of the Americas. As Father Cyprian Davis has written of those early years of African history:

> Long before Christianity arrived in the Scandinavian countries, at least a century before St. Patrick evangelized Ireland, and over two centuries before St. Augustine would arrive in Canterbury, and almost seven centuries before the conversion of the Poles and the establishment of the kingdom of Poland, this mountainous Black kingdom [Ethiopia] was a Catholic nation with its own liturgy, its own spectacular religious art, its own monastic tradition, its saints, and its own spirituality.[4]

This cherished heritage must, once again, be brought forth, exposed to the light of a new day, and shared with all of the church catholic.

Arguably one can say that the continued presence of Black Catholics in the Catholic church in the United States serves as a subversive memory, one which turns all of reality upside-down, for it is a memory of hope brought forth from pain, of perseverance maintained in the face of bloody opposition, of faith born of tortured struggle. It is the memory of a people forced to bring forth life from conditions conducive only to death, much as Christ himself was restored to life after a scandalous death. Ours is a memory of survival against all odds. It is the memory of a people, born in a strange and often hostile land, paradoxically celebrating Christ's victory over death as a sign of God's promise of their eventual liberation from a harsh servitude imposed by their fellow Christians. Today, Black Catholics are affirming that we are no longer sojourners, we are no longer just passing through; we are here to stay and intend to celebrate our presence as only we can.

THE PERSISTENT PRESENCE OF RACISM

This memory becomes even more challenging when we recognize the demographic shifts taking place both in the United States and in the Roman Catholic Church as we enter the third millennium. The most recent U.S. Census statistics present a picture of a very different American society and American Catholic Church, one in which persons of color, as a whole, are the majority rather than the minority. African American Catholics will be a part of this majority, which can be seen, depending upon one's perspective, as threatening to the very stability and identity of both church and state or simply as a sign of the changing times that must be dealt with.

These changes do provide a critical challenge for us as church today as we seek to affirm the new understandings of theology, ministry, and liturgy that are already emerging from persons heretofore marginalized on the church's periphery. Black Catholic theology is only one example of these shifts in understanding that must be acknowledged and placed in dialogue. This theology was born out of the struggle to maintain both our Catholic faith and our Black culture in the face of the racism that still besets our church, institutionally and individually. The Pontifical Peace and Justice Commission noted in 1989:

> Today racism has not disappeared. There are even troubling new manifestations of it here and there in various forms, be they spontaneous, officially tolerated or institutionalized. . . . The victims are certain groups of persons whose physical appearance or ethnic, cultural or religious characteristics are different from those of the dominant group and are interpreted by the latter as being signs of innate and definite inferiority, thereby justifying all discriminatory practices in their regard.[5]

Racism is a fact of life that continues to torment Black Americans regardless of their particular faith. It has its roots in the very foundations of our society, where, in drafting the Constitution, the enslavement of Blacks was recognized and accepted. The revolutionary phrases of the Founding Fathers, proclaiming liberty and justice for all and declaring the equality of all "men," ignored the condition of Black humanity. As the late Supreme Court Justice Thurgood Marshall noted, "The famous first three words of that document, 'We the People,' did not include women who were denied the vote, or blacks, who were enslaved."[6] The intent was clearly expressed in the notification that Blacks counted as only three-fifths of a white person and then only for the purpose of white male representation in the new Congress. The Constitution was developed not as a color-blind document but as one assuring the hegemony of white, propertied males over all others living in the newly formed union.

Racism has changed its face, however. Rather than the blatant overt racism of prior years, today we are confronted with a more sinister, because less visible, form of covert racism. Institutional racism "originates in the operation of established and respected forces in the society and thus receives far less public consideration."[7]

As such, institutional racism is more than a form "sanctioned by the Constitution and laws of a country," as the Vatican commission suggests.[8] For even after the Constitution has been expunged of its color bias, and the laws mandating segregation and second-class citizenship have been removed, the aura of institutionalized racism still persists. It persists in the very warp and woof of that society which has, for so long, been imbued with an ideology supported all too often by an erroneous interpretation of the teachings of Sacred Scripture.

The 1960s and 1970s saw significant changes in the laws governing American society with regard to African Americans. Yet, today, many of those changes are being nullified and labeled as preferential treatment, thereby ignoring the centuries of slavery and second-class citizenship that have hindered the descendants of African slaves from attaining equal opportunity before the law. All too often persons of faith have been silent in the face of these assaults against the human dignity of persons of color.

Racism still persists. It is a mindset that flies in the face of Sacred Scripture and the teachings of the Christian church. It is a distortion of the teaching that "all are endowed with a rational soul and are created in God's image."[9] Racism is incompatible with God's design. It is a sin that goes beyond the individual acts of individual human beings. Racism, to be blunt, is sin that is incorporated into and becomes a constituent part of the framework of society, sin that is the concentration to the infinite of the personal sins of those who condone evil.

The U.S. Catholic bishops have affirmed this understanding:

The structures of our society are subtly racist, for these structures reflect the values which society upholds. They are geared
to the success of the majority and the failure of the minority.
Members of both groups give unwitting approval by accepting
things as they are. Perhaps no single individual is to blame.
The sinfulness is often anonymous but nonetheless real. The
sin is social in nature in that each of us in some measure are
accomplices. . . . The absence of personal fault for an evil does
not absolve one of all responsibility. We must seek to resist and
undo injustices we have not caused, lest we become bystanders
who tacitly endorse evil and so share in guilt for it.[10]

REFLECTING ON THE JOURNEY

Theology, in its simplest understanding, can be seen as "God-talk."
We, as African American Catholics, often become intimidated when
asked to reflect theologically on a matter of importance to us, such
as our relationship with God or how we see our role in the church,
because we see ourselves as academically unqualified. There are too
few of us with academic degrees in systematic theology.[11] Yet, when
asked simply to talk about God's action in our lives or the working
of the Holy Spirit in our midst, our reaction is quite different.
    Although academe may not recognize our reflections as such, we
are indeed speaking theologically when we do this. And as African
Americans, we have been doing so for all of our existence. What we
have done, as a holistic people in whom the sacred and secular are
intertwined rather than alienated, is simply to talk about God, about
Jesus Christ, about the Holy Spirit and about their importance in
our lives, a God that you can lean on, a brother you can depend on in
your darkest hours, a Spirit that walks with you and brings peace to
a troubled soul. We have not put our theology down in dry, dusty
tomes that no one can or really wants to read; we have lived it in the
midst of our daily lives. That theology has been expressed most clearly
in our songs, in our stories, in our prayers. We talk of a God who
saves, a God who preserves, a God who frees and continues to free
us from the "troubles of this world."
    Theology also can be seen as "interested conversation." In other
words, theology is talk, dialogue, discussion, conversation about God

and God's salvific action in the world, not from an objective, unbiased stance—because no such stance truly exists—but from the perspective of one who is "involved," one who is caught up in that discussion, one whose involvement is "colored," as it were, by his or her own history, heritage, and culture. We cannot speak about the church, Jesus Christ or anything else except from within the context of who we are, a people caught in a daily struggle to survive despite the constant assaults of racism, prejudice, and discrimination from the institutional structures of both our society and our church.

This is to say, on one hand, that there are as many different theologies within the church as there are persons talking about God, but, on the other hand, that all of these theologies have, as their foundation, the context of Roman Catholicism with its particular teachings, traditions, and faith beliefs. Our theology as African American Catholics is "interested conversation" about that "ultimate reality" which is central to the core of our being, our faith in Jesus Christ. As such, our theology cannot be understood or conceived of apart from our being and the place in which we find ourselves. All theologies are particular, rooted in and arising from a particular context, the context of the people engaged in their development. Theology arises out of their loves and their angers, their joys and their sorrows, their sufferings and their hopes for a better tomorrow as they express these in the light of their faith.

Today, we, as an African American Catholic people, are engaged in the development of a theology that speaks truly to us and expresses who we are and whose we are for the enlightenment of the entire church.

We are African Americans: a people with roots deeply sunk in the history and culture of our African homeland yet also a people with a long and proud history in these United States. Both strands of our heritage are important in defining who we are. Neither can be denied without denying an important part of our very selves. That understanding of "who we are and whose we are" affects our theologizing. It "colors," quite simply, our concept of God, our faith in Jesus Christ, our existence in the Holy Spirit, our total understanding of what it means to be truly Black and authentically Catholic. Our reflections are not abstract or objective; they are particular because they are grounded in the particular context of African American history, which is a history of slavery, of second-class citizenship, of discrimination, both in U.S. society and in our mother church as well. More important, it is also a history of struggle, of perseverance, of hope, of faith, and of survival against all odds and all obstacles placed in our path.

As a holistic people, however, the pain does not outweigh the hope, the struggle does not diminish the faith. We rejoice in the intertwining, rather than the separation, of the many strands of our life, for we are a people for whom religious faith has been and remains an integral part of who and what we are. Thus, the context of our theologizing is a grounding in our faith, examined in the light of Christ's teachings and a religious tradition dating back to the early church. Accordingly, our lives must be a witness to the ongoing and pervasive presence of the gospel within us and must reflect that presence back into the world in which we live.

We therefore cherish our memories, painful though they may often be, for they serve as subversive memories, memories that turn all of reality upside-down, as Jesus Christ did in his life, death, and resurrection. These memories transform that which is seen as worthless to that which is of the highest value. We remember, not with an eye toward revenge but in order to prevent faintheartedness in the struggle. We remember that we, as a people, survived and continue to survive despite it all. The apostle Paul's words have a particular significance for us: "God chose what is foolish in the world to shame the wise, God chose what is weak in the world to shame the strong, God chose what is low and despised in the world, even things that are not, to bring to nothing things that are" (1 Cor 1:27-28).

We have been, and too often continue to be, seen as the "low and despised" in the world in which we find ourselves, but paradoxically we see ourselves also as that chosen race and priestly people commissioned to overturn the inaccurate education of ourselves and all Americans regarding African Americans. Knowledge and understanding of our chosenness come to us from our God, who nurtured and sustained us like a bridge over the troubled waters of our sojourn here. It is from God that we received our faith, and it is to God that we turn in the bosom of our church, the Roman Catholic Church. For it is the church that our foremothers and forefathers nurtured and sustained long before many who now claim total ownership of it even knew of its existence.

Black Catholics have remained in the church, feeling love and hate, forgiveness and frustration, concern and impatience. We, too, the darker brothers and sisters of this country, are a vital and vibrant part of the Roman Catholic Church. We, too, have gifts of song, story, and praise to offer the church universal. And we know that those gifts are not only needed but welcomed by the number of our Catholic brothers and sisters who attend our services of worship and even join our gospel choirs, recognizing, perhaps, the absence in their lives of a joy-filled praise of God that brings a comforting peace.

Yet, still, we wonder at the coldness with which we are so often received, and at the anger that is directed toward us. How do we prove that we are who we say we are? Why must we even do so? As W.E.B. Du Bois recognized almost a century ago, African Americans, and especially African American Catholics, are often caught in a quandary. He states:

> It is a peculiar sensation, this double consciousness, this sense of always looking at one's self through the eyes of others, of measuring one's soul by the tape of a world that looks on in amused contempt and pity. One ever feels his twoness—an American, a Negro; two souls, two thoughts, two unreconciled strivings; two warring ideals in one dark body, whose dogged strength alone keeps it from being torn asunder.[12]

This has been our quandary in the four hundred years of our sojourn in this land. But the confusion is now at end; the turmoil is over; the strivings are reconciled. There is evidence throughout this nation that our Catholic African American sisters and brothers are taking down their harps from the walls, they are taking them out of the dark trunks and closets where they have been gathering the dust of the ages and are proclaiming, as our poetic brother did years ago, that we, too, sing America.

We are proclaiming to the church and the world at large that to be Black and Catholic is not a paradox; it is not a conflict; it is not a contradiction. To be Black and Catholic is correct, it is authentic, it is who we are and have always been. For, ironically, it must also be recognized that questions about our faithfulness have come not just from our Catholic family but from the greater Black community. This is further evidence of the critical need for the full history of the African presence in early Christianity as well as in the United States predating the English-speaking Protestant colonies to be told. For in the telling, naysayers will have to acknowledge that there have been African peoples in the Catholic church as long as that church has existed. Black faith is not and cannot be limited to one church or one expression. But it does share in a richness of heritage that predates Christianity and continues to shape and form it into a new creation.

The time finally has come for African American Catholics fully to articulate our self-understanding and to present that articulation not only to our brothers and sisters in the Roman Catholic Church but to all with whom we come into contact. If theology is "God-talk," if it is "interested conversation," then we must become full and active participants in that conversation, one which has been going on for too long a time without our input.

In our gatherings, discussions, dialogues, days of reflection, re-vivals, and congresses we are developing a theology, a way of speaking about God, Jesus, the Holy Spirit, the church and all that pertains to them in a way that is indigenous to us, that is Afri-centric, that is truly Black and authentically Catholic. Our way of doing theology stems from our understanding of and faith in a God who is an active, interested and loving participant in our history.

We say this not to be divisive, not to deny the truths and teach-ings of our Catholic faith, but simply to acknowledge for ourselves and to demand from others the recognition of our distinctive Catho-licity, a Catholicity with African roots and myriad branches.

SPEAKING THE TRUTH

It is time to "speak the truth to the people."[13] It is time for the history of the darker peoples of the Catholic church to be set forth so that all can learn not only of the dark days of colonization and enslavement but also of the days of civilizations ancient and re-nowned throughout the world. Instead of others' stories, we must learn of and share our stories so that we see ourselves as a new people empowered by our knowledge to take our rightful place in the ranks of peoples of the world. Pope Paul VI noted when in Africa that we, as Africans and people of African descent, are now missionaries to ourselves. He stated further: "You must now give your gifts of Blackness to the whole church,"[14] a sentiment reaf-firmed by Pope John Paul II in his meeting with Black Catholics in 1987.

We must learn of ourselves and then share that knowledge with others. "We have come this far by faith," in the words of our gospel heritage, and we will and must continue to explore and uncover the truth of our past so that we may move forward into the future.

African American Catholics have retained, despite the strains of slavery, segregation, discrimination, and second-class citizenship, a steadfast faith in God. Remaining unseduced by the distortions of Christianity force-fed to them during slavery, they have always believed in a God who saves, one who is on the side of the poor and oppressed, like them. This steadfast faith in a God who promised eventual deliverance grounds all that is said and done, providing thereby a freedom, both spiritual and physical, for there is no dichotomy between the life lived on earth and the life to be lived with the coming of the Kingdom.

In order to learn about ourselves, in order to understand and accept "who and whose" we are, we must reflect on both faith and its praxis, seeking to understand for ourselves, in language of our own choosing, the constant presence of God within our lives while recognizing with St. Anselm that theology in its truest sense is "faith seeking understanding." We must then share that understanding with all of the church. For it is in learning the "truth" of ourselves that we are empowered to continue the struggle, "leaning on the everlasting arms" of our God.

PLENTY GOOD ROOM

We are all called to defend the faith that is ours (1 Pt 3:15). This is especially true on the local level, for it is in the parish setting that we are called upon to spread the gospel of Jesus Christ, both inside and outside of the church itself. We are all called as Christian faithful who have been anointed in baptism to share in the mission and ministry of Christ (canon 204). It is our responsibility and our joy to evangelize, to spread the good news of the life, death, and resurrection of our Lord and Savior Jesus Christ to all around us. This must be done for those outside the church but even more so for those within. We must rekindle the spirit of love within the hearts of our brothers and sisters in Christ. But we must do so in a way that is uniquely ours. As a people of God, we are called to witness to the working of the Holy Spirit within us, while recognizing the different gifts the Spirit has bestowed.

It is the Spirit of God that has empowered us as African American Catholics to speak of our faith and to present that faith without shame, recognizing that as African American Catholics we are "no longer simply recipients of the ministry of others, [but] are called to be full participants in the life and mission of the Church, on both the local and national levels."[15]

It is now time for African American Catholics to take ownership of this church in which they have for so long lived marginalized and often alienated lives. We are called to express that ownership in all that we say and do, in our workshops, programs, liturgies, parishes, and every part of our lives.

Today we recognize and affirm that to be both Black and Catholic is not a contradiction but a proclamation of historical pride, for to be truly Black and authentically Catholic means that we, as an African and American and Catholic people, have, indeed, come of age and are beginning to act in accordance with our adulthood. It means that we are challenging the all-too-prevalent understanding of Roman Catholicism as a Western, Euro-centric religion. We are proclaiming by our presence in the church that there is, indeed, "plenty good room" in our Father's Kingdom for a diversity of expressions of the Catholic faith. We are challenging the church catholic to acknowledge that recognition and acceptance of the cultures and heritages of the many peoples who make up the church, as they are lived out in the faith and worship of these people, are no longer luxuries but necessities. Otherwise, there is the risk of preaching not the transcendent Christ but a cultural Christ, one who is embodied in a particular time, a particular context, a particular culture.

As the church finally opens itself to the contributions of peoples of every race and ethnicity, it must also expand its understanding and expression of God and Jesus Christ. This correlates with our understanding of the incarnation of Jesus Christ. If God became incarnate in a human being, a male, a Jew, taking on all of the characteristics and appearances of that humanity, so must the church, expressive of Christ's body, incarnate itself today in the peoples and cultures with whom it has come in contact. This is not optional; it is mandated.

There is "plenty good room" in God's Kingdom. We must only choose our seats and sit down. As African American Catholics, however, we must ensure not only that we are doing the choosing but that the seats actually "fit" us, that we have participated fully in their construction and placement at the center, not the periphery, of our church.

As Black Catholics we are full members of the Catholic communion. We have struggled for a long time, but the journey is nearing its end. As we continue toward that end, we take as our mandate the words of the prophet Isaiah: "They who wait upon the Lord shall renew their strength, they shall mount up with wings like eagles, they shall run and not be weary, they shall walk and not faint" (40:31). Our faith has not faltered, and our Spirit has been renewed. We are truly Black and authentically Catholic. As we continue to deepen our own understanding of ourselves, we offer the gift of ourselves to the Roman Catholic Church, acknowledging that there is still much work to be done. Yet, we have come this far by faith, and that faith will in time lead us home.

The essays included in this work evidence the coming of age of Black Catholics in the United States. The individual authors—lay, religious, and clergy—have addressed issues of great concern not only to African American Catholics but to all people of faith. The language and styles of presentation may differ, but all are rooted in their common African ancestry and affirm their American and Catholic heritage as well, resulting in the development of a Black Catholic theology that both challenges and affirms us all.

NOTES

[1] Cincinnati, Ohio: St. Anthony Messenger Press, 1984.

[2] Ibid., p. 2.

[3] In this work the terms *African American Catholic* and *Black Catholic* will be used interchangeably to depict Catholics of African descent now living in the United States, whether their arrival in this country lies in the distant past or in the present.

[4] Cyprian Davis, O.S.B., "Black Spirituality: A Catholic Perspective," in *One Faith, One Lord, One Baptism: The Hopes and Experiences of the Black Community in the Archdiocese of New York*, vol. 2 (New York: Archdiocese of New York, Office of Pastoral Research, 1988), p. 45.

[5] "The Church and Racism: Toward a More Fraternal Society," *Origins* 18:37 (February 23, 1989), p. 617.

[6] In Janet Dewart, ed., *The State of Black America 1988* (New York: National Urban League, 1988), p. 6.

[7] S. Carmichael and C. V. Hamilton, *Black Power: The Politics of Liberation in America*, (New York: Vintage Books, 1967), p. 4.

[8] "The Church and Racism," p. 617.

[9] Vatican II, *Gaudium et Spes*, no. 29

[10] National Conference of Catholic Bishops, *Brothers and Sisters to Us: The U.S. Bishops' Pastoral Letter on Racism in Our Day* (Washington, D.C.: United States Catholic Conference, 1979), p. 3.

[11] At this time, there are six Black Catholic theologians with terminal degrees in systematic theology. They are the Most Reverend Edward Braxton, S.T.D.; M. Shawn Copeland, Ph.D.; Diana L. Hayes, S.T.D.; Philip Linden, S.S.J., S.T.D.; Jamie Phelps, O.P., Ph.D.; and Reverend

Bryan N. Massingale, S.T.D. The number of Black Catholics with degrees in other theological/religious studies areas is growing, however.

[12] W.E.B. Du Bois, "Of Our Spiritual Strivings," in *The Souls of Black Folk* (New York: NAL [Signet Classic], 1969), p. 45.

[13] Mari Evans, "Speak the Truth to the People" in *Trouble the Water: 250 Years of African-American Poetry,* ed. Jerry W. Ward Jr. (New York and London: Mentor, Penguin Group, 1997), pp. 217-19.

[14] "To the Heart of Africa" (address to the bishops of the African Continent at the closing session of a symposium held in Kampala, Uganda), in *The Pope Speaks* 14 (1969), p. 219.

[15] "Here I Am, Send Me: The U.S. Bishops' Response to the Evangelization of African Americans and the National Black Catholic Pastoral Plan," *Origins* 19:30 (December 28, 1989), p. 487.

PART I

HISTORICAL CONTEXT

1

God of Our Weary Years

Black Catholics in American Catholic History

CYPRIAN DAVIS, O.S.B.

Sometime in the first half of the fourteenth century, the Arab historian Ibn Fadl Allah al-'Umari recounted the visit to Cairo of the emperor of Mali, Mansa Kanku Musa (1307-1337), on his way back from the pilgrimage to Mecca. Mansa Musa came with a caravan of sixty thousand porters, carrying eighty bags of gold dust, and five hundred golden-clad slaves bearing staffs of gold, so much gold that he depressed the gold market. His wealth became legendary, and he became the most famous of the black African monarchs of the Middle Ages. The maps of the time showed the bearded African monarch contemplating a gold nugget held in his hand.

Al-'Umari recorded an incident described by Mansa Musa regarding his predecessor, Muhammed, whom he had succeeded as ruler of Mali. According to Mansa Musa, his predecessor's curiosity about the Atlantic was intense. Obsessed with the desire to know what was on the other side, he outfitted two hundred ships with men and provisions and sent them off; not hearing from them for a long time, they were deemed lost.

> The son of the Emir . . . has related: "I asked the Sultan Musa how the power had come to him." He told me: "We belong to a family in which the power is inherited. He who was before me did not believe that the [Atlantic] Ocean was impossible to cross. He wished to reach the furthest end and was obsessed [by this project]. He equipped 200 pirogues which were filled with men

17

and as many others filled with gold, water and provisions suffi-
cient for several years. He then said to those who were proposed
for these boats: "Do not return until you have attained the limits of the ocean or if you have exhausted your provisions or
your water."

Finally, a lone ship from the expedition returned to report that the
flotilla had reached land and most of the ships had ventured into a
river, which some have assumed might have been the Amazon. This
one ship that returned had not ventured in. None of the others returned. Mansa Musa's predecessor seemingly refused to give up. A
second expedition was outfitted. This time the king himself joined
the expedition.

> [The sultan] prepared . . . 2,000 pirogues, 1,000 for himself and
> his men who would accompany him and 1,000 for the water
> and provisions. Finally, he installed me as his replacement, he
> embarked with his companions and left. This was the last time
> that we saw either him or his companions, and thus I became
> the sole master of power.[1]

The fate of this expedition became a mystery.[2]
Unfortunately, there are no corroborating facts to support the
notion that this report by Mansa Musa is substantially correct. Without contemporary reports from the American side, there is no clear
indication that black Africans had arrived in the western hemisphere
some two centuries before Columbus. What this historical account
does do is corroborate the facts already known about African maritime traffic along the Atlantic coast. As a result one is left simply
with the question, Did an African and his maritime expedition arrive in South or Central America in the fourteenth century?[3] What
is certain is that Africans did arrive in chains two hundred years
later in the transatlantic commerce known as the slave trade.

THE AFRICAN SLAVE TRADE

In the ancient world slavery was a recognized institution in nearly
every society. This was as true on the African continent as it was in
European or Asian societies. Slavery was as varied in forms as it
was universal in its extension. Sub-Saharan Africa was itself a land

rich in its variety of social systems, such as kingdoms, city states, and tribal entities. In most of these cultures slavery was part of the social fabric. From the beginning, it seems, trade in slaves played a prominent part in commercial enterprise. By the end of the Middle Ages, African slaves had begun to appear in large numbers in southern Europe for the first time since the end of the Roman Empire.[4] Catalonian and Genoese merchants sold African slaves. In the third quarter of the fifteenth century African slaves were being imported into Portugal and the various regions of Spain. By and large many African slaves were needed because of the increase of sugar cane plantations. African slaves worked not only in agriculture but also in the mines, in the construction of buildings, in the military, as messengers, stevedores, and in many other types of menial service and intensive labor.[5] Some became priests and religious. Juan de Latino, a renowned black scholar of the sixteenth century, was attached to the University of Granada.[6]

In 1455 John II, viceroy of the kingdom of Aragon, recognized an association of black freedpersons and slaves in Barcelona, that is, a *cofradia* established at the Church of St. James in Barcelona. Drawn up in Latin and Catalan, the foundation charter stipulated that each member was to pay a certain amount of dues every Saturday. Money was collected for the future burial of each member. Regulations prescribed the presence of members at the funerals of the respective members as well as offerings for Mass on the anniversary of the day of death. The indigent among them were to receive aid and medication. Money was set apart for acts of piety such as the offering of a candle for the Corpus Christi procession and for the candles at the funeral liturgy.[7]

A similar document was drawn up in 1472 for another black *cofradia* in Valencia by Ferdinand II, the future husband of Isabella the Catholic, the queen of Castile. The *cofradia* was in honor of Our Lady of the Blacks and numbered some forty free Blacks, who every year offered a candle in the chapel of Our Lady of Grace belonging to the Augustinian friars. Their rights and privileges were also set forth in a royal document by Ferdinand II.[8] These confraternities are a reminder that Africans were part of the landscape of the southern European world. It is a reminder also that the Iberian entry into the New World was a biracial and bicultural event.

The American slave trade, nevertheless, would become a worldwide, multinational phenomenon bringing suffering and division to the African continent. This New World institution of slavery would be particularly inhumane and cruel. It would result in a gigantic displacement of persons and the creation of one of the most wide-ranging diasporas in human history. The age of discovery and the age of the Reformation was most emphatically also the age of oppression and inhumanity.

AMERICAN SLAVERY

The importation of African slaves into the newly founded colonies of Spain and Brazil began at the onset of the sixteenth century. The official introduction of African slavery into Brazil came in 1549. By this time, however, African slaves were already present. By 1570 several thousand were present in Brazil. The increase of sugar cane plantations demanded an ever greater number of laborers. Slaves were imported mainly into the Spanish possessions of Peru, Mexico, Venezuela, Colombia, and Cuba shortly after 1500. Most slaves entered the Spanish possessions by way of Vera Cruz in Mexico and Cartagena in Colombia. The African slaves soon became an integral part of the Spanish colonial community. Most of the slaves coming into Latin America came at first from the Iberian peninsula and later from the area between Senegal and Nigeria and the Congo and northern Angola.[9]

The first Africans to arrive in what is now the continental United States were Spanish-speaking and Roman Catholic. The Spanish government introduced in 1565 the colony of St. Augustine in northern Florida to serve as a northern defense for its empire in the Caribbean and Mexico. The baptismal registers, which began with the colony and are the oldest ecclesiastical documents in American history, witness to the presence of Blacks among the first inhabitants of St. Augustine. In these registers, Blacks and mulattoes are clearly designated as such, along with the indication whether the individual was slave or free. Other types of information were also provided. The names of the sponsors were given, serving as precious indications of the relationships between Blacks and whites in this Spanish colonial town. The place of birth was supplied, the identity of parents given, if known. The place of birth is significant for historians because after 1700 the colonial officials made known that all slaves in the English colonies who found refuge in the Floridas and converted to Catholicism would be freed.

In 1738, the Spanish governor of St. Augustine, Manuel de Montiano, established two miles north of St. Augustine the town of

Gracia Real de Santa Teresa de Mose as a *palenque*, or a town of freed slaves, to receive fugitive slaves. This first all-black settlement in what is now the United States was a Catholic town. The only white person in this community of roughly a hundred people was the Franciscan chaplain. The head of the community was Francisco Menéndez, a former slave escaped from South Carolina, who because of his bravery had been made head of the slave militia that was established in 1726 by the Spanish authorities to fight against the British. Menéndez and the other black militiamen, all slaves, fought with ferocity alongside the Yamassee Indians, the tribe that was allied with the Spaniards against the British. After the establishment of Santa Teresa "the free black militia of Mose worked alongside the other citizenry to fortify provincial defenses. . . . They also provided the Spaniards with critical intelligence reports."[10]

One year after the founding of Santa Teresa, there was a slave revolt in Stono in South Carolina, close by Charleston. It was one of the first well-known slave revolts in what was an English colony. The authors of the revolt were a nucleus of twenty slaves, seemingly well disciplined in warfare, who had a predetermined plan to make their way to St. Augustine. Although the numbers increased after the initial foray, Professor John K. Thornton has shown that more than likely the leaders of the rebellion were Roman Catholics from the Kingdom of the Congo in present-day Angola.[11] Unfortunately, the insurgent slaves were defeated by the British.

Thanks to the sacramental registers kept by the Spanish we know a lot about the early Black Catholics in America. From 1784 to 1821, when Florida became United States territory, the baptisms, marriages, and deaths were recorded in separate books for Blacks, free and slave. It is these death records that reveal the fact that Spanish Florida had black soldiers garrisoned at St. Augustine. The announcements often mentioned Cuba as the place of origin, although some were also from Africa. Unlike the British and the Americans, the Spanish had a long tradition of arming Blacks, both slave and free.

In the Spanish southwest, Spanish-speaking Blacks were also to be found. Many of them were also soldiers. In 1781 the present city of Los Angeles was founded by eleven families coming from the northern Mexican villages of Sonora and Sinaloa. They were brought to southern California by the Spanish governor, Felipe de Neve, to encourage the settlement of California by farmers and artisans from Mexico in order to prevent further encroachments on the territory by the Russians or the Americans. The census of 1781 indicates that only two of the forty-odd persons who settled in Los Angeles were white, but they were all Catholic and a little over half were of African ancestry.[12]

The French settled Louisiana and much of the territory along the Mississippi in Missouri and Illinois. The slaves they held were mostly black and to a large extent Catholic. The ecclesiastical records in these areas of French settlements reveal that most French-speaking Catholics had their slaves baptized in the Catholic church. In many instances, however, information regarding the pastoral care of these slaves is far from abundant. The same was true in the English colonies. In a letter to Cardinal Antonelli in 1785, John Carroll, at the time superior of the Roman Catholic clergy of Maryland, spoke about the pastoral situation of black slaves in the state of Maryland where they were one-fifth of the Catholic population, numbering about three thousand. He expressed his concern about the ministry available to them.[13]

Shortly before the Civil War, William Henry Elder (who would later become archbishop of Cincinnati), wrote about his diocesan ministry in Natchez, Mississippi, for the Society of the Propagation of the Faith in Lyons, France. He observed that 50 percent of the population was slaves. "These poor negroes form in some respects my chief anxiety . . . for learning and practising religion, they have at present very little opportunity indeed." Undoubtedly, Elder had real concern; but sharing in the common attitude of many well-meaning whites of the period, he saw Blacks as overgrown children.

> The poor negroes very often have at first a fear of a Catholic Priest, or imagine they can never understand him; but they are not ill disposed towards religion. Indeed, they often have a craving for its ministration. Having few comforts and no expectations in this world, their thoughts and desires are the more easily drawn to the good things of the world to come. I say often because often again they are so entirely animal in their inclinations, so engrossed with the senses, that they have no regard for any thing above the gratifications of the body.[14]

The Catholic church was implicated in the institution of slavery to an extent far greater than its numbers. Members of religious orders as well as diocesan priests were slave owners. The Carmelite nuns in Port Tobacco, Maryland, the oldest community of contemplatives in the United States, possessed slaves. "A portion of the property of the nuns . . . consisted of slaves. Many of the novices, on entering the community, brought their slaves with them."[15] In 1790, when the community was established in Maryland, the slaves were about thirty in number.

Other sisters owned slaves. In Kentucky the Dominican sisters at St. Catherine's, the Sisters of Loretto, and the Sisters of Charity at Nazareth were all slave holders, as were the Visitation nuns in Washington, D.C., and the Ursulines in New Orleans. The Maryland Jesuits sold almost three hundred of their slaves to dealers in the South in 1835 because slave holding was no longer financially sound.[16] The Vincentians and the Sulpicians both had slaves in their seminaries. Not only did well-known priests, like Father Badin (1768-1853) in Kentucky[17] and Father Gibault in Vincennes (1735-1802),[18] own slaves, but so did bishops like Carroll of Baltimore, Flaget of Bardstown/Louisville, Portier of Mobile, and others. It can truly be said that the Catholic church, especially in the South, owes its material existence to black labor and black toil.

In general the American bishops shied away from any pronouncements on the issue of slavery. While many Protestant churches were divided over the question, American Catholics were never divided. In fact, while many Protestants became avid Abolitionists, Roman Catholics tended to distance themselves from the Abolitionists. The Abolitionists tended to come from the same Protestant milieu, well educated and upper class, that was the most opposed to Catholicism, seen by them as an obscurantist religion contrary to American ideals. Immigrant Catholics, moreover, found instant sympathy with the Democratic Party and saw the African Americans as rivals in their attempt to find employment and a place in American society.

In 1839 Pope Gregory XVI, a stern conservative pontiff, condemned in no uncertain terms the slave trade, stating

> that no one in the future dare to bother unjustly, despoil of their possessions, or reduce to slavery *(in servitutem redigere)* Indians, Blacks or other such peoples. Nor are they to lend aid and favor to those who give themselves up to these practices, or exercise that inhuman traffic by which the Blacks, as if they were not humans but rather mere animals, having been brought into slavery in no matter what way, are, without any distinction and contrary to the rights of justice and humanity, bought, sold and sometimes given over to the hardest labor.

Then Pope Gregory XVI prohibited any member of the church from defending or promoting the slave trade:

> We then, by Apostolic Authority, condemn all such practices as absolutely unworthy of the Christian name. By the same Authority We prohibit and strictly forbid any Ecclesiastic or lay person from presuming to defend as permissible this trade in Blacks under no matter what pretext or excuse, or from publishing or teaching in any manner whatsoever, in public or privately, opinions contrary to what We have set forth in these Apostolic Letters.[19]

By this time the opinion of the American South was totally engaged in defense of slavery and was totally opposed to any contact with an opposing point of view or the slightest hint of abolitionism. From 1840 to 1841, John England, the Irish-born bishop of Charleston, South Carolina, wrote a series of eighteen public letters to John Forsyth of Georgia, former secretary of state, who as a loyal Southerner had charged the pope with being an abolitionist. England rose to the pope's defense in these letters published in his diocesan newspaper—the first in the country—whereby England pointed out that the Catholic church had never condemned slavery; and he thereupon proceeded to show by historical precedent and theological reasoning that slavery was not necessarily an evil and could be a good. England never concluded his series of letters. He died in 1842 after admitting that he was personally opposed to slavery but saw no way in which it could be abolished.[20]

Auguste Martin, the first bishop of Natchitoches in Louisiana, went even further than England in his defense of slavery. Originally from Brittany in France, he was ordained priest in 1828 and came to the United States, first to Indiana and then to New Orleans, where he was made the first bishop of Natchitoches, the northernmost French settlement in Louisiana (later it became the diocese of Alexandria). When the Civil War began in April of 1861, Auguste Martin wrote in French a pastoral letter to the Catholics of Natchitoches. Martin wrote to console his people about the war, to give support to the Confederacy, and to defend its cause. He defended the institution of slavery using theological reasons for his stand. His letter was delated to Rome. Martin insisted that slavery was a good thing for Africans:

With the admirable provisions taken in His Providence, the Lord, the Father of us all, God who loves the souls for whom He gave his beloved . . . Son . . . for centuries has been snatching from the barbarity of their ferocious customs thousands of children of the race of Canaan, upon whom the curse of an outraged Father continues to weigh heavily.

According to Martin, God commits these children of Canaan "to the care of the privileged ones of the great human family for His own purposes and these people must be their shepherds and their fathers rather than their masters." In a sense, according to this, slavery is a part payment for real benefits.

The manifest will of God is that, in exchange for a freedom which they are unable to defend and which will kill them, and in return for a lifetime of work, we must give these unfortunate people not only the bread and the clothes necessary to their material life but also . . . their just share of truth and of the goods of grace, which may console them for their present troubles with the hope of eternal rest in the bosom of their Father, who calls them as well as us. From this point of view . . . slavery, far from being an evil, would be an eminently Christian work . . . the redemption of millions of human beings who would pass in such a way from the darkest intellectual night to the sweet . . . light of the Gospel.[21]

This theology of slavery by a nineteenth century Catholic bishop was considered erroneous by the curial officials of Pope Pius IX. The Dominican Vincenzo Gatti, who would eventually become Master of the Sacred Palace, carefully marked the erroneous and dangerous opinions in this letter. It was to be condemned, but Martin was to be allowed time to correct his errors. The letter was given to the Prefect of the Congregation *Propaganda Fide* in 1894. Before Martin's response could be given the war ended and with it slavery. We can only conjecture as to how a public explicit condemnation of slavery would have affected attitudes toward race in the contemporary period. As Caravaglios points out, "A small revolution was effected in the Curia's thinking on the subject of human rights."[22]

THE RESPONSE OF AFRICAN AMERICAN CATHOLICS

The history of the Catholic church in the United States is not merely the story of an ecclesiastical institution implicated in the slavery system. It is more than a question of slave-holding priests and people, of sisters and their bond servants, of a system that ultimately entrapped the consciences of the individuals; it is the revelation of a universal and inclusive church that flourished among Blacks and that generated a much richer Catholicism. This richer Catholicism can be termed a black response to a white Catholic world.

Two documents found in the Sulpician Archives in Baltimore give a look into Black Catholicism before the Civil War. The first is a small, handwritten notebook entitled "Records of Confraternities." It contains the list of members of three confraternities plus the rite for the conferring of the scapular, and the census list for Ward 11, Baltimore City, in 1850. The confraternities are Our Lady of the Scapular, Our Lady Help of Christians, Our Lady of the Rosary, and a fragment of the Confraternity of the Sacred Heart established in the chapel of the Visitation nuns in Georgetown, D.C.[23]

The names of members of the respective confraternities were entered under the date on which the member was received into the confraternity. The earliest date in any of the lists is January 1, 1796; the latest is 1856. Because the lists give the names of some very prominent Roman Catholic laypersons, religious, and clergy, the lists are certainly significant. Their membership in the confraternity was a sign that they had accepted certain pious obligations such as wearing the brown scapular of Our Lady of Mount Carmel and reciting the rosary or other prayers. These sects were normally considered as supplementary acts of devotion. The largest confraternity, that of Our Lady of Mount Carmel, had over a thousand names. The director of this confraternity was John Carroll, the bishop of Baltimore. Significantly for us, this study reveals that over a third of the individuals were black men and women, both slave and free. In fact, this is true for most of the confraternity lists. The notices were written in French because French-speaking Sulpicians kept the record. Blacks appear therein from the beginning. The first page begins on January 1, 1796 as follows:

1796

January 1	Has been received Marie La Combe Fortunée, Negro woman of Mr. Dennis
	Sophia, free Mulatto woman
	Veronique, Negro woman of Madame La Lammie (?)
September 11	Alzire, free Mulatto woman
	Lucile, free Mulatto woman
October 9	Jean Batiste, Negro of Mr. Gearity
	Marie Theophile, Mulatto woman of Mr. Clery
	Emilie, Mulatto woman of M. Autrissean
	Marie Louise, Negro woman of Madame Creusat

1797

February 11	Elizabeth Brigitt Kempe
February 16	Demetrius Augustin Gallitizin, named Smith
February 19	Anire, Negro woman of Madame Ponce

The majority are clearly black women, most of whom were slaves. On the same page is the name of one of the first American priests ordained in this country, Prince Gallitzen.[24] Further research on these records may very well reveal more about the African Americans listed here. Inasmuch as some of the Blacks were free persons, this may indicate that membership in the confraternity was without coercion and was simply an act of personal piety. The presence of Blacks in such large numbers would seem to suggest that piety and devotion were not alien to their lives.

The second document in the Baltimore Sulpician Archives is a notebook in longhand entitled *Journal of the Commencement And of the proceedings of the Society of Colored People; with the approbation of Most Rev. Archbishop Samuel [Eccleston] and of the Rector of the Cathedral Rev. H. B. Coskery.*[25] From the end of 1843 to the fall of 1845, some two hundred or so black men and women met in the basement of Calvert Hall, next to the cathedral of Baltimore. Father Hickey, a Sulpician, seemingly the only white person in regular attendance, kept the minutes each Sunday evening at the weekly meeting. At the first meeting in December 1843 they decided to name themselves the Society of the Holy Family, and they chose as president John Noel. Two lists of the members were given. They paid dues of six and a quarter cents per month. Meetings began at 7:00 P.M. and lasted about two hours. They sang about four hymns each session. Singing was very important. One member is mentioned as indulging in spontaneous prayer. The members recited the rosary and evening prayers. At each meeting Hickey gave a conference. They raised money to buy books for a lending library and for a bookcase. Many of the books were catechisms and lives of the saints. Two Masses were celebrated for the soul of a deceased member. The members disbursed funds, meager as they were, for designated charitable purposes. They seemed to be a thriving institution, but on September 7, 1845, it was announced that there would be no meeting of the Holy Family Society. The Brothers of Christian Doctrine had taken over Calvert Hall. It was subsequently decided to dissolve the society.

There are some indications that the Holy Family Society did not cease to exist but that it moved to what had become the center of Black Catholics in Baltimore, the convent chapel of the Oblate Sisters of Providence. Grace Sherwood, the historian of the Oblate Sisters of Providence, pointed out in the centennial history of this congregation that there were two organizations that were called the Society of the Holy Family. One had been an organization to which students in St. Mary's College, operated by the Sulpicians, had belonged, and was opened up to the worshipers in the basement chapel of St. Mary's Seminary.[26] Another Holy Family Society was established in 1852 at St. Frances Chapel by Thaddeus Anwander, the chaplain of the Oblate Sisters of Providence. This was a society originally established in Belgium in 1844.[27]

As early as 1787, Richard Allen, the founder and first bishop of the African Methodist Episcopal Church, founded the Free African Society in Philadelphia, the first known mutual aid society for Blacks in the United States. Soon there would be others. The Society of the Holy Family in 1843 is one of the earliest known mutual aid societies among Black Catholics. Its formation, however, is an indication that Black Catholics had as much initiative and organizational ability as Black Protestants. In fact, recent research has shown for the first time that burial societies and other mutual aid societies existed among Black Catholics. For example *The Metropolitan Catholic Almanac* for 1839 lists "the Tobias Society, established in Baltimore, January 1, 1828. . . . This charitable association has for its object the decent burial of Catholic coloured persons. It is governed by excellent regulations tending to the practice of religion and the special exercise of fraternal charity." On the same page in the very next entry, there is the mention of several mutual aid societies.

Mutual Relief Societies for Coloured Persons in Baltimore. The monthly contributions of those who belong to these societies form a fund which is applied to the relief of the members in the time of sickness, and after death, to the payment of their funeral expenses. There are two institutions of this kind among the Catholic coloured people of Baltimore.[28]

This would seem to indicate that there were two other mutual aid societies and the Tobias Society. The same three societies were mentioned in the almanac of 1843.[29]

Baltimore, however, was not the only city that had Black Catholic mutual aid societies. New Orleans had several, some with French titles, such as the *Société des Artisans de Bienfaisance et d'Assistance Mutuelle*, which was established in 1834, and *Dieu Nous Protège*, established in 1844.[30] More extensive research in this area of Black Catholicism will no doubt reveal much more about lay initiative than was formerly known.

CONGREGATIONS OF BLACK SISTERS

Despite racial prejudice and suspicion, two orders of black religious women were established in the United States in the period of slavery. That they lasted is a tribute to the faith of the Black Catholic community. Their perseverance, however, came at a price.

Blacks had worshiped in the lower chapel of St. Mary's Seminary from the beginning of the century. In 1793 a boatload of Blacks from Haiti had docked in Baltimore harbor. These Black Catholics formed the nucleus of the community that worshiped in the lower chapel. In 1827, Jacques Joubert (an ex-soldier and former government official in Haiti who had migrated to Baltimore at the beginning of the century, had entered the seminary, and had been ordained in 1810) became the pastor for this community. Joubert saw the need for education for the children of the community. Searching for teachers, he found four young women, Haitian by birth or by parentage, who not only desired to teach but also to lead the religious life: the foundress, Elizabeth Lange, along with Rosine Boegue, Marie Madeleine Balas, and Almeide Maxis Duchemin.[31] Almeide, later known as Therese, was born in the United States of a Haitian slave mother and an English military officer. Many years later this talented woman was herself the foundress of the Sisters, Servants of the Immaculate Heart of Mary in 1845 in Monroe, Michigan.[32] Despite the outright hostility of some toward the idea of a religious community of black women, James Whitfield, the archbishop of Baltimore, gave his full support and blessing to the new foundation in 1829. Two years later Pope Gregory XVI gave his approval. The community opened a school for young black girls, then a school for boys, and an orphanage.

The Catholic Directory of 1839 had a notice stating that

> the Sisters of Providence are a religious society of coloured women. . . . They renounce the world to consecrate themselves to God and the Christian education of coloured girls. . . . Besides the care bestowed on their religious education, girls of colour are taught English, French, Cyphering and Writing, Sewing in all its branches, Embroidery, Washing and Ironing.[33]

In New Orleans, two women of color, Henriette DeLille and Juliette Gaudin, began a second congregation of black religious women. The vicar general of the diocese, the Abbé Etienne Rousselon, aided the two women to begin their life of service to the poor and needy among the black population. In 1842 they founded the Sisters of the Holy Family. A third woman, Josephine Charles, joined them in 1843. At first they had to have an association with lay people for legal purposes. They were not regarded as nuns for a long time. Only in 1872 were they able to wear their religious habit on the streets. From the beginning, they taught young girls of color, while they taught catechism to the slaves in the evening.

The community grew very slowly. In 1852 the sisters made their public vows for the first time. The community was now recognized as sisters. Because of their heroic service to the sick during the Yellow Fever epidemic of 1853, the Sisters of the Holy Family received a grudging gratitude from the citizens of New Orleans.[34] Henriette DeLille died at the age of fifty in 1862.

In an era when black people were accorded little or no respect or esteem, in a time when black women were degraded by slave holders or abused by white employers, in a society where black women were considered to be weak in morality, black sisters were a counter sign and a proof that the Black Catholic community was rooted in faith and devotion, for vocations arise from a faith-filled people. Lest it be forgotten, the two black sisterhoods were not European transplants; they were very much American in origin.

AFRICAN AMERICAN PRIESTS

Black sisters antedated black priests in the United States by a quarter of a century. The call to the priesthood, however, was also felt by Blacks even before the end of slavery. William Augustine Williams, a black man and a convert to Catholicism born in Virginia, entered Urban College attached to the Congregation of the Propaganda as a seminarian in 1855 on the recommendation of Thaddeus Anwander, the chaplain of the Oblate Sisters in Baltimore. It was impossible, however, to find an American bishop willing to sponsor him. Archbishop Hughes of New York informed the Congregation that the American public would be violently opposed to black priests. Archbishop Kenrick of Baltimore urged the Congregation to ordain Williams and send him to Liberia; a second bishop suggested Haiti. As a result Williams had to leave Urban College. He returned to the States, continued to dream of priesthood, made an unsuccessful attempt to begin a religious community of black brothers, and eventually became for a while a librarian at the Catholic University of America in Washington.[35]

The first black priest in the history of the United States also became America's first black bishop. James Augustine Healy was born a slave in Georgia in 1830. He was the eldest of ten children, all children of Michael Morris Healy, who came from Ireland to the United States having served in the British army in the War of 1812. Michael Morris Healy carved out for himself a plantation in the center of Georgia with the assistance of his slaves. Never married, he had ten children by Eliza Healy, a light-skinned slave. Although legally slaves, Michael Morris Healy was determined to send his children north to eventual freedom. With the assistance of John Fitzpatrick, later bishop of Boston, Healy sent his four oldest sons to Holy Cross College in Worcester, Massachusetts. James Augustine was the valedictorian for the first graduating class at Holy Cross. Three of the seven Healy sons became priests and two of the three daughters nuns. James Augustine studied first in the seminary at Montreal and later at Saint Sulpice in Paris, where he was ordained for the diocese of Boston in 1854. Another brother, Alexander Sherwood, studied in Rome and was ordained in 1858. He would later accompany his bishop, John Williams of Boston, to the First Vatican Council in 1870. Alexander was talented and gifted with much promise, but he died in 1875. In that same year James Augustine became the second bishop of Portland, Maine, and America's first black bishop and the only American bishop to have been born a slave.

Patrick Francis Healy, the third son of Michael Morris Healy, entered the Jesuits and studied at the University of Louvain in Belgium. In Belgium he was ordained a priest in 1864. In 1874, he became the head of Georgetown University in Washington, D.C., the oldest Catholic university in the country. He would be the first to have the title of president, well merited because it was he who raised funds for the university, expanded it, and enlarged its departments. Of the Healy brothers, he seems to have been the only one who passed as white. His sister Eliza became Sister St. Mary Magdalen of the Congregation of Notre Dame in Montreal. She would become superior in several of the convents of her order in the United States. A younger brother, Michael, was a member of the merchant marine and had a colorful career as an officer in the United States Revenue Marine Service, forerunner of the Coast Guard, and as a captain of a ship in the Alaskan waters.[36]

Brilliant as they were, the Healys did not really identify themselves with the Black Catholic community. The priest whom all Blacks would look to for inspiration and with pride was a tall, black-skinned man born a slave of Catholic slave parents in 1854 in northern Missouri. Augustus Tolton's father had escaped slavery and sought service in the Union Army in St. Louis, but he died at the beginning of the war. Martha Tolton, Augustus's mother, escaped slavery with her three children by crossing the Mississippi in a rowboat. She brought up her children in the midst of poverty and racial animosity in Quincy, Illinois.

Augustus early developed a desire for priesthood but could find no American seminary to accept him. The account of how an ex-slave became a priest after finding a place to study in Rome is the stuff of miracles. Tolton was that ex-slave. Thanks to the influence of the Minister General of the Franciscans, Tolton became a student at Urban College in 1880. As mentioned earlier, William A. Williams had gone to that college in 1855 but had to give up his studies because no bishop in the United States would sponsor him. Tolton was to go to Africa, but times had changed since the period of Williams. The prefect of the Congregation of the Propaganda, Cardinal Simeoni, was determined that the United States should have a black priest. Tolton was sent back to the diocese of Alton (later Springfield) in Illinois.

Ordained in Rome in 1886, Tolton received a tumultuous and triumphant welcome in Quincy, where he sang his first Mass in 1886. He was made pastor of a black parish to which many white Catholics came. Because of the jealousy and the racist attitudes of a neighboring pastor, Tolton found his life at Quincy unbearable and sought a change. In 1889 he was welcomed into the Chicago archdiocese by Archbishop Feehan and placed in charge of the Black Catholics. Eventually a black parish was formed, St. Monica's, and a church was in the process of construction. It was never finished.

One of those who gave financial aid toward the construction of St. Monica's was Blessed Katherine Drexel (1858-1955), the Philadelphia heiress, who founded the Sisters of the Blessed Sacrament for the evangelization of both Blacks and Native Americans.[37] Thanks to her inheritance Katherine Drexel was able to give financial aid for the construction of churches and the establishment of schools for Indians and Blacks. Tolton not only wrote her for aid, but he also poured out his heart to her:

> One thing I do know and that is it took the Catholic Church 100 years here in America to show up such a person as yourself. That is the reason why you have so much bother now and so many extending their hands to get a lift. . . . As I stand alone as the first Negro priest of America so you Mother Catherine stand alone as the first one to make such a sacrifice for the cause of a downtrodden race, hence the south is looking on with an angry eye, the north in many places is criticising every act, just as it is watching today every move I make; I suppose that is the reason why we had no Negro priests before this day. They watch us, just the same as the Pharisees did our Lord. They watched him.[38]

Tolton felt his loneliness and his isolation. He apparently knew nothing about the Healy brothers. He was admired and sought after by the black community but was seemingly cut off from white priests. He died at the early age of forty-three from heat exhaustion on July 9, 1897. His body was buried in Quincy, Illinois, where his ministry had begun.[39]

The first black priests in the United States had an extremely harsh life. The Mill Hill Fathers, established as a missionary society in England in 1866 by Herbert Vaughan, future cardinal archbishop of Westminster, came to the United States in 1871. In 1893 the Mill

Hill Fathers in the United States separated from the society in England and became known as the Society of St. Joseph of the Sacred Heart or Josephites. In 1891 Charles Randolph Uncles, the first Black to become a Josephite, was ordained a priest in Baltimore. He was the first African American ordained in the United States.[40] In 1902 John Henry Dorsey, also a Josephite, became the second black priest to be ordained in this country and the fifth in the history of the nation. He would become the first Black to serve as a pastor in the South. He would be the victim of racist attitudes in his two-year service as pastor of St. Peter's Church in Pine Bluff, Arkansas, from 1905 to 1907. Although highly successful as a preacher, the relationship between Dorsey and the Josephite superiors was never satisfactory. He died broken in health in 1926.[41]

Perhaps the most tragic figure of all was John Plantevigne (1871-1913). Born in Pointe Coupée Parish in Louisiana, he was ordained a Josephite priest in 1907. The specter of racism followed him throughout his short priestly career. Forbidden to have a public first Mass on a Sunday in his home parish; thwarted in his efforts to have a Catholic school opened for Blacks in his home parish at Chenel, Louisiana, because the pastor did not believe in education for Blacks; and finally, forced to cancel a scheduled mission at a black parish in New Orleans because Archbishop James Blenk (1856-1917) believed that the white Catholics of the city would not accept a black priest as preacher; Plantevigne became progressively disenchanted with what he felt was the oppressive racism in the American church. In the end his health deteriorated, and he died in January of 1913 at the age of forty-two.[42] After his death, the Josephites stopped ordaining African Americans. By 1910 when Father Stephen Theobald, originally from British Guiana, was ordained for the archdiocese of St. Paul, there were only four other black priests living in the United States. There would be no more than a dozen until 1933.[43]

AFRICAN AMERICAN LAITY

Unlike most Catholic ethnic groups, the Black Catholic community lacked a strong clerical component within its midst that could provide inspired leadership and guidance. Black Catholics were proud of the black priests, but their presence was rarely felt. Many dedicated white priests served as pastors and provided leadership. Not all, however, were capable of identifying themselves with a segment of the American population that was generally despised and forgotten. Those that did paid a price.

Leadership, on the other hand, emerged from the Black Catholic laity. This phenomenon of lay leadership is almost unparalleled in Catholic church history. At the end of the nineteenth century it was the work of the members of the Black Catholic congresses. At the time of the First World War it was the activity of a well-organized pressure group under black leadership.

Daniel Rudd (1854-1933), born a slave in Bardstown, Kentucky, was an unlikely candidate for national leadership. He was a slight, dark-skinned man with a vision and an incredible spirit of optimism. Addressing an all-white convention of Catholic young men in Cincinnati in 1888, Rudd acknowledged, "I hardly expected when a little boy, in the State of Kentucky, that at this early day of my life—and I am a young man yet—I would be standing before a Catholic convention . . . to lift my voice in the interest of my race and of my church." Rudd briefly spoke to the assembled youth on the number of Black Catholics in the United States at that time (two hundred thousand out of seven million), and the project that he had in mind for the growth of this number. "We have been led to believe that the church was inimical to the negro race, inimical to the genius of our Republic. . . . I feel that I owe it to myself, my God, and my country to refute the slander." Rudd spoke of his newspaper, a projected convention of Black Catholics, and a projected mass conversion of Blacks to Catholicism. "I believe that within ten years, if the work goes on as it has been going on, there will be awakened a latent force in this country."[44]

Daniel Rudd began a black weekly newspaper in 1884; it became a Black Catholic weekly newspaper, *The American Catholic Tribune*, in 1886. It would be the first newspaper of its kind and the longest lasting. Rudd believed passionately in the Catholic church and its civilizing mission. He believed just as passionately in the necessity for Blacks to embrace Catholicism, which would transform the race and elevate its position in American society. The newspaper was one way of broadcasting this message. Rudd also lectured all over the country. Finally, he conceived the idea of a national congress.

In the summer of 1889 Rudd was afforded the opportunity of a trip to Europe to participate in an anti-slavery congress organized by Cardinal Lavigérie (1825-1892), the great French missionary of Africa, to be held in Lucerne, Switzerland. The congress was postponed, but Rudd met and embraced Lavigérie. On his way back to the States he was welcomed by Cardinal Manning (1808-1892) in London. These two events were a highlight in Rudd's life, but the great achievement of Rudd was the convoking of five Black Catholic lay congresses. The first was in Washington, D.C., in January of 1889; the second in Cincinnati in 1890; the third in Philadelphia in 1892; the fourth in Chicago in 1893; and the last in Baltimore in 1894.[45]

These congresses were made up of male delegates elected from the black parishes and parish organizations across the country. It does not seem that there were more than two hundred delegates each time. The only whites present were members of the clergy. Many of the delegates were leaders in their respective local communities. None was a nationally known leader. As the meetings progressed, the delegates became more outspoken and more definite about the needs of the Black Catholic community and its own agenda. In fact, they began to articulate the beginnings of what can be called a Black Catholic theology. At the fourth congress, held in Chicago in 1893 as part of the Columbian Exposition, the delegates published a lengthy statement to their fellow Catholics:

> The Catholic Church, guided by the spirit of truth, must always preserve inviolate the deposit of faith, and thus she cannot err in proclaiming the rights of man. . . . From the days of Christ it has been her mission to inculcate the doctrine of love, and not of hate; to raise up the downtrodden, and to rebuke the proud. It has been her mission to proclaim to the ends of the earth that we all have stamped on our immortal souls the image of God. . . . For ages the Church has labored to break down the walls of race prejudice, to teach the world the doctrine of the meek and humble Christ, that man should be gauged by his moral worth; that virtue alone, springing from grace, truly elevates a man; and that vice alone, springing from the malice of the heart, degrades him.

The address, which was seemingly the work of a committee, expressed in eloquent terms the love and devotion for the church that was no doubt typical of Black Catholics of the period.

> We know that the Roman Church, as she is One and Apostolic, is also Catholic and holy. With thorough confidence in the rec-

titude of our course in the enduring love of Mother Church, and the consciousness of our priesthood, we show our devotion to the Church, our jealousy of her glory and our love for her history in that we respectfully call the attention of the Catholic world . . . to those wrong practices which mark the conduct of those . . . who have yielded to the popular prejudice.[46]

In an age when little was written on social justice in the United States, these Black Catholics made social justice the centerpiece of their ecclesiology. At the same time that they spoke of their pride in their church, they spoke of the consciousness of their priesthood. They closed the statement with an invitation for evangelization efforts for fellow African Americans.

Should the clergy . . . see to it that in all instances and in all places the truth of Catholic doctrine, which knows no distinction of races or previous condition, be maintained, the day will yet come when the whole colored race of the United States will be knocking at her doors for admittance, anxious to be of that faith which teaches and practices the sublime essence of human rights in the sight of God and our fellow man.[47]

To some extent the congress movement was both a success and a failure. For reasons that are not clear, the 1894 congress would be the last until 1987. Many of its demands were not met. Nevertheless, the congresses gave a cohesiveness to African American Catholics and gave them a sense of responsibility to their faith. It is no surprise that many of the leaders in the movement continued their activities long after the last meeting. Nor is it surprising that three decades later another lay-directed movement came into being.

Thomas Wyatt Turner was born in 1877 in Charles County, Maryland, son of Catholic sharecroppers. Turner was reared in the Catholic faith and even turned down the chance for a scholarship if he converted to enter an Episcopal school. In fact, Turner studied at Catholic University in the nation's capital at a period prior to the prohibition against Blacks studying there. Turner eventually received his doctorate in biology from Cornell University in 1921. While teaching at Howard University in Washington, D.C., Turner formed a committee in 1913 of Black Catholic laymen to lobby the National Catholic War Council on behalf of Black Catholic soldiers, who were totally ignored by the major religious organizations that ministered to the needs of white soldiers and Black Protestant soldiers. The necessary changes were made, but Turner's committee began its evolution as a movement of Black Catholic protest, to become known first in 1916 as the Committee for the Advancement of Colored Catholics and later in 1924 as the Federated Colored Catholics. Turner wanted an organization that would be action-oriented, with lay leadership by Blacks; that would work for an increased black participation in church organizations, particularly the reception of black applicants as students at Catholic University in Washington and the access of Blacks to all sectors of Catholic education; and finally, the admission of Blacks to the ranks of the priesthood. In the end, he called for the elimination of racism from the policies and the attitudes of the United States church.

Turner was very much ahead of his time with his sense of black consciousness and black pride. Some interpreted his ideas as a surrender to another form of racial discrimination. This was especially the conclusion of two Jesuit priests who were among the most widely known advocates for racial equality in the country. William Markoe (1892-1969) had devoted himself to the evangelization of Blacks from his days as a Jesuit scholastic at Florissant, near St. Louis. Once ordained he became the pastor of St. Elizabeth's church in St. Louis. William Markoe was determined, dogged, intense, and sometimes arrogant. He was convinced that Turner had created a "Jim-Crow organization" and was determined to turn it around. To do this he engaged the help of a fellow Jesuit, John LaFarge.

John LaFarge (1880-1963) was the most widely known Catholic priest serving the cause of racial justice in the period before the Second World War and for a period after it. LaFarge's was the voice of reason, moderation, civility, and social concern. Although he sympathized with Turner, he too believed that it was more important for the races to mingle, to converse, and to become educated about each other. The Jesuits had one vision; Turner had another. The Jesuits sought to steer in their direction the Federated Colored Catholics and the many Blacks whose sympathy lay with Markoe and LaFarge. The result was a split in 1932. LaFarge began the New York Catholic Interracial Council in 1934, a movement of interracial study groups and cooperative efforts that gradually spread to other cities. The Federated Colored Catholics ceased in 1952.[48]

THE GROWTH OF THE AFRICAN AMERICAN
CATHOLIC COMMUNITY

In the year 1930 African Americans numbered eleven million and African American Catholics numbered two hundred thousand. Ten years later Black Catholics numbered three hundred thousand out of a black population of twelve million. In 1920 a German missionary congregation, the Society of the Divine Word, had opened a seminary in Mississippi for black students for the priesthood. In 1934 four black Divine Word students were ordained. By 1934 a third religious community of black sisters, the Franciscan Handmaids of Mary, moved their motherhouse from Savannah, where they had been founded in 1916, to Harlem, where they taught school and ministered to the poor. In 1931 Xavier University in New Orleans, established by the Sisters of the Blessed Sacrament, became the first Black Catholic university.

The numbers of Black Catholics increased in northern cities, thanks especially to the increase in Catholic schools for black children. In many urban areas energetic white pastors increased social services—like night school, credit unions, and different fraternal organizations in their parishes—but the parish school was the parish centerpiece. By the 1950s the numbers of black priests had begun to increase, and in 1966 Harold Perry, S.V.D., became the second black bishop in the United States when he was ordained auxiliary bishop of New Orleans in 1966.

AFRICAN AMERICAN CATHOLICS AND CIVIL RIGHTS

In the beginning the Catholic church in the United States did not play a central role in the movement for civil rights. In fact, it was only in 1958 that the United States bishops spoke out as a body against racial discrimination in American public life.[49] There had been individual actions by certain bishops. Archbishop Ritter, later cardinal, of St. Louis did away with racial discrimination in Catholic schools in 1947 despite sharp opposition from many lay Catholics. Archbishop O'Boyle did the same in Washington, D.C. in 1948. The first massive participation of Catholic priests and sisters in the Civil Rights movement was the outpouring of priests and religious into Selma, Alabama, at the request of Martin Luther King Jr. in 1965.

The first organized protest of African American priests took place in Detroit in 1968, following the assassination of Martin Luther King Jr. and the wave of inner-city violence that ensued. Meeting apart from the white priests assembled for the Catholic Clergy Conference on the Interracial Apostolate, black priests organized themselves into a caucus, the first of its kind in American church history. The National Black Catholic Clergy Caucus, as it was called, presented a list of grievances to the American bishops. Black sisters formed the National Black Sisters Conference that same year. Shortly thereafter came the Black Catholic Lay Congress and the National Black Catholic Seminarians' Association. The action by these priests, although confrontational in the beginning, sparked a change that would permanently affect the position of African Americans within the United States Catholic church. In 1971 the National Office of Black Catholics was organized with its headquarters in Washington, D.C. It would serve as a clearing house and spokesperson for the four major black caucuses and conferences.[50]

In 1973 Joseph Howze was ordained bishop and became the first black ordinary for the see of Biloxi in Mississippi in 1977. In 1988 Eugene Marino, S.S.J., became the first black archbishop when he was named to the see of Atlanta. Upon his resignation in 1990, James Lyke, O.F.M., succeeded him as the second black archbishop. In 1979 the American bishops published a pastoral letter, "Brothers and Sisters to Us," in which racism was clearly designated as an evil and which called upon "the Church [to] proclaim to all that the sin of racism defiles the image of God and degrades the sacred dignity of humankind which has been revealed by the mystery of the Incarnation . . . a terrible sin that mocks the cross of Christ and ridicules the Incarnation. For the brother and sister of our Brother Jesus Christ are brother and sister to us."[51] Five years later the African American bishops issued their first pastoral letter, "What We Have Seen and Heard," in which they reminded their fellow African American Catholics "that the Black Catholic community in the American Church has now come of age" and that now is the time "to reclaim our roots and to shoulder the responsibilities of being both Black and Catholic."[52]

Within the two decades since Black Catholics had brought the issue of civil rights for the African American community to the United States church, diocesan offices for Black Catholics were set up all over the country to give voice and assistance to Black Catholics in their respective dioceses. In 1986 the National Council of Catholic

Bishops established the Secretariat for African American Catholics. In 1980 Black Catholic intellectuals established the Institute of Black Catholic Studies as a summer institute at Xavier University in New Orleans. In 1987 the Sixth Black Catholic Congress was held in Washington, D.C. Two years later, in 1989, a black priest of the archdiocese of Washington, George Stallings, established his own autonomous parish, the Imani Temple. He, along with Bruce Greening, S.D.S., broke from the Catholic church and formed a schismatic body with Stallings ordained a bishop by a bishop of the American Independent Orthodox Church. Bruce Greening, who subsequently broke from Imani Temple, formed his own independent church and was also ordained a bishop. Both religious bodies have kept the outward signs of Roman Catholic liturgy expressed in an African idiom. Contrary to the fears of some, there was not a massive exodus of Black Catholics. In 1992 the Second Black Catholic Congress in this century was held in New Orleans.

CONCLUSION

At the end of the twentieth century the African American Catholic community numbers close to two and a half million or more members. With a number that is about equal to the total membership of the Episcopal church in the United States, Black Catholics are the fifth largest Black church in this country. Of all the ethnic groups that make up American Catholicism today, Black Catholics have been here the longest, having antedated every other non-native American group with the exception of the Spaniards, with whom they must be counted. But, like Native Americans and Hispanics, they have been among the forgotten and the neglected children of this ancient church. Still, if the history of Black Catholics has any validity for tomorrow, it is that as a community Black Catholics will continue to be as vocal and persistent within the church of the twenty-first century as they have been since the sixteenth.

NOTES

[1] *Masaklik al-Absar Fi Mamalik al-Amsar (742-749/1342-1349)* by al-'Umari in *Recueil des Sources Arabes concernant l'Afrique Occidentale du VIIIe au XVIe Siècle (Bilad al-Sudan)*. Edited by Joseph M. Cuoq and Raymond Mauny. Sources d'Histoire Médiévale (Paris: Éditions du Centre National de la Recherche Scientifique, 1975), pp. 274-75. This is an

English translation from the French version of the Arabic. The title of the original Arabic text is *Tour of the Civilized Kingdoms.*

[2] The Arab historian and official al-'Umari, born in Damascus in 1301, served most of his life as a high-ranking civil servant for the Mameluk dynasty in Cairo, dying in Damascus in 1349. His writings are important sources of information during the Mameluk period. See *The Encyclopedia of Islam* (Leiden: Brill, new edition, 1971). See also Ibn Fadl Allah al-'Umari. Information regarding Mansa Musa I and his predecessor's Atlantic expedition is found in chapter 26: "Africa in Intercontinental Relations," by J. Devisse and S. Labib, in *General History of Africa*, 4:664-65. See also in the same volume pp. 150-51.

[3] Ivan Van Sertima in *They Came Before Columbus* presents several hypotheses that would indicate the arrival of Blacks in the western hemisphere before the fifteenth century. Van Sertima asserts that the ships from Mali were not the only African arrivals. He indicates that there is reason to believe that Nubian-Egyptian voyagers arrived in pre-Columbian America in the ninth century before Christ. He also postulates a regular traffic of African tradesmen and fishermen by Mandingo people in the fifteenth century and probably centuries before. Van Sertima rests his arguments upon a vast array of sources, including the Negroid characteristics of Olmec sculpted heads (Olmec civilization in southern Mexico 1100-800 B.C.) and other pre-Columbian sculpted figures, the various ocean currents in the South Atlantic, the evidence of the transfer of cereal plants, even linguistic similarities. In 1987 was published *African Presence in Early America*, ed. Ivan Van Sertima, and the entire issue of *Journal of African Civilizations*, December 1986. A dozen articles examine some aspect of the question of pre-Columbian African presence in the Americas. Some new evidence is presented. In some instances the hypotheses presented are very persuasive. Unfortunately, there seems not to be enough corroborative evidence to support conclusively the idea of African presence in pre-Columbian America. It would seem, however, that some of the Van Sertima conclusions should be taken seriously. He has opened up new possibilities for research.

[4] Both serfdom and slavery existed during the high Middle Ages. The Slavic nations supplied most of the slaves during this period, hence the origin of the word *slave*. From the twelfth century black African slaves were imported into Sicily, Italy, the kingdom of Aragon, and other Mediterranean countries. See J. Devisse and S. Labib, "Africa in Intercontinental Relations," *General History* 4:651-52.

[5] See J. E. Harris, chapter 5, "The African Diaspora in the Old and the New Worlds," *General History* 5:113-14.

[6] For the life of Juan Latino, see V. B. Spratlin, *Juan Latino: Slave and Humanist* (New York: Spinner Press, 1938).

[7] Prospero de Bofarull y Mascaró, ed., *Colleccion de Documentos Inéditos del Archivo General de la Corona de Aragon* 7:109, pp. 463-71.

[8] Miguel Gual Camarena, "Una Cofradia de Negros Libertos en al Siglo XV," *Estudios de Edad Media de la Corona de Aragon* 5:457-63. Consejo Superior de Investigaciones Cientificas. Escuela de Estudios Medievales. Estudios XXIII (Xaragoza, 1952).

[9] *The Cambridge History of Latin America*, vol. 2: *Colonial Latin America*, ed. Leslie Bethel. Maria Luiza Marcilio, "The Population of Colonial Brazil," pp. 52-57, and Frederick Bowser, "Africans in Spanish American Colonial Society," pp. 357-75 (Cambridge University Press, 1984). See also Frederick Bowser, *The African Slave in Colonial Peru: 1524-1650* (Stanford: Stanford University Press, 1974), pp. 26-50.

[10] Jane Landers, "Gracia Real de Santa Teresa de Mose: A Free Black Town in Spanish Colonial Florida," *The American Historical Review* 95 (1990): 19-20. In her doctoral dissertation, "Black Society in Spanish St. Augustine, 1784-1821" (University Microfilms International, 1988), Landers describes the rich and varied layers of society in Florida during this period.

[11] John K. Thornton, "African Dimensions of the Stono Rebellion," *The American Historical Review* 96 (1991): 1101-13. Peter H. Wood, *Black Majority: Negroes in Colonial South Carolina from 1670 throughout the Stono Rebellion* (New York: W.W. Norton and Co., 1974), pp. 314-23.

[12] Cyprian Davis, *The History of Black Catholics in the United States* (New York: Crossroad, 1990), pp. 33-34. See also Jack Forbes, "Black Pioneers: The Spanish-Speaking Afroamericans of the Southwest," *Phylon* 27 (1966): 233-46. Forbes lists Esteban or Estevanico, the black guide of Fray Marcos de Niza on his famous expedition to the seven cities of gold, as a Muslim. He does not support the assertion. It would be unlikely that a Muslim would have a Christian name. It is more probable that he was Catholic as were practically all of the Spanish-speaking Blacks.

[13] "To Leonardo Antonelli," in *The John Carroll Papers*, vol. 1, ed. Thomas Hanley (Notre Dame, Ind.: University of Notre Dame Press, 1976), pp. 179-254.

[14] "Bishop Elder on the Apostolate to the Negro Slaves in Mississippi, 1858," *Documents of American Catholic History*, ed. John Tracy Ellis (Wilmington, Del.: Michael Glazier, 1987), pp. 325-29.

[15] Charles Warren Currier, *Carmel in America: A Centennial History of the Discalced Carmelites in the United States*, 200th anniversary ed. (Darien, Ill.: Carmelite Press, 1989 [orig. publ. John Murphy and Co., 1890]), p. 83.

[16] See Emmett Curran, "'Splendid Poverty': Jesuit Slaveholding in Maryland, 1805-1838," *Catholics in the Old South: Essays on Church and Culture*, ed. Randall M. Miller and Jon L. Wakelyn (Macon, Ga.: Mercer University Press, 1983), pp. 125-46.

[17] Stephen Theodore Badin was the first priest ordained in the United States and was the pioneer missionary priest in what is now the Middle West.

[18] Pierre Gibault was a French Canadian pioneer missionary in the Louisiana territory.

[19] "Gregory XVI: *In Supremo*, December 3, 1839," trans. and ed. Joel S. Panzer, in *The Popes and Slavery* (New York: Alba House, 1996), pp. 97-102.

[20] *The Works of the Right Rev. John England*, 5 vols. (Baltimore: John Murphy, 1849), vol. 3, pp. 106-91. Davis, *Black Catholics*, pp. 46-48.

[21] Maria Caravaglios, "A Roman Critique of the Pro-Slavery Views of Bishop Martin of Natchitoches, Louisiana," in *Records of the American Catholic Historical Society of Philadelphia* 83 (1972): 71.

[22] Ibid., p. 70.

[23] "Records of Confraternities," SAB, RG 1, Box 17, Sulpician Archives, Baltimore, Maryland.

[24] Demetrius Gallitzen (1770-1840) was the son of a Russian prince and became the first priest to study as a seminarian in the United States. He was ordained in 1795.

[25] RG 42, Box 2, Sulpician Archives, Baltimore.

[26] Grace Sherwood, *The Oblates' Hundred and One Years* (New York: The Macmillan Company, 1931), p. 65.

[27] Ibid., pp. 122-23. At present there seems to be no way in which one can distinguish between the three Societies of the Holy Family. It may be that the Society of the Holy Family that had Hickey as its director could have eventually joined with the group established by Anwander. This might very well have been the one that had members present at the centenary celebration of 1831.

[28] *The Metropolitan Catholic Almanac and Laity's Directory, for the Year of Our Lord 1839* (Baltimore: Published by Fielding Lucas Jr., 1839), p. 98.

[29] Ibid., 1843, p. 66. The Tobias Society is mentioned very briefly this time, and two mutual relief societies are briefly added in the following entry.

[30] See Steven J. Ochs, "A Patriot, a Priest and a Prelate: Black Catholic Activism in Civil-War New Orleans," *U.S. Catholic Historian* 12 (1994): 58.

[31] See Sherwood, *The Oblates*, pp. 8-31. Also see Sister M. Reginald Gerdes, O.S.P., "To Educate and Evangelize: Black Catholic Schools of the Oblate Sisters of Providence (1828-1880)," *U.S. Catholic Historian* 7 (1988): 183-99.

[32] Margaret Gannon, I.H.M., ed., *Paths of Daring Deeds of Hope: Letters by and about Mother Theresa Maxis Duchemin* (Scranton, Penn.: Congregation of the Sisters, Servants of the Immaculate Heart of Mary, 1992).

[33] *Catholic Almanac*, pp. 94-95.

[34] Sister Mary Francis Borgia Hart, S.S.F., *Violets in the King's Garden: A History of the Sisters of the Holy Family of New Orleans* (New Orleans: Sisters of the Holy Family, private printing, 1976), pp. 13-14.

[35] Stephen Ochs, *Desegregating the Altar: The Josephites and the Struggle for Black Priests, 1871-1960* (Baton Rouge: Louisiana State University Press, 1990), pp. 29-31.

[36] For information on the Healy brothers, see Albert Foley, *Bishop Healy, Beloved Outcaste: The Story of a Great Man Whose Life Has Become a Living Legend* (New York: Farrar, Straus, 1954) and *Dream of an Outcaste: Patrick F. Healy. The Story of the Slave-Born Georgian* (Tuscaloosa, Ala.: Portals Press, 1989). Also see Davis, *The History of Black Catholics*, pp. 146-52.

[37] Consuela Duffy, *Katherine Drexel: A Biography* (Cornwell Heights, Penn.: Mother Katherine Drexel Guild, 1966).

[38] Letter of Augustus Tolton to Katherine Drexel. June 1891. Archives of the Sisters of the Blessed Sacrament, Cornwell Heights, Pennsylvania. The passage has been slightly corrected.

[39] See Sister Caroline Hemesath, *From Slave to Priest: A Biography of the Rev. Augustine Tolton (1854-97), First Afro-American Priest of the United States* (Chicago: Franciscan Herald Press, 1973).

[40] Ochs, *Desegregating the Altar*, pp. 81-82.

[41] Stephen Ochs, "The Ordeal of the Black Priest," *U.S. Catholic Historian* 5 (1986): 45-66.

[42] Ibid., pp. 164-74.

[43] See Ochs, *Desegregating the Altar*, p. 456; and Albert Foley, *God's Men of Color: The Colored Catholic Priests of the United States, 1854-1954* (New York: Farrar, Straus, 1955.)

[44] Thomas McMillan, "With Readers and Correspondents," *The Catholic World* 47 (1888): 711-13.

[45] *Three Catholic Afro-American Congresses* (Cincinnati: American Catholic Tribune, 1893; reprint New York: Arno Press, 1978). Thomas Spalding, "The Negro Catholic Congresses, 1889-1894," *Catholic Historical Review* 55 (1969): 337-57. Joseph Lackner, "Daniel Rudd, Editor of the *American Catholic Tribune*, from Bardstown to Cincinnati," *Catholic Historical Review* 80 (1994): 258-81.

[46] Cyprian Davis, "Two Sides of a Coin: The Black Presence in the History of the Catholic Church in America," *Many Rains Ago: A Historical and Theological Reflection on the Role of the Episcopate in the Evangelization of African American Catholics* (Washington, D.C.: Secretariat for Black Catholics, National Conference of Catholic Bishops, 1990), pp. 57-58.

[47] Ibid., p. 58.

[48] For information regarding the relationship of Turner, Markoe, and LaFarge, see Marilyn Nickels, *Black Catholic Protest and the Federated Colored Catholics, 1917-1933: Three Perspectives on Racial Justice,* The Heritage of American Catholicism (New York: Garland Publishing, 1988). For LaFarge and the interracial apostolate, see Martin Zielinski, "Working for Interracial Justice: The Catholic Interracial Council of New York,

1934-1964," *U.S. Catholic Historian* 7 (1988): 233-60; and David Southern, *John LaFarge and the Limits of Catholic Interracialism, 1911-1963* (Baton Rouge: Louisiana State University Press, 1996).

[49] "The American Catholic Bishops and Racism, November 14, 1958," in Ellis, *Documents*, 2:646-52.

[50] Joseph M. Davis, S.M., and Cyprian Rowe, F.M.S., "The Development of the National Office for Black Catholics," *U.S. Catholic Historian* 7 (1988): 265-89.

[51] "Brothers and Sisters to Us," U.S. Bishops' Pastoral Letter on Racism in Our Day (Washington, D.C.: United States Catholic Conference, 1979), p. 9.

[52] "What We Have Seen and Heard," A Pastoral Letter on Evangelization from the Black Bishops of the United States (Cincinnati, Ohio: St. Anthony Messenger Press, 1984), pp. 2, 17.

PART II

ASPECTS OF BLACK CATHOLIC THEOLOGY

2

Through the Eyes of Faith

The Seventh Principle of the Nguzo Saba *and the Beatitudes of Matthew*

DIANA L. HAYES

In 1619, almost 380 years ago, a small group of African men and women set foot on the eastern shores of what is now the United States. They were not the first, nor would they be the last Africans to come to this land. They came, not as slaves, but as indentured servants; they eventually earned their freedom and were able to buy land and acquire wealth like all others around them.

Before them, around 1536, came Estevanico, who accompanied the Spanish conquistador Cabeza de Vaca in his exploration of the Southwest.[1] It is asserted that before him there were others, and certainly after him came countless other Spanish- and French-speaking Blacks to the lands now known as Florida and Louisiana. Many of them were free; others were indentured servants, like those who arrived in Jamestown, Virginia, in 1619. Many others, however, especially those nameless hundreds of thousands who were brought over in the next two hundred plus years came against their will, as slaves. They were people allowed no right to their own lives, or the lives of their children, or any claim to their own destinies. But they retained one thing that enabled them to survive: the freedom of their souls and their faith in a power higher than themselves and higher than those who enslaved them. It was this freedom and strength of spirit that gave them the capacity to withstand all that was to come.

A PARADIGM SHIFT

The early years of the colonizing of what is now the United States caused a paradigm shift in time, in understanding, and in history, resulting in centuries of lies, distortion, deceit, and misleading education perpetrated and perpetuated by one people against another, with Sacred Scripture usually brought in solely as an afterthought.

Slavery, as it emerged in the Americas, caused a dramatic shift in human history. It marked the coming together of a "Christian and civilized" people as a dominant and destructive force over against a "pagan and uncivilized" people as their subjects. It thereby marked the end of an era in which all people—regardless of color, class, or economic status—were accorded certain rights and responsibilities, in keeping with their humanity. It forecast the beginning of a new and horrific era in which skin color became the mark by which one was granted rights and privileges or no rights at all, and all for the purpose of cheap labor. Yet this era also signaled the emergence of a new people, African Americans, with an ancestry rooted in their African homeland but a destiny that was to become intertwined with that of a new nation, the United States of America.

The Sermon on the Mount, as related in Matthew 5:1-12, also marks the end of one era and the beginning of another. Jesus' words proclaimed the end of Jewish-Greco-Roman history and the beginning of a new history, Christian history. It was a shift from the Mosaic law of the Old Testament to the new law of Jesus Christ. It was a dramatic shift in understanding from a law mandating "an eye for an eye and a tooth for a tooth" to the calling down of God's healing grace upon those who suffered trials and tribulations for the sake of the Kingdom of God—the righteous ones of God.

The Beatitudes are paradoxical in their message; they are subversive, even revolutionary, for they contradict all that had once been acceptable. Some interpret Matthew as "spiritualizing" the bolder proclamations that Luke sets forth in his presentation of the same Sermon on the Mount. Where Luke proclaims straightforwardly, "Blessed are the poor," Matthew seems to murmur, "Blessed are the poor in spirit." Where Luke announces, "Blessed are you that hunger *now*," Matthew suggests, "Blessed are those who hunger and thirst for *righteousness*." Yet, both are reporting the words and can be said to be revealing the meaning of Jesus accurately. But each had his own audience to whom he was speaking.

Luke was addressing a Gentile audience of non-Christians, seeking to emphasize Jesus' words to the poor gathered on the plains before him. Those poor were the Jews, a persecuted, oppressed people who were forbidden nationhood, forbidden the free worship of their God, forbidden even personhood, in many ways, much as Black Americans have been persecuted and oppressed in the United States for so long a time.

Matthew, however, is speaking to Jewish-Christians, those who have already begun their journey of faith in Christ. His audience is predominantly poor, many of them slaves or former slaves, and he is calling upon them to realize that Jesus' words apply equally to them now just as they did when Jesus first spoke them. His spiritualizing of the message is an attempt to help them to understand that it is not only their material status that is of significance but also their internal attitude. He is calling them to reconceptualize their very way of life as they live out their faith in the world. For as poor, oppressed, and marginalized as the early Christians are, they are in the unique position of having the freedom to see clearly what is good, what is just, what is righteous before God, because they have *no* vested interest in the outcome. They are already martyrs; they are already poor and despised; what more can they suffer for the sake of the Kingdom?

Thus, Matthew is not speaking to those who, although materially rich, are somehow lacking in spirituality, although that is too often how he is read today to the comfort and solace of many. Nor is he speaking about those who, though wealthy, are in some way spiritually detached from their wealth. We know this because of Jesus' other teachings, which state bluntly that you cannot serve both God and wealth (Mt 6:24) and that it is easier for a camel to slip through the eye of a needle than for the rich to enter the Kingdom of God (Mt 19:24).

Matthew is calling upon *all* Christians to live the life God has called them to live, one radically different, even paradoxical in nature, because it goes against all that had been understood (or perhaps misunderstood) as living the good life. Matthew is calling *us* to understand that Jesus' message in the Beatitudes and throughout the gospel sets the basis for a revolutionary change in which the materially poor of this world, and those who make a preferential option toward them, are promised the grace of God not only in the next world but, even more important, in this world as well.

FAITH AND THE *NGUZO SABA*

The principles of the *Nguzo Saba* provide an excellent lens through which the faith of African American Catholics and the teachings of Jesus Christ can be interpreted. These seven principles were developed in the late 1960s by Ron Karenga as a means to help African Americans become reacquainted with their African heritage and also to learn and to affirm what is needed for the health and survival of the Black community. The principles, both singly and as a group, have become a central focus for African Americans seeking to renew their faith and spirituality.[2]

THE *NGUZO SABA*—THE POWER WITHIN

Umoja—Unity
 Unity means to come together, to work and to struggle together.

Kujichagulia—Self-Determination
 Self-determination means to name ourselves. We as African people define ourselves, being what we say we are, and we express ourselves. When we do, whatever we do, we know what we are doing.

Ujima—Collective Work and Responsibility
 To *collect* means to gather together many things or people in one group. To *work* means to expend energy and get something done. *Responsibility* means to take care of, to maintain, and to be accountable for.

Ujamma—Familyhood and Cooperative Economics
 Familyhood means to extend to all our people the respect and co-operation due brothers and sisters. *Cooperative* means to work together in peace and harmony. *Economics* is the ownership, production, distribution, and consumption of goods and services. *Cooperative economics* is the establishment and ownership of businesses on a one-member one-vote basis, with limited dividends on investments and patronage return.

Nia—Purpose
 Our *purpose* is to work together and to struggle together for the unification, liberation, and independence of all people of African descent by gaining, maintaining, and using power.

Kuumba—Creativity

Creativity enables us to do always as much as we can in the way we can, in order to leave our community more beautiful and beneficial than we inherited it.

Imani—Faith

Faith means to believe in something with all our hearts. We believe in African people and the *Nguzo Saba. We believe that we can and must do the impossible,* that is, to unify, liberate, and free all people of African descent, especially those where we live.

In this chapter I will concentrate on the seventh principle, *Imani/* Faith, with the understanding that, as with the African world view, all of the principles are united, thereby bringing about a wholeness that is life-giving and life-sustaining.

To have faith means to believe in something or someone unseen and usually unverifiable by human means. Faith is a gift from God, freely given as a grace that both sustains and nurtures one, not something to be sought after or achieved.

African Americans are and have always been a faith-filled and faithful people. To paraphrase Zora Neale Hurston, our eyes have always been watching God, attempting to discern God's working in and throughout our lives. We have been put to the test many times, but our faith in a God unlike any other, a God who is a "way maker" and "obstacle breaker" has enabled us to be steadfast in our journeying. We recognize that God has promised us eternal salvation if we but keep the faith, and our God has *not* failed us yet.

Thus, our faith exemplifies that paradoxical faith, that subversive faith, which Jesus himself lived so long ago. It is a faith that refuses to acknowledge the so-called limitations placed on African Americans and their personhood by those who don't know us or care to understand us. Ours is a faith that shatters all of reality, that shatters all of time, because it goes beyond this world to find its home in the next.

This does not mean, however, that this faith is simply a "pie in the sky when you die" ideology, although that temptation is constantly present and, at times, may even be necessary for self-preservation. Gayraud Wilmore speaks of Black faith manifesting itself historically in terms of a dialectical tension between what he calls the Black religion of the institutional church, which tends toward a more passive, at times, ethereal mode of being in the world, and Black radicalism, our lived-out faith in the world, an active, ever revolutionary proclamation of the gospel truths.[3] That tension is alive, constantly in flux, shifting according to the unconscious and sometimes conscious needs of the time, pushing forward then retreating, biding its time as it seeks to conserve, maintain, and set forth the truth of Black being and the needs of the Black community.

Marable Manning also speaks of this tension, this constant balancing act, which runs like an elastic cord through the lives of all Black folk from throughout the African Diaspora.[4] He notes: "The Black conception of God is alternately and simultaneously a distant heavenly representation of an ultimate spiritual redemption and a creative symbol of emancipation in the present."[5]

This tension, often revealed as a "double consciousness," is clearly depicted in the spirituals and slave narratives. These oral articulations of Black faith and an emergent Black theology originate in African religious traditions. These traditions were then meshed with Christian doctrine as seen through the sharply focused lens of the Black historical experience in the United States rather than the distorted teachings of Euro-American Christendom.

For African American Catholics, in particular, this faith required, at times, that they go to Mass on Sunday mornings and to "church" (usually a Protestant service at a relative's church) in the afternoon in order to be not only fed by the Body of Christ but also inspired by the Word of God exuberantly proclaimed and sung.

FAITH AND THE HOLY SPIRIT DURING SLAVERY

God's grace came to African slaves in and through the Holy Spirit, fostering a faith that has withstood the test of time. The Spirit of God nurtured and guided us through the ordeals of slavery and the torments of Jim-Crowism and continues to do so today despite constant assaults on every side. The African American understanding of the Spirit is clearly African in its origins, for it is grounded in "an attitude that sees all of life in the context of the encounter with the Divine, and the all-embracing vision of the Divine-human encounter."[6]

The source of this understanding, as briefly mentioned above, is the African world view, with its marks of (a) belief in a Supreme Being; (b) belief in the ancestors; (c) belief in spirits and powers; and (d) belief in the fullness of the present life and its foundation in the community formed by those who suffer and struggle with them for justice and righteousness.[7] We do not know how many of the Africans brought to this country were already Christian and probably Catholic, having been converted with the first invasion of Portuguese and Spanish Catholic explorers in the fifteenth century. What is known, however, is that Catholicism was particularly attractive to the Africans' inclusive understanding of religion. They found much in Catholicism that was reminiscent of their traditional faith, and they were open to its ritualized formality and the symbolism of statues, incense, holy water, fast days and feast days, and other aspects of the faith.[8]

Coming to this strange new world did not destroy either our world view or our sense of community. Our slave ancestors adapted, for the most part, to their new situations by re-creating community among all who were oppressed because of their African ancestry or origins, regardless of tribe or language. They also refused to accept the lie of the distorted Christianity being taught them. As can be seen in their own stories, prayers, and songs, they were able to do for themselves what their "Christian" teachers did not do for them: discern the kernel of truth in Jesus' message that God was a God for all and that all that God had created was good, including the African people. The narratives of slave conversion experiences confirm this goodness within in ways that dramatically contrast their physical state of enslavement with their spiritual breaking of the chains that bind them.[9]

For the slaves, to be converted meant "getting religion," being "slain in the Spirit," being "struck dead" by the hand of God and revived as a new being. It was usually a physical rather than a passive act, leading them to shout, speak of visions of God, heaven, or freedom; and engage in often frenzied behavior that "manifested the Holy Spirit's presence in their midst."[10]

They believed that one's true (rather than slave) identity was revealed through conversion, the revelation that one was a child of God, a human being, one of the redeemed of God, and that it was and still is today the Spirit of the Lord Jesus Christ who showed them the path to that new identity. George Cummings notes:

The Spirit's presence . . . entailed the affirmation of independence and selfhood; sustained hope for freedom as embodied in their prayer life; served as the basis of love within the slave community; and even assisted slaves in their desire to escape to freedom. The Spirit's sustaining power/presence was nurtured in the secret meetings where black slaves disobeyed their masters' orders to serve God, sustained their sense of personal identity and well-being, and provided mutual support for each other by giving meaning and hope to their tragic existence.[11]

Sarah Rhodes, a former slave, speaks of those "hush-arbor" meetings in this way:

We used to steal off to de woods and have church, like de Spirit moved us—sing and pray to our own liking and soul satisfaction—and we sure did have good meetings, honey—baptize in de river like God said. We had dem spirit-filled meetings at night on de bank of de river and God met us there.[12]

Theirs was a defiant faith, born of the Spirit, which moved them to disobey their masters in order to obey their God, a God who they knew had created them as free men and women in God's own image. This Spirit-grounded faith enabled them to flee plantations, plot and carry out escapes and rebellions, and silently but obstinately refuse to participate in their own dehumanization, often to the consternation and fear of their masters.

The slave narratives also reveal an eschatological hope reflective of "a connection between the presence of the Spirit of God and the hopes and aspirations of the slave community."[13] Theirs was a hope born of their burning desire for freedom and their determination to one day be free. It was an eschatological hope born of the Spirit's movement within them, and its sustaining and nurturing presence in every aspect of their lives was exemplified in their steadfast and persistent faith in a God who saves, a God who liberates. Theirs was the faith of those who hunger and thirst for righteousness; who know their reward will be great (Mt 5:6).

The slaves, our ancestors, looked forward to a reversal of the status quo, a shift in time and situation for them and for those who oppressed them, expressed in the belief that "everybody talking about heaven ain't going there." They knew that the future was promised them if they but kept the faith (Mt 5:3), and this gave them the ability to stay strong, knowing that it was not a future "way off somewhere." It was at one and the same time here but not yet in its fullness; the "eschaton was not an opiate; . . . the 'home over yonder' and the 'promised land' they sang of in the spirituals were for the slaves both an 'otherworldly' promise and a 'this worldly' hope for freedom"[14] (Mt 5:10-11).

THE SPIRITUALS AND BLACK FAITH

The spirituals spoke of a future freedom to come in heaven, but one that could also be achieved by their actions in escaping to the North and to Canada and in fighting against their oppressed status. So they sang of Canaan and ran away to Canada. The spirituals are the voice of the Spirit of God expressed in the words of an illiterate yet faith-filled people. They sang "Steal Away to Jesus" while they stole away North, and "Wade in the Water" while they walked across the Ohio, the Delaware, and the Mississippi Rivers. The masters and overseers may have been fooled, but the slaves were not. They knew and believed in the freedom that they were singing about, and they acted accordingly.

James Cone sees the spirituals as

God himself breaking into the lives of the people, buildin' them up where they were torn and proppin' them up on every leanin' side. The Spirit was God's presence in the people and his will to provide them the courage and the strength to make it through.[15]

They could, therefore, sing in affirmation of that presence that "everytime I feel the Spirit moving in my heart, I will pray." For it *was* a feeling, a feeling reflected in rhythm, in song, and in a lived-out, active faith. "This song invites the believer to move closer to the very sources of black being and to experience the black community's power to endure and the will to survive."[16]

All the believer has to do is to respond to the divine apocalyptic disclosure of God's revelation and cry, "Have mercy, please." This cry is not a cry of passivity, but a faithful, free response to the movement of the Black Spirit. It is the black community accepting themselves as the people of the Black Spirit and knowing through his presence that no chains can hold the Spirit of black humanity in bondage.[17]

Cone concludes that "the spiritual, then, is the Spirit of the people struggling to be free."[18] He continues:

Black history then is the stuff out of which the black spirituals were created. But the "stuff" of black history includes more
than the bare historical facts of slavery. Black history is an
experience, a soulful event. And to understand it is to know
the being of a people who had to "feel their way along the
course of American slavery," enduring the stresses and strains
of human servitude but not without a song. *Black history is a
spiritual.*[19]

Black history is the sung memory of a hope sustained against all
odds for a freedom that *will come*, in God's own time and their own.
This eschatological hope, this undying faith in a liberating God and
their acting upon it, had the effect of transforming them not just
spiritually but even in physical ways. As Harriet Tubman noted:

I looked at my hands to see if I was de same person now I was
free. Dere was such a glory ober de fields and I felt like I was in
heaven.[20]

This experience was also portrayed in song, "I looked at my hands
and they looked new; I looked at my feet and they were too."

This experience of the working of the Spirit continues to be a part
of Black America's understanding of how God acts in its history. It
calls forth "a spirituality that is not the classic *imitati Christi*, but is
rather the *participati Christi*, through performance, drama, emotion,
and ritual.[21]

This faith arose out of a community of believers, a people who
knew that together they could withstand all things, who recognized
that alone they had no identity but that in community they were
indeed somebody to be reckoned with. It is a faith that persists to
this day and is being reclaimed by Black Catholic Christians, who, in
attempting to affirm their Catholicity, were too often forced to deny
their Blackness. We are reclaiming our Black past today, recognizing the critical role it plays in our self-identity and self-consciousness.
In so doing, we are liberating both ourselves and our Catholic faith
in the truest sense of liberation theology, freeing ourselves of the
artificial restraints and restrictions placed upon our expression of
faith and freeing our church from a false sense of universality that
has been imposed upon all Catholics.

Through our faith in a God who loves, saves, and liberates, we as
African American Catholics have been given the courage and the

ability to believe in and to *do* the impossible. Against all odds, against the persistent efforts of those who sought and continue to seek to dehumanize, demonize, and destroy us, both body and soul, we have survived, and, in company with our Black brothers and sisters of every faith, we continue to *survive*. But in so doing, we have been able to do even more, by giving new meaning to the liberating message of Jesus Christ.

A FAITH OF PASSION

Christianity is a passionate religion; it is truly a slave religion, not in the ways understood by those who urge all Blacks to move away from it into other more "suitably black" faiths, but in its original and most radical sense. For in its beginnings Christianity was a religion predominantly of slaves, of the outcast, of the despised, of those who mourned the injustice in the world and sought to bring about peace; of those persecuted for righteousness' sake, that is, for being right with God as the prophets define such righteousness, hating evil and loving good, taking care of the widowed and orphaned, seeking the empowerment of all, demanding justice in God's name.

This passion, however, has been lived out differently in this country by those oppressing and by those oppressed. Manning speaks of two Christianities, one white and one black, recognizing that practitioners of the former may also be people of color and that those of the latter may be Euro-Americans. He states:

> The passion of white Christianity transfers critical thought to an idealist or supernatural plane, removing individual Christians from making moral decisions within the secular world, allowing the "sadistic extermination of the weak" to continue. The purpose of white Christianity as a popular philosophy, therefore, is not to change the world, but to offer the prejudices and emotions of those who dwell within the world to tolerate their real conditions. . . . White Christianity is limited to the realm of the pulpit and the pews; it would not nor could not take an aggressive stand on secular issues, such as human rights of Blacks, Indians, or other ethnic minorities. . . . White racism became a faith in which millions subconsciously or willingly shared, because the orthodox religious institutions took *no positions* in favor of Black humanity.[22]

Although many have become aware of the truths to be found in this statement, others are still unaware of this failure of faith on the part of the institutional Catholic church. Further research and writing are needed to counter the many compilations on the social teachings of the Catholic church that discuss the church's stance on issues of abortion, economics, peace, justice, and even sexuality and gender, while remaining silent on issues of racial and ethnic hatred, prejudice, and discrimination, which continue to plague this land and which still form the bases for too many social, political, economic, and even ecclesial decisions.[23]

Black Christianity, on the other hand, in its more radical manifestation calls forth a vision of faith that, rather than providing an "intellectual shield through which the oppressive essence of . . . economic and political systems are made virtually invisible,"[24] points instead toward a higher vision for all humanity. It points toward that vision proclaimed by Jesus himself in the Beatitudes: to be peacemakers, to hunger and thirst for righteousness, to mourn injustice, to be merciful to those less fortunate, to stand up for what is right in the face of persecution and prejudice (Mt 5:1-12).

BLACK FAITH AND BLACK CATHOLIC THEOLOGY

This radical consciousness is "the consciousness of oppression, a cultural search for self-affirmation and authenticity," which is, Manning continues, "the impetus toward political activism and the use of religious rhetoric to promote the destruction of the white status quo."[25] It calls forth a response that is community based and grounded, the essence of *Imani* as it has been and must once again be lived out in the Black Catholic community.

This consciousness is the Black historical experience from which all expressions of Black theology, whether Protestant or Catholic, male or womanist, flow. Such a theology liberates not only African Americans but *all* who are oppressed from the shackles of a false theology that holds humanity in thrall to race hatred and prejudice. It is also liberating in that it frees us to become true members of the beloved community of Jesus Christ, true neighbors to each other, loving God and one another as equals.

Just as Black theology is a recognition that Black faith and Black power are not opposites but work hand in hand to rebuild family and community in the here and now, so too Black Catholics in their theologizing are realizing that they too must reach back into the depths of their lost history in order to reforge the tools needed to rebuild their families and communities. Our theology is a recognition of the truth of Black Catholic existence in this country today, which requires, if we are to continue to survive as a people and as a church, that we must all learn, regardless of our race or ethnicity, to speak the *truth* to the people: the truth of Black Catholic history, which predates that of almost all now present in the church, the truth of Black Catholic lives and contributions not just to our church but to this country's status in the world. We must speak the truth, acknowledging that the laity are themselves capable of choosing the good, for they have done so in the past, and are capable of doing what is right for themselves today *as* a people. It is an affirmation that the People of God are a Black and beautiful people who truly model this empowering understanding of church. To speak the truth calls for a recognition that "our [young] people will not be frightened into heaven out of fear of burning in hell. . . . [They are] not looking for saviors but for solutions. They are not looking so much for princes of peace as they are for pioneers in protest."[26]

Thus, the time has come not so much to return to the early church but to update that church and bring its vision of a beloved community to renewed life today. We must see in Jesus' words a message not just of hope but of a radical and revolutionary praxis that announced the tearing down of the religious, social, and political status quo of his day and its replacement with a new world of justice, righteousness, and empowerment of the lowest of the low. We must revive our Catholic faith by recognizing and affirming it in all of its richness and diversity. It is necessary to align ourselves on the side of those who suffer, not for their faith or lack thereof, but for their skin color, poverty, and gender.

The time has come to recognize that Black faith is indeed by itself the real Christianity, for it is, in its revolutionary, radically liberating form, the true bearer of the gospel, the good news, of Jesus Christ. This means that in the Roman Catholic Church we must all become ontologically Black, in our very being, in our innermost selves. We must rid ourselves of the alienating, dualistic understandings of faith, life, and humanity that emerged from the church's cooption by the Roman state, which resulted in a Christendom that allowed, if not encouraged, the slave trade and the destruction of peoples, and that has kept us divided in our very selves within the church. Rather, we must align ourselves with the revolutionary faith of African peoples, the faith called forth by Jesus Christ, himself a product of the Afro-Asiatic world of the Middle East of his time; recognizing that the church catholic is not only multicolored but multicultural. It is in Jesus that Blacks see the validation of their humanity; Jesus is, therefore, Black, because we, as the oppressed, are Black, and Jesus abides with us. As James Cone has affirmed, it is because the Black community is an oppressed community, because and only because of its blackness, that the christological importance of Jesus Christ is found in blackness.[27] As Jesus is Black so must the church become Black, recognizing that in blackness lies the profound response of God to God's people, a response, a preferential option, which has been manifest throughout human history. To say that we must all become Black, then, means taking up the cross of Black Christianity, the cross of Black faith, a faith rooted in trials and tribulations.

> Faith is, *after all*, reliance upon the trustworthiness of God to support us and do well by us. Faith is trust in God, openness to his world and what he is doing in it. It is the willingness to align ourselves with him and participate in his liberating work.[28]

African American Catholics maintain that faith today. The liberating work of God is taking place in our very midst. It is not an easy task, but one fraught with peril, one which will cause people, as Matthew notes and Jesus prophesied, "to revile you and persecute you and utter all kinds of evil against you falsely, on my account" (Mt 5:11).

BLACK FAITH, THE BLACK COMMUNITY, AND THE BLACK CHURCH TODAY[29]

We are living in very difficult times. There are few better witnesses to that fact in the United States than African Americans. We see the evil that exists because we come into daily contact with it— in our streets, in our schools, in our work places, and even in our churches. As a result, we *know* God and how God works from experience. We know the temptations that are present in life, for we deal with them on a daily basis—the lures of drugs, sex, materialism, consumerism, individualism.

We name ourselves both Black and Catholic, and we are raising challenging questions for our church today, questions that emerge from that deeply held faith we have maintained for so long. The response that we—and all who are marginalized and victimized—need to hear from the church today is where it stands in the struggle, on the side of the oppressor or that of the oppressed? There can be no middle ground. We seek to know whether and how the church understands what it means to be Black in this land and in the church; whether and how the church knows what it means to be marginalized, invisible, ostracized, ignored, victimized, heavy-laden, over-burdened, and tired. Jesus knew what it was like, for he was one of us. Jesus knew what it was like, and he called for a change, a revolutionary change, and he was killed for doing so. Jesus was lynched, hanged on a tree, like so many African Americans down through the years. Today the lynchings have ceased, at least the physical ones, but psychologically they continue. How does our church respond?

This is why the Sermon on the Mount, especially the Beatitudes, fits so well with the *Nguzo Saba*. Jesus knew the importance of community; he had one, women and men who walked with him all the way to Calvary. Jesus knew the importance of faith, hope, and love, and he shared them with all he came into contact with. No persons were spurned because of the work they did, or the amount of money they had, or the clothes they wore, or the illnesses they suffered from, or the language they spoke, or the color of their skin, not even because they were male or female. He cherished them all. Jesus knew how hard it was to be poor, for he was poor; to thirst after justice, for he did, and he died still thirsting; to mourn the loss of loved ones, for he brought Lazarus back to life. *Jesus knew,* but does our church?

CONTINUING OUR PILGRIM JOURNEY

Today, Black Catholics have come of age. We see ourselves as the People of God, whom the Second Vatican Council proclaimed. We acknowledge our call to ministry, which evolves from our baptism, as a true call to serve not just our own but all who are in need. The challenge before us, as the People of God, is to affirm the tasks that we, as Catholic faithful, must be about today. These tasks arise out of our understanding of theology as "God-talk," which both liberates and is liberating, and our understanding of the Sermon on the Mount as it is interpreted in and through the Black lens of the *Nguzo Saba*.

What is it that our faith, affirmed in this way, calls us to do? First, we must all reflect critically on our church and the People of God who are its living manifestation, as well as on the society in which our church is located. Are we living up to Christ's liberating message of salvation promised to all God's people? Or are we preaching a message that divides and frustrates, angers and isolates, one that denies the reality of sin within our very midst? As Martin Luther King Jr. noted in *Letter from Birmingham Jail:*

> I have watched so many churches commit themselves to a completely other worldly religion which made a strange distinction between body and soul, the sacred and the secular.
>
> So here we are moving toward the exit of the twentieth century with a religious community largely adjusted to the status quo, standing as a taillight behind other community agencies rather than a headlight leading men to higher levels of justice.[30]

Are we, as church, as Christians, now in the waning years of the twentieth century, still guilty of this? How do we transform ourselves? How do we live out our faith, a radically Black faith, in today's world?

Second, what is the praxis of our church and the People of God? Are we living as though we truly believe the Beatitudes, the gospel message of Christ, or are we simply giving it lip service? How do we live out our radical Black faith in a world that seems to be totally preoccupied with material wealth and a culture of death?

These tasks of reflection and praxis can only be done from within the context of a lived out, actualized, forged in the fire, faith. Faith *(Imani),* the faith of Jesus, the faith of our ancestors, must be the foundation for both the critical reflection and the praxis that grows out of that reflection and is then in turn critiqued and reflected upon itself. It is an unending spiral of faith that comes from God and returns to God as a constant and ongoing lived-out prayer of the Spirit.

> What good is it, my brothers and sisters, if you say you have faith but do not have works? . . . So faith by itself, if it has no works, is dead (Jas 2:14, 17).

Faith without works, without action grounded in that faith, is like a house built on sand, quickly washed away in times of crisis. Works without faith, done merely for self-aggrandizement, are of temporary value, like a granary full of wheat that is quickly burned down and lost. But faith *with* works, praxis in the light of one's faith, constantly reflected upon and critiqued, both positively and negatively, can truly move mountains. It is God's grace that grants us faith, but it is our response that brings that faith to life fully in the communities in which we live out our lives.

We as African American Catholics have understood this, for we have spent our lives having to move mountains in order not just to survive but also to move on up a little higher. It is our faith in God, our commitment to the liberating message of Jesus within us, that has brought us this far, and it is that same Black faith that will continue to carry us on. We have acknowledged our faith in many ways, but the most telling for me is verbalized in yet another spiritual: "We've come *this far* by faith. *Leaning* on the Lord. *Trusting* in his Holy Word. He's never failed me yet."

This is our faith as African American Christians. This is the faith that we as Black Catholics have kept as a smoldering coal deep within our bosoms, one now free to burst forth fully enflamed, fully passionate, as we claim our rightful place as Black and Catholic.

This is *Imani,* the faith in our ability, as a people of God, to "unify, liberate, and free all people of African descent" and, in so doing, to free all of humanity from its bondage, regardless of race. It is fitting because we are all of humanity; our Mother Africa is the source of all life.

We have mourned, but now we are comforted. We have been meek, but now we claim our rightful inheritance. We have hungered and thirsted for righteousness and now we are being filled. Today we rejoice and are glad, for God has promised us the victory. And we know, through faith, that in God's time, that victory will come.

NOTES

[1] Estevanico (or Esteban) was an Arabian black from Morocco, a Spanish-speaking slave, the first of many Black Catholics in the Americas. For more, see Cyprian Davis, *The History of Black Catholics in the United States* (New York: Crossroad, 1990), pp. 28-29.

[2] The seven principles are based upon Karenga's understanding of the African world view as holistic and sacred. Each term is in Swahili and is accompanied by an affirming statement that deepens the understanding of the specific principle. Today they are of especial importance in the celebration of Kwanzaa, an African American holiday celebrated between Christmas and New Year and based on an African harvest festival. It is a time of thanksgiving and reaffirmation.

³ See Gayraud S. Wilmore, *Black Religion and Black Radicalism*, 2d ed. (Maryknoll, N.Y.: Orbis Books, 1983), introduction and chap. 9.

⁴ Marable Manning, "Religion and Black Protest Thought in African American History," in *African American Religious Studies: An Interdisciplinary Anthology*, ed. Gayraud S. Wilmore (Durham, N.C.: Duke University Press, 1989), pp. 318-39.

⁵ Ibid., p. 324.

⁶ Jamie Phelps, O.P., "Black Spirituality," in *Spiritual Traditions for the Contemporary Church*, Robin Maas and Gabriel O'Donnell, O.P. (Nashville: Abingdon Press, 1990), pp. 332-51, quotation at p. 332.

⁷ Ibid., p. 335; see also John S. Mbiti, *African Religions and Philosophy* (New York: Doubleday Anchor Books, 1970).

⁸ See Diana L. Hayes, *And Still We Rise: An Introduction to Black Liberation Theology* (Mahwah, N.J.: Paulist Press, 1996), chap. 2, pp. 24-53; see also Davis, *History*.

⁹ See Albert Raboteau, *Slave Religion: The "Invisible Institution" in the Antebellum South* (New York: Oxford University Press, 1978).

¹⁰ George Cummings, "The Slave Narratives as a Source of Black Theological Discourse: The Spirit and Eschatology," in *Cut Loose Your Stammering Tongue: Black Theology in the Slave Narratives,* ed. Dwight Hopkins and George Cummings (Maryknoll, N.Y.: Orbis Books, 1991), p. 48.

¹¹ Ibid., p. 49.

¹² James Mellon, ed., *Bullwhip Days: The Slaves Remember* (New York: Weidenfeld & Nicolson, 1988), pp. 194-95.

¹³ Cummings, "The Slave Narratives," p. 54.

¹⁴ Ibid., p. 58.

¹⁵ James Cone, *The Spirituals and the Blues: An Interpretation* (New York: Crossroad/Seabury Press, 1972), p. 2.

¹⁶ Ibid., p. 5.

¹⁷ Ibid.

¹⁸ Ibid., p. 32.

¹⁹ Ibid., p. 33.

²⁰ Sarah Bradford, *Harriet Tubman: The Moses of Her People* (New York: Corinth Books, 1961), p. 30.

²¹ Robert E. Hood, *Must God Remain Greek?: Afro Cultures and God-Talk* (Minneapolis: Augsburg Fortress, 1990), p. 205.

²² Manning, "Religion and Black Protest," p. 320.

²³ For example, see John Coleman, S.J., ed., *One Hundred Years of Catholic Social Thought: Celebration and Challenge* (Maryknoll, N.Y.: Orbis Books, 1991), which lists sections on the family, work, and peace but has no sections on racism, despite the few but important documents issued by both the bishops of the United States, *Brothers and Sisters to Us* (Washington, D.C.: USCC, 1974), and the Vatican, *The Church and Racism: Towards a More Fraternal Society* (Vatican City: Pontifical Commission

on Justice and Peace, 1988). The only discussion of racism appears in two brief paragraphs in an essay entitled "Family as Domestic Church" (p. 123).

[24] Manning, "Religion and Black Protest," p. 327.

[25] Ibid., pp. 327-28.

[26] Ibid., p. 334

[27] See James Cone, *God of the Oppressed* (New York: Crossroad/Seabury, 1975).

[28] Warner Traynham, *Christian Faith in Black and White* (Wakefield, Mass.: Parameter Press, 1973), p. 23.

[29] When speaking in terms of the church, I am speaking in terms of the Christian churches as a whole and also, as a Catholic myself, of the Roman Catholic Church in particular. The issues and concerns are similar for both Black Catholics and Black Protestants, especially those in predominantly white denominations.

[30] Martin Luther King Jr., quoted in James Melvin Washington, ed., *A Testament of Hope: The Essential Writings of Martin Luther King, Jr.* (San Francisco: Harper & Row, 1986), p. 299.

3

Inculturating Jesus

A Search for Dynamic Images for the Mission of the Church among African Americans

JAMIE T. PHELPS, O.P.

INTRODUCTION

As the United States reaps the whirlwind of its secularization at the end of the twentieth century, it is necessary for theologians to provide new images of the human encounter with the risen Christ, which will deepen the faith of believers and engender new faith for nonbelievers. Three a priori assumptions undergird my research. First, that belief in Jesus Christ can still provide life-engendering hope to Blacks and all peoples who are the victims of oppression within the dominant social and ecclesial institutions of the United States.[1] Second, that belief in Jesus Christ and Christian discipleship can provide a life-engendering way of life for those Blacks who are marginalized and oppressed within the black community and black church in the United States.[2] Third, critically interpreting the good news manifest in the preaching, ministry, and way of life of the earthly Jesus of history provides a model for church mission among the poor and marginalized today.

Using a social-historical approach combined with a method of correlation, I will reference selected findings from sociological, psychological, and popular literature that document the oppressive experiences of African Americans and bring these into dialogue with biblical scholarship[3] and theological interpretations of Jesus. This approach is an anthropocentric one in that it starts "from below."[4] It is employed to keep the focus on humanity—the humanity of the historical Jesus and the historical experience of the human groups whom Jesus encountered and transformed in his ministry of preaching, healing, and building community. Such correlation should expand our understanding of the meaning and significance of Jesus for contemporary African Americans.[5] The goal is to provide new insights, interpretations, and images of the historical or pre-Easter[6] Jesus and his way in order to make faith in Jesus Christ and a life of Christian discipleship a viable and reasonable life-option for African Americans searching for a constructive response to our individual and collective experience of oppression.

By using this approach I do not wish to suggest that belief in Jesus was or is merely a survival tactic, or that Jesus was or is only a charismatic prophet indistinguishable from other such prophets. Jesus' unique identity as God is of primary importance for an understanding of who Jesus is and was, but most African American Catholics and other African American Christians affirm his truly human and truly divine designation without contention. However, the secular nature of our dominant society and the dulling of the religious sense among Blacks, alienated from traditional black socialization or intellectually blinded by embracing the rational extremism of modernity, demand that we be able to give a rational account for our faith. Such a rational accounting can be made without abandoning the eye of faith. Jesus' divinity was not and is not apparent to either believers or nonbelievers. Indeed, only the post-resurrection eye of faith makes the affirmation of the divinity of Jesus possible. However, in an increasingly secular milieu we must be able to explain why and how belief in and the following of Jesus are reasonable. For nonbelievers we must explain why encountering and believing in Jesus are significant for our grappling with the existential questions that confront the African American community. For believers, the approach "from below" deepens the understanding of the call as Christians to participate in a holistic approach to church mission, a mission concerned about the spiritual and social well-being and life of all human beings.

Briefly stated, this chapter explores the meaning of Jesus Christ for African Americans who are struggling with questions of identity and purpose in the complex context of a nation and a church that have exhibited alternating and ambiguous patterns of indifference, hostility, and acceptance toward citizens and members who are black. Secondarily, it will articulate some implications for Catholic church mission as a consequence of this interpretation for black people in the United States.

The biblical witness viewed through a social-psychological lens suggests that the first Christians encountered and responded to Jesus' call to discipleship because he offered them a way of life that affirmed their human dignity and identity. As a social prophet, Jesus' preaching and lifestyle called for the establishment of new patterns of social relationships.[7] He transformed the lives of his followers by proclaiming a new order and way of life.[8] As the earthly Jesus encountered those on the margins of society, he forgave their sins, healed their infirmities, revealed their inner worth to them, gave them hope, and invited them to participate in his mission as his disciples.[9] The Way of Jesus provided an alternative to the patriarchal, economic, and ruling class–peasant divisions characteristic of the society of his time.[10]

THE OPPRESSIVE DYNAMICS THAT AFFECT AFRICAN AMERICAN LIFE

THE EXTERNAL OPPRESSION OF THE BLACK COMMUNITY IN THE UNITED STATES

"Jesus Is the Answer" was a popular gospel hymn during the late sixties and seventies. The refrain stated boldly and with great certitude: "Jesus is the answer for the world today, above him there's no other. Jesus is the way!" *Is* Jesus the answer to the existential questions about identity and purpose arising in the complex social cultural matrix of the black community and black individuals in the United States of America? If he is the answer to the questions that lie at the heart of African Americans' search for meaning, what is the nature of this answer and how is it manifested historically within the context of the oppressive conditions that characterize the milieu in which contemporary African Americans struggle for life? What new patterns of social relationships portend a hopeful future for Black Americans? Jesus' proclamation of the reign of God was central to his mission. Jesus not only proclaimed the reign of God, but he embodied it for the poor, the marginalized, and the oppressed peoples of his day. Those professing to be followers of Jesus and participants in his continuing mission must seek to understand how the reign of God can be proclaimed and embodied for the poor of today, including the poor and marginalized within the black community of the United States.

GENERALIZED SOCIAL-ECONOMIC OPPRESSION

Let me begin by drawing a verbal portrait of life-threatening conditions that give rise to some fundamental questions about the future of black people and the black community that disquiet the minds and hearts of many African Americans. Andrew Billingsley identifies a "cluster of conditions with devastating consequences" that the African American community faces. Black life in America is plagued by poverty, unemployment, stress, marital conflict, domestic violence, divorce, single parenting, teen pregnancy, school failure, high infant mortality, latchkey children, substance abuse, sexually transmitted diseases, including AIDS, other physical illness, mental illness, homicide, suicide, criminal behavior, accidents, and homelessness.[11]

Julius Wilson extends the description by suggesting that the majority of African Americans within the United States are oppressed by an economic poverty conditioned by poor education, unemployment, and social marginalization predicated on racial-ethnic, gender, and class stereotypes. Many African Americans live in socially alienated, segregated, urban communities that isolate them from primary relationships with other American ethnic-racial groups. We are confronted daily with the dynamics of marginalization, hostility, and indifference within dominant cultural, social, and ecclesial institutions. These structural, psychological, and emotional dynamics condition the cross-cultural interactions of African Americans in their ordinary lives of work and play.[12] As a consequence, in most dominant culture institutions the life and well-being of African Americans are treated as auxiliary or ancillary to the well-being of members of the dominant society.

Poor African American men, women, children, and youth living in urban centers are devalued because they are perceived as threatening presences. African American urban neighborhoods are seen by both insiders and outsiders as places of drug-related crime and violence dominated by fear. Outsiders consider most Blacks to be a group of lazy and dependent persons who lack high moral integrity and intellectual capacity.[13] Many are unprepared to relate to African Americans in other than their stereotyped image of Blacks as poor, violent criminal elements within society.

Even Blacks who do not suffer the ravages of poverty are devalued. Despite demonstrated intelligence, integrity, and skills in their
areas of professional and technological expertise, many black middle-
class and upper-class educated men and women are confronted with
barriers to inclusion and promotion in their work environment. They
are often denied access to the social networks that facilitate promo-
tions and full participation. Progressive changes are not the result of
institutional self-critical social transformation on the part of government and private institutions but rather the result of "improvements
in blacks' economic, social and political status ... [founded upon]
black initiative and identity."[14] Today efforts are being made to roll
back even those progressive changes that have taken place as attacks
on affirmative action, falsely labeled preferences and quotas, seek to
close doors to further achievement by Blacks.

THE TRIPLE OPPRESSION OF BLACK WOMEN IN THE UNITED STATES

The condition of black women has a complexity that is distinct
from that of black men. Like black men, most African American
women do not and have not had access to the same educational,
economic, and job opportunities as their European counterparts.[15]
Unlike black men, poor black women have been forced to live lives
of coerced or voluntary surrogacy, in which they are abused sexually, psychologically, and physically by both black and non-black men.
They are often marginalized and dehumanized as domestics in households under the control of white and other women, and they continue
to serve as surrogate parents to white and other women's children.[16]
In addition, black women who are employed as domestics and in the
mainstream have had to be both mother and father in their own
single-parent households. In the past the physical and emotional
energy needed to fulfill these double roles was eased by the existence of the extended family of grandparents, aunts, and uncles who
assisted single black women in raising their own children. However,
as extended family networks disappear, poor black women carry
heavier and heavier burdens of responsibility while being made the
target of public and interpersonal hostility; indeed, hostility against
welfare-recipient mothers is increasingly intense. One must note also
that even those black women who have escaped the worst ravages of
economic poverty by employment in mainstream corporations and
academic institutions do not escape from subtle and sophisticated

forms of social domination, similar to that which oppresses their sisters who work as domestics.[17]

THE INTERNAL OPPRESSION OF THE BLACK COMMUNITY

One might conclude from the above that African Americans are solely victims of an externally oppressive society.[18] This would be an oversimplification. Truth demands that we clearly acknowledge that many of the current problems that militate against the life and well-being of African Americans are internal ones. On one hand, some Blacks have adopted the U.S. drive toward the accumulation of wealth, with its concomitant materialism, rugged individualism, greed, violence, crime, cultural arrogance, and patterns of social domination; on the other hand, some Blacks live a marginalized ghetto existence, having internalized the negative expectations of others. For the latter, a life of unconscious hopelessness prevails. Born into economically and morally depressed communities of despair, they are unaware of their human potential. Opportunities for the development of their humanity and of their skills are minimal. Many lack the internal and external incentives to live productive lives in the dominant and oppressive social order. Out of necessity they have constructed alternative modes of living. They live lives focused on daily survival, with little or no hope for a future. Economically poor Blacks are not alone in their experience of social malaise; many middle-and upper-class Blacks, who choose assimilation or choose to live in separate, economically elite enclaves of black "high culture," have succumbed to the current social crises and have embraced lives indicative of moral and social despair. "Psychological depression, personal worthlessness, and social despair are widespread in Black America," according to Cornel West. Collectively these conditions pose a "nihilist threat to [African American] existence."[19]

In summary, one can say that the lives of many African Americans are threatened daily by continued *institutionalized oppression*, internalized self-hatred, and nihilistic despair. This human dilemma is the result of a complex mixture of structural, psychological, and spiritual crises rooted in the persistent historical struggle of African peoples in America. The social despair that threatens black life is a response to current institutionalization of racism, sexism, and classism, which marginalizes, devalues, and consequently makes expendable the lives of African Americans and other oppressed peoples in the United States.

Several existential questions about the future of the life of Black Americans arise within such a devaluating and life-threatening context. First, how and when will we Blacks, as a community, be released from the marginalizing power of dominant social and ecclesial institutions? Second, how and when will we Black Americans, as a community, abandon our collective self-hatred?[20] Third, how and when will the full humanity of Black Americans, as a community, be recognized and honored as a gift from God for the benefit of the whole human community?

The remainder of this chapter addresses these questions, after exploring an interpretation of the life, ministry, and death of the earthly Jesus of history as it relates to the existential condition of structural, psychological, and spiritual oppression of African Americans within the United States. In the process we hope to articulate some old and new dynamic images of Jesus that can be used in the course of ministry to engender hope in a milieu of despair.

JESUS AND OPPRESSION

JESUS AND INSTITUTIONAL OPPRESSION

The cry of African Americans for liberation from sins of violence, greed, despair, and all that oppresses us echoes that of the poor and marginalized people in Jesus' time.[21] Hearing this cry, Jesus challenged the interpretations of both Roman and Jewish laws, which perpetuated the oppression of the Jews and the poor and marginalized within Judaism.[22] The power elite among the Roman and Jewish leaders erroneously identified the national interests with their own desire to secure positions of power and authority. Protecting the well-being of their status was equated with protecting the well-being of the nation. They were blinded to the impact of their laws upon the life and humanity of those whom they deemed to be on the insignificant margins of the society.[23]

Though generally law abiding, Jesus' life and ministry embody the principle that love and compassion for the neighbor must be the standard by which social, political, and religious customs and laws are measured. Jesus' legal transgressions were aimed precisely toward protection of the life of those whose well-being was perceived as irrelevant, marginal, or a threat to the well-being of Rome and that of the nation compromised by Roman domination. Where existing religious and civic laws actually threatened the lives of the poor and marginalized, Jesus had recourse to the higher law of the universal love of God and neighbor.

As a social prophet, Jesus "engaged in radical social criticism" that resulted in his entering into conflict with the political, economic, and religious elites of Rome and first-century Jewish Palestine.[24] His vision of the future of the society contrasted with that of the status quo upheld by these elite.[25] Jesus' preaching of the reign of God challenged many of the existing norms, mores, and patterns of relationship legalized by Roman and Jewish law. The parabolic preaching of Jesus constantly illustrated this contrast. His listeners were often offended by what seemed unjust or unfair according to the prevailing customs and laws.[26] His proclamation of the reign of God demanded radical love and compassionate solidarity with the poor, the outcast, the hungry, the unemployed, the sick, the discouraged, the suffering people who were oppressed and humiliated as non-persons, subhumans.[27] Jesus cured on the Sabbath, ate with known sinners and outcasts, spoke with the Samaritan and other "foreign" women, and occasionally ignored the demands of the laws of ritual purity.

African Americans who read the Bible from the perspective of their situation of oppression find hope in Jesus' challenge to political and religious laws that benefit the power elite at the expense of the poor and the marginalized.[28] Such laws are contrary to the moral law of love of God and neighbor that Jesus proclaimed and embodied. Such laws set up barriers between diverse groups of God's people and divide their spiritual and social communion ordained by God's act of creation. Such laws militate against the loving compassionate solidarity that characterized Jesus' relationship to the poor and outcast.

The patterns of inequality initiated during slavery persist in the social arrangements that characterize Blacks' interaction with whites and other ethnic racial groups in the United States. Historically, the life, well-being, and civil rights of Black Americans have consistently been considered marginal or secondary to those of the colonizing goals of their English, French, and Spanish enslavers. The laws of the founding fathers protected the well-being of their white, propertied male descendants at the expense of the native peoples, African slaves, and women both slave and free. The alliance of the Roman-

Jewish leadership protected the political and economic self-interest of the power-elite of Jesus' day at the expense of the lives and well-being of the poor and marginalized of Israel. Analogously, the laws of racial segregation protected the self-interest of all whites, particularly the privileged, propertied white males, at the expense of the poor of the nineteenth century. Non-propertied males, women, and children, including the free Blacks and slaves, had few rights.[29] Black men and women were restricted from voting, education, adult religious formation, and participation in the development of society and church. These restrictions were legitimized by social convention and laws whose aim was to protect the status quo.[30] Christians theologically justified the enslavement of the Africans and African Americans under slavery and colonialism. The legal practice of segregation regulated by Jim Crow laws and a "separate but equal" philosophy in many instances contributed to the misleading education and under-development of African Americans and other oppressed and marginalized peoples of color within the United States.

Current political and legislative debates about national taxes, medical care, welfare, women's rights, and affirmative action clearly continue the legacy of protecting the interests of the economic and power elite. Appeals to the idealized American traditions of "rugged individualism" and "self-made men" protect the status quo, which privileges a few economic elite and their immediate families with little regard for the masses of the poor and marginalized people from all ethnic-racial groups. It also masks the fact that such "self-made men" rose to wealth and power by exploiting the labor of the masses through slavery, unjust wages, long work hours, and so on. Blacks, the poor, women, and other oppressed groups have been legally disenfranchised and denied their right to full participation in the responsibilities and benefits of citizenship. Racial, class, and gender restrictions were legitimized by social custom and unjust laws.

At the end of the twentieth century African Americans are witnessing a resurgence of social distancing and hostility toward the masses of poor people in general and the black poor in particular. The current political debates in the United States are a struggle of the rich against the poor, similar to that of the biblical community described in the gospel of Luke. The struggle for the human liberation of African Americans within the United States is, however, simultaneously a social-cultural struggle against institutionalized systems of class stratification, racial-cultural domination, and gender devaluation. The preservation of racial caste systems, economic apartheid, and a gender hierarchy continue to dehumanize and de-value black people in America.

The link between economic class and racial and gender oppression was clearly indicated in the 1986 U. S. bishops' pastoral letter, "Economic Justice for All":

Who are the unemployed? Blacks, Hispanics, Native Americans, young adults, female heads of households, and those who are inadequately educated are represented disproportionately among the ranks of the unemployed. The unemployment rate among minorities is almost twice as high as the rate among whites. For female heads of households the unemployment rate is over 10 percent. Among black teenagers, unemployment reaches the scandalous rate of more than one in three (no. 140).

Stats need updating

Perhaps most distressing is the growing number of children who are poor. Today one in every four children under the age of six, and one in every two black children under six, are poor (no. 176).

More than one-third of all female-headed families are poor. Among minority families headed by women the poverty rate is over 50 percent (no. 178).

Most poor people in our nation are white, but the rates of poverty in our nation are highest among those who have borne the brunt of racial prejudice and discrimination. For example, blacks are about three times more likely to be poor than whites. While one out of every nine white Americans are poor, one of every three blacks and Native Americans and more than one of every four Hispanics are poor. While some members of the minority community have successfully moved up the economic ladder, the overall picture indicates that black family income is only 55 percent of white family income, reflecting an income gap that is wider now than at any time in the last fifteen years (no. 181).[31]

Despite the continued reality of institutional and structural oppression, which is evident in both church and society, African Americans have traditionally found a source of hope in Jesus' compassionate love for the poor and marginalized and the call of the early Christian community to unity. Socio-historically, Jesus died because the desire for power and privilege blinded the religious and political elite to the moral and spiritual vision of the reign of God that Jesus preached. Life under the rule of God requires that the community recognize all as the children of God without cultural compromise. Our patterns of cultural, gender, and class relationships must give evidence of this understanding. In a community united by faith in the God of Jesus Christ, who is father and mother of all, the cultural distinctions of ethnicity, gender, and religion are no longer perceived as barriers but are transformed into gifts to solidify and enrich the community (Gal 3:28; Cor 12:12).

A significant core of sermons, hymns, and literary sources created by African Americans calls attention to God's universal care for all peoples. Such music and literature prophetically call for the transformation of the oppressive patterns of our prevailing socially constructed relationships.[32] This oral and written tradition of African American ethics found clear expression in the legacy of Dr. Martin Luther King's Christian call for the recognition of a worldwide or global "revolution" of human values:

> Our values must become ecumenical not sectional. Every nation must now develop an overriding loyalty to mankind as a whole in order to preserve the best in their individual societies.
> . . . This call for a worldwide fellowship [or community] that lifts neighborly concern beyond one's tribe, race and class and nation is in reality a call for an all embracing unconditional love for all men.[33]

Jesus' table fellowship was a dramatic symbol of his call for social unity. He ate with sinners and tax-collectors, who were among the despised of the community, as well as with the wealthy.[34] Many times, the economic, social, and religious privileges that the power elite exercise make it difficult for them to adapt to new patterns of relationships consistent with Jesus' vision of the reign of God. The self-denigration and low self-esteem of the poor often supports their reluctance to cross racial, cultural, and class boundaries. The reign of God fully realized demands that human beings form inclusive communities of people brought together in compassionate solidarity of love because of their common origin in and love of God. The primacy of the law of love of God and love of neighbor demands the building of new social and ecclesial communities in which the rich and prominent and poor and marginalized gather in a spirit of compassionate solidarity. Race, class, and gender distinctions no longer lead to social fragmentation but to a unity born of the recognition of the giftedness of all. Only then can Black Americans fully encounter the risen Christ imaged as Jesus the Liberator, Jesus the Social Prophet, and Jesus the Social Equalizer.[35]

JESUS AND PSYCHOLOGICAL OPPRESSION

God, in the person of Jesus, did not enter human history and die for the poor and marginalized only for them to be consigned permanently to a life of oppression. Jesus' death and resurrection were aimed at the liberation of all peoples. Accordingly, liberation from institutional oppression must be accompanied by liberation from one's psychological oppression and personal/social sin, which alienates one from God and the community. The external conversion of structures of exclusion to structures of inclusion in the first Christian communities is necessarily accompanied by the internal conversion of one's intellectual, psychological, and spiritual self-understanding. Conversion entails attitudinal and behavioral change. Those who joined the Jesus movement were invited to a radical change in their way of life. They were encouraged to embrace a new set of values and new patterns of living (Mt 19:20-22 et al.).

The Civil Rights and Black Power movements in the United States during the 1960s were the catalyst for the intellectual, psychological, and spiritual self-understanding of many Blacks. Black civic and religious organizations nurtured the emergence of the black social, political, and theological voice of men and women.[36] These events signaled the paradigmatic break of the black community's collective negative self-image, which was the product of years of internalized self-hatred. The black community entered into a stage of critical study and retrieval of the history and culture of black people in America and Africa. The "Black is beautiful" epigram of the 1960s and the theories of the 1990s symbolize this shift from self-hatred to self-affirmation.

Psychologist William E. Cross has outlined the psycho-social aspects of this shift in four stages categorized as *pre-encounter*, *encounter*, *immersion*, and *internalization*.[37] The stages chart the movement of black individuals and communities from negative self-images and self-hatred to a positive black consciousness. Prior to the sixties many Blacks in the United States had slowly succumbed to the view of themselves promulgated by the dominant culture, which viewed African Americans as morally and intellectually inferior and bereft of culture. In this first of Cross's stages, the *pre-encounter stage*, Blacks suffer from self-hatred and low self-esteem manifested by a "strong anti-black bias." They think of other Blacks as untrustworthy and consider their identity as black persons insignificant.[38] During the *encounter stage* African Americans have an emotionally transforming negative experience of the white system that forces them to recognize that denial of their own cultural identity will not in fact lead to full inclusion as members of the dominant society. The shattering of this previous unspoken and sometimes unconscious assumption leads to the *immersion stage.* In this stage persons seek to discover more about their cultural identity and history as black and African people, a rediscovery of the history and culture of African Americans that they had previously ignored or considered insignificant because of its omission from the pages of U.S. American history. During the *immersion stage* Blacks explore and reevaluate positively the richness and gifts of the African and African American cultural and historical past, with a commitment to place the well-being and life of African peoples at the center of their value system. The final stage of mature black consciousness, the *internalization stage,* is manifested by persons who have attained a positive and critical view of themselves and African and African American cultures. Their concern for the life and well-being of African and African American peoples remains a central point of their value system, but this is augmented with a concern for all oppressed peoples and all peoples in general. An African American who successfully navigates these four developmental stages has moved through stages of self-denial, self-hatred, self-affirmation, and affirmation of others. The clearest sign of a black person's maturity in black consciousness is the ability to esteem the experience of others as equal to his or her own while being able to be critical of self and others. The mature black-conscious person has replaced the hatred of self or others with an interest and concern for the well-being of peoples of all cultures including his or her own.[39]

In the pre–Vatican II and pre–Civil Rights U.S. Catholic church, most Catholic associations and institutions were predominantly white.[40] Leadership and power were exercised by persons who had little knowledge or concern about the history and culture of African Americans within the United States. As a consequence, black Catholics and Christians were marginalized and treated as objects of charity in most Catholic institutions rather than as full brothers and sisters having a common origin and a common faith. Racism, sexism, and classism within predominantly white churches continue to act as barriers to full participation by members of the community even with regard to the exercise of lay and official ministries of the church.[41] Such barriers can have a negative psychological and spiritual impact on many black men, women, teenagers, and children.

The formation of black Catholic associations during the sixties provided a context in which those black priests, sisters, brothers, laymen, and laywomen who were stymied by black self-hate or denial discovered their authentic African American identity and thus were enabled to act more fully as subjects rather than objects of ministry. These organizations assisted their members to enter into ministries aimed at helping other black Catholics discover their role as disciples called to minister to the church and the society within and beyond the black community. Such associations mitigated the negative impact of the alienation experienced within the dominant institutions of the church and society. They served as nurturing oases in the midst of social and institutionalized hostility. In the milieu of such organizations African American men, women, and children developed an inner strength based on a critical self-knowledge that was psychologically and spiritually healthy. Thus strengthened, they successfully navigated between the denial and rejection of their full humanity encountered in the psychologically hostile dominant institutions and the culturally affirming associations and churches. Thus fed, they continue to make major contributions to their churches and associations and to the broader society.

The affirmation and nurturing of positive self-esteem of peoples who have been marginalized and devalued can rightly be conceived of as a continuance of the healing ministries of Jesus. African Americans as an ethnic-racial group have been despised, devalued, and marginalized within the social structures and institutions of the church and the society of the United States. Christian communities continue the mission of Jesus Christ when they mediate the friendship of the risen Christ who continually extends God's very self to those who are despised and devalued.[42]

> You are my friends if you do what I command you, I do not call
> you servants[43] any longer, because the servant does not know
> what the master is doing; but I have called you friend, because
> I have made known to you everything that I have heard from

my Father. You did not choose me but I chose you. And I appointed you to go and bear fruit, fruit that will last, so that the Father will give you whatever you ask him in my name. I am giving you these commands so that you may love one another. If the world hates you, be aware that it hated me before it hated you (Jn 15).

Becoming aware of one's identity as a friend of Jesus provides inner healing for a mind torn with feelings of isolation and the low self-esteem characteristic of self-hate.[44] Experiences of the friendship and love of God within the social context of the community of believers and/or the mystical encounter of the risen Christ in prayer have a healing effect that leads to the realization of one's irrevocable and empowering identity as a child of God.[45] The intense desire to belong, which lies deep within the African American psyche, is fulfilled as one realizes that he or she is never alone because of the loving presence and indwelling of the God of Jesus Christ within both self and community. Howard Thurman noted that one's status as a child of God and friend of Jesus assures one that God, who sustains all nature and life itself, will sustain the life of those whose backs are against the wall.[46] The self-destructive emotions of fear, hatred, and deception of others and oneself need not triumph. Love of self, neighbor, and enemy is made possible by the overwhelming power of the Love of God, given as gift to each of us. The indwelling Spirit and risen Christ can transform us and through us transform the community into sacraments of God's unconditional love.

The Civil Rights movement under the leadership of Dr. Martin Luther King is a prime example of this reality. The Civil Rights movement was a prophetic movement in which King's personal transformation enabled him to challenge and transform the agenda of the churches and society by his appeal to an all-inclusive love.[47] Jesus Christ calls those who have been healed of the psychological scars of social marginalization and devaluation by the transformative power of friendship and prayer found in community to live with an absolute trust, hope, and all-encompassing love of God and neighbor because God has first loved us. Having overcome the debilitating effects of self-hatred, Blacks and other oppressed peoples must become sacraments of God's unconditional love. As such, we must help others recognize their encounter with the risen Christ imaged as Jesus as Friend, Jesus the Heart Fixer, and Jesus the Mind Regulator. All of these images are found active in the common black worship, song, and preaching as these interpreted the biblical messages and counsels of Jesus (Jn 15:1; Jn 14:1; Mt 6:31-32).

JESUS AND SPIRITUAL OPPRESSION

African American Christians, united by the bonds of a common oppression and a common hope, have traditionally found the story of the life, death, and resurrection of Jesus a source of strength and hope in their struggle for liberation. Reading history from this religious perspective, the Civil War, the passage of the constitutional amendments, the Civil Rights movement, the establishments of social and religious institutions and associations to address their spiritual and material needs are all seen as evidence of God's revelation of love and concern in history. The religious history of black Christians in the United States reveals that God has sent prophets of hope among us to nurture and sustain us through our journey of oppression within the churches and social institutions of the United States.[48]

Despite this rich history and reality, today, many rich, middle-class and poor African Americans in the United States find themselves disconnected from our black religious traditions, the good news of the gospel, and the religious cultural values that placed God at the center and as the source of black hope. The moral crises of values and the diminishing concern for the common good, a widening shadow in American culture, have infected the African American community. Many have become isolated and estranged from one another by the prevailing social culture, which promotes individualism, a narcissistic desire for immediate gratification, social isolation, and the search for financial wealth at the expense of interpersonal and community well-being. In the United States intellectual and functional atheism has accompanied technical advancement and the centering of life around the accumulation of wealth. Many walk in the spiritual confusion of economic and material idolatry, while others, having come to the abyss of nihilism and despair, are seeking to discover or reclaim their connection with a higher spiritual power.

While many working, middle-class and upper-class African Americans continue to enjoy the protection and nurturing provided by the traditional African American support systems identified earlier in this chapter, others have not been immune to the lure of false security and a sense of belonging promised by a false sense of prestige and power born of drugs and money. African Americans, who are economically and socially disadvantaged, are often beyond the reach of ordinary programs provided by the black or white churches, public or church-related schools, and other social agencies. Their family and social networks have disintegrated because of drugs, unemployment, and the lack of basic resources. The existing welfare programs and social programs do not provide the economic, moral, or psychological nurturance necessary for positive self-esteem, confidence, and hope in the future. Senior citizens, adults, teens, and children among the poor underclass are left to grapple for the meaning of life in the isolation of the margins of the marginalized.[49]

Children from the depressed areas of the cities witness domestic and social violence as commonplace. Some of the underclass, poor adults and their children, have sought and found community among those who have seduced them with promises of an immediate sense of belonging, power, prestige, and money through participation in well-established gangs, which engage in the violence of organized crime that accompanies drug trafficking, prostitution, murder, and theft. Those disconnected from normal constructive socialization agents live in a culture bereft of enduring hope. Large numbers of children do not anticipate living past their teen years because of the culture of violence that surrounds them.

In a book on gang life in the South Central district of Los Angeles, California, a journalist tells a true story that illustrates this point. Leon Bing witnessed a gang class conducted by Mr. Jones in a classroom at Camp Kilpatrick for about fifteen gang members, two of whom are Hispanic, the rest black. Mr. Jones wrote the word *kill* on the board and asked the participants to give him "a real good reason to kill somebody." In a brainstorming-like fashion amid a lot of playful teasing the gang members created the following list:

For the fuck of it
Cause he's an enemy
Put in work for the hood
For revenge
Cause he said something wrong
Cause he looked at me funny, gave me that mad dog look
Cause I don't like him
Cause he wearing the wrong color
Cause he gonna hurt a member of my family
For money
So I can jack somebody for dope

Cause he gave me no respect
Cause he a disgrace, he a buster
For his car
Cause he try to get my lady
Cause he a transformer[spy] in my hood
In self-defense
Cause he try to jack you—take yo' shit
For a nickel
For the way he walks
If he got something I want and he don't wanna give it to me
Cause I'm a loc
For his association
Cause he called me a baboon—dis me
Cause he fuck with my food—you know, like took one of my
    French fries or something
Cause I didn't like his attitude
Cause he said the wrong thing—he wolf me
Cause I'm buzzed—you know, all like, high and bent
Just playing around
Cause he funked up my hair at the barbershop
Cause he's a snitch
Cause he hit up my wall, cross'[out] names and shit writing
    R.I.P
If a lady don't give me what I want, you know, the wild thing
Cause they ugly
Cause he try to run a drag [con] on me.[50]

After completing the list, Mr. Jones asked: "Okay. Now, which of this shit would you die for?" After some stunned silence, one member suggested that they erase the whole list. The group participants discuss some of the items on the list for which they might be ready to die. After much discussion around each item the members agreed to erase all the reasons except three. All the participants were willing to die "for his association . . . family, and self-defense."[51] The counselor continued the exercise, demonstrating the difference between "normal" thinking and "sprung" [irrational] thinking. He helped the participants to see the irrationality of their earlier thinking, which yielded thirty-five reasons to kill someone.[52]

To say that this is a sobering account is an understatement, but it illustrates clearly a youthful segment of our U.S. African American culture, a segment that is deprived of any sense of the value of human life, their own or others. Without support of family, community, church, or school, it is extremely difficult to introduce youth and others to the reality of Jesus or sustain long-term hope. Many of these children anticipate an early death and as a consequence live in a constant state of anxiety or suicidal abandonment to immediate gratification.

What can be done to make the option of following Jesus a real option for life for these young men and women caught up in gang life? Biblical scholarship affirms that Jesus' ministry was directed toward the poor and those on the margins of society. Somehow, Christians have to find ways of engaging our sisters and brothers who live in the abyss of nihilism and despair to drink of the spiritual waters of inner peace and hope born of faith in a risen Christ. Faith in the presence of the God of Jesus Christ has been the source of life-transforming powers that sustained Africans Americans through slavery, segregation, Jim Crow laws, lynching, and the Civil Rights movement. The encounter of the risen Christ in community and prayer has sustained us physically, mentally, and spiritually. How do we lead those who are succumbing to the nihilistic threat of despair to that inner stillness where they can encounter God? How do we introduce young men and women who are gang members, or who are confused by the nonbelieving milieu of post-Enlightenment society, to Jesus? How do we help these young men and women choose life instead of death?

A review of the ministry of Jesus reveals above all that his preaching, miracles, and formation of a community of disciples brought a sense of hope in the midst of hopelessness to those who were poor and marginalized in the current social and religious structures of Jesus' day. The good news of Jesus Christ evoked a response because hearers heard words that told of God's love and concern for their well-being. They discovered in the actions, words, and message of Jesus their true identity as children of a God who loved them with an everlasting love. Through Jesus their lives were turned from journeys of despair to journeys of hope. They discovered that, though they were devalued and marginalized outcasts in social and religious circles of the power elite, they were not worthless. As friends and followers of Christ their lives had new value, purpose, and meaning. Prior to Jesus' crucifixion his apostles and disciples were called to embrace a way of community life characterized by a compassionate love that transcended the economic, social, and religious barriers of their society. In the post-resurrection communities of Christians, those who had walked with Jesus called others to share the words and Way of Jesus. Homes, skills, time, friendship, wisdom, and prayer were to be shared. Similarly, Christian churches must reach out to gang members and others who have become isolated and alienated from the community to begin the struggle to help them overcome their estrangement from their spiritual and social identity as human beings made in the "image and likeness of God" and called to live life in all its fullness in communion with all those created by our loving God. Those who are lost by the confusion of the fragmentation and disintegration of common social mores and customs in our post-modern world can find hope in an Old Testament image of God applied to Jesus. "In the desert I make a way, in the wasteland rivers" (Is 43:19). They may find hope in the recognition of their encounters with the risen Christ when others help them discover their way at a point where they were without hope and nearing despair. In these encounters they meet the risen Christ as Jesus the Waymaker, who makes a way out of no way: "I am the way, the truth and the life; no one comes to the Father but through me" (Jn 14:6). Gang members who live in the midst of hopelessness as the marginalized within the marginalized may find hope in an encounter with the risen Christ mediated by Christian disciples or a community who commit themselves to unswerving fidelity as a companion on the Way. Through these ministers of hope gang members will come to know Jesus the Homeboy, who is always covering their backs and who risked and embraced death that they might live (Jn 10:10; 17:12).

IMPLICATIONS FOR CHURCH MISSION
AMONG AFRICAN AMERICANS IN THE UNITED STATES

Given the devaluation and marginalization of African Americans within the dominant structures of the church and society within the United States, Christian churches concerned with continuing the proclamation of the good news of Jesus Christ among African Americans must address the social alienation experienced by many. Churches that wish to engage in *effective* ministry within the African American community must address the three fundamental debilitating realities of black life in America—the persistent institutional, psychological, and spiritual oppression of black people.

First, the churches themselves must engage in a self-critique followed by the intentional formation of just and inclusive communities that welcome African Americans and other marginalized and alienated ethnic-racial groups into a community of friends committed to being followers of Jesus Christ. Being affirmed as friends of Jesus and children of God contradicts the social denial of their full humanity and dignity. African American Christians must be assisted in their spiritual growth through study, prayer, and the exercise of their ministries. No ministerial roles within the church—whether as lay ministers, deacons, catechists, priests, religious men and women, or bishops—must be understood as beyond possibility for African American Catholics because of their race, class, or gender. Their roles must be determined by mutual discernment of God's call by the individual, the church community, and church officials. Strengthened by their community of faith and study of the life and mission of Jesus Christ, African American Catholic Christians will discover the rich social-justice traditions of Catholicism as a firm foundation for their continued faith and ministry.

They must not only be active participants in the specifically ecclesial ministries directed toward the church community but must as members of a believing community bring their understandings of social co-responsibility to the places where black people gather. Like the pre-Easter Jesus, we must "come out from behind the stained-glass walls and dwell where mothers are crying, children are hungry, fathers are jobless"[53] and our large numbers of youth are lost to the violence of the streets. We must go into the barber shops, beauty shops and board rooms, the playgrounds, the exercise gyms and shopping malls.

We must direct church mission and ministry toward the holistic fulfillment of the physical, psychological, and spiritual aspects of human life. Catholic Christian congregations and local churches must provide opportunities, build housing, maintain schools, and establish small businesses for those who are locked out of the existing socio-economic structures. Historically many African Americans have been enabled to hurdle the socio-economic obstacles of the past by the moral, social, and academic education provided by Catholic schools. This ministry to African Americans, particularly those in the inner city, must not be abandoned just at a time when public education in those areas is struggling against failure because of overcrowding, inadequate faculties, and insufficient materials. Catholic archdioceses, parishes, and schools must enter into partnership with small and large corporations and other fields of employment to provide job training for the emerging technological industries and corporate world as well as the traditional services industries of education, nursing, medicine, and law.

In the political arena we must challenge political and religious laws that sacrifice the common good of Blacks and other oppressed people for the benefit of a political or religious elite. We must challenge those social and ecclesial structures that act as stumbling blocks for the poor rather than as universal sacraments of God's unconditional love.[54]

Second, the churches must be attentive to the psychological healing and personal affirmation of their humanity which many African Americans need. The liturgical assembly and strong religious education programs for children and adults are primary arenas for this work. The efforts of black Catholics to develop liturgical rituals, symbols, and music that interpret God's revelation through the risen Christ manifest in the life, history, and culture of African Americans affirm the African American psyche and continue the healing ministry of Jesus. The pioneer work of liturgical inculturation begun by Clarence Rivers[55] and continued by other African American musicians and liturgists celebrates the God of Jesus Christ risen and manifest in the daily life and struggles of African Americans. Within the context of these inculturated liturgies the African American community places before Jesus its life and struggle for blessing and transformation. Preaching interprets the meaning and message of the Jesus of history in a manner that helps contemporary African Americans be faithful to their lives as disciples of Jesus Christ participating in his mission in the particular context of the U.S. community with all its social-cultural diversity. Inculturation of the liturgy affirms the good that God has made manifest in African American history and culture and challenges the community to continue to transform its customs and mores to conform with the good news of Jesus.

There is much work to be done to develop curriculum and religious education and formation models to expand the knowledge and foster the spiritual development of the Catholic faithful, adults and children, through study of the biblical, theological, spiritual, and social-justice traditions of our church. Many Catholic parishes in the United States have done a poor job in providing ongoing religious education for adults beyond the elementary and secondary levels. Strong parish education programs for adults and children must be structured so that our Catholic heritage and traditions are presented in a way that makes them viable sources for moral decision making, spiritual growth, and social transformation. To be effective, all religious education programs in a nation characterized by its racial-ethnic pluralism must be inculturated in such a way that this ethnic-racial plurality is reflected in its stories, images, and history. The story of African American Catholics must be an integral part of the U.S. Catholic story. U.S. Catholics from diverse ethnic-racial backgrounds should not continue to be misinformed about the religious history, spiritual journey, and beliefs of their brothers and sisters from distinct ethnic-racial cultures. Indeed, we all need to be enriched by the manifestation of God's revelation and presence in extraordinary cultural variety. Such knowledge can serve as a basis of U.S. Catholic unity in the midst of cultural and religious diversity within the church and as a springboard for Catholic ecumenism and interreligious dialogue.

Black Catholic parishes must become vibrant centers of psychological healing and social transformation rooted in prayer and study. In the liturgy the praying community brings before God and the assembly those concerns and issues that threaten black life. Listening to God's word the community finds comfort and strength to engage in authentic action on behalf of justice. Through religious education and formation community members learn how to relate within their families, their communities, and with all those created by God for God's glory. Receiving God's body in eucharist they acknowledge their communion made whole by the redemptive life, death, and resurrection of Jesus. Such praying communities affirm that the world is God's body and that every person and creature of creation is their brother and sister with God as their common Father and Mother. Transformed by the celebration they go forth to be agents of social transformation inviting all to patterns of right relationship characteristic of those who have embraced the Way of Jesus as they await the full realization of the reign of God.

Third, I cannot overemphasize the church's need to focus on the spiritual growth and development of African Americans and other Catholic Christians. Currently the cultures of death and the cultures of wealth are waxing strong within U.S. society. There is potential for national collapse or national rebirth. National rebirth will be predicated upon a spiritual rebirth in which U.S. citizens forsake the death offered by the god of wealth accumulation and embrace the God who offers us the communion of all-embracing love. The fragmentation and violence of U.S. society affects all its members. Many, acknowledging the fragmentation and violence that threaten the future of the black community, have called for a retrieval of traditional religious and spiritual values as an antidote to community despair. One dimension of the Afrocentric movement, which focuses its concern exclusively on the well-being of black people, is a return to the holistic spirituality that characterized traditional African communities. Christian churches must enable their members and those they serve to discover how their relationship to God and others has been nourished and can continue to be nourished by drinking of the river of black Christian spirituality, which is fed by the life-engendering aspects of our non-Christian Black African *and* our worldwide Catholic Christian religious traditions and practices.

Jesus was historically, culturally, and spiritually a member of the oppressed community of Jews that was critical of the Jewish religious traditions, which seemed to hold the graciousness of God in captivity. His Way of life called for a transformation of Judaism and the social-political conventions that excluded those on the margins. In a similar fashion, African American Christians must be critical of those aspects of African and Christian traditions that hold God's graciousness toward African and African Americans in captivity and separate us from the communion of our brothers and sisters from other ethnic-racial cultures. Embracing our rich African American cultural and religious traditions as gifts from God, we must unite them with our African and non-African brothers and sisters within and beyond our worldwide Catholic communion. Jesus is the answer for African Americans today, if and only if their encounter with the earthly Jesus of history and the risen Christ within and beyond the church serves to bring them a realization of their full humanity and destiny as members of the human community called to communion with God. Jesus came that we might have life and live it to the full (Jn 10:10). Through study, a deep spiritual communion with God in prayer, and active participation in the community of believers engaged in ministry we meet our Great Ancestor, the God of Jesus Christ, who came that we might have life and live it to the full. As a fruit of these encounters African Americans and others will be able to preach and embody Jesus as the Social Prophet, Liberator, Social Equalizer, Heart Fixer, Mind Regulator, Waymaker, and "Homeboy," who continuously covers our backs and watches over us in order to save our lives on earth as well as in heaven.

It is through the full realization of our identity as those called by the God of Jesus Christ to an all-inclusive love and participation in the mission of Christ directed toward all humanity, including the poor, oppressed, and marginalized of this world, that African American Catholics and other African American Christians can be released from the marginalizing power of the dominant social and ecclesial institutions. Our identity as children of God and disciples of Christ participating in his ministry enables us to abandon our collective self-hate and to celebrate and share the contributions of our African American gifts with church and society. It is only the realization of the full humanity of Black Americans and our constructive and positive contributions to church and society that will enable others to recognize us as a community gifted by God to participate in the social and spiritual transformation of the world into the community living in accord with the reign of God.

NOTES

¹ U.S. Catholic Bishops, "Brothers and Sisters to Us: U.S. Bishops Pastoral on Racism in Our Day" (Washington, D.C.: United States Catholic Conference, 1979).

² The term *black church* is used to designate the traditional churches established by African Americans as denominations and congregations separated from their parent European-American denominations in the eighteenth and nineteenth centuries as well as those black congregations and organizations within predominantly European-American Christian denominations. See C. Eric Lincoln, *Race and Religion and the Continuing American Dilemma* (New York: Hill and Wang, 1984), pp. 73-78. Lincoln suggests four sources of internal division within the black church: (1) Many slaves internalized the value system of the dominant culture and "felt the need to be white" in order to be recognized as fully human. (2) The division of the black slaves into house slaves or field slaves led to a social hierarchy and potential for conflict within the slave community. The house slaves had close contact with "the master or members of his family" and were perceived as belonging to "an elite with certain privileges and opportunities." Among these privileges was the opportunity to become skilled artisans and professionals in virtue of their responsibilities. The field slaves, in contrast, had very little contact with the master's family, and their skills, other than those of using a plow and hoe, remained undeveloped. (3) The development of a skin-color hierarchy in which lighter skinned slaves were thought to be superior to darker ones coupled with the role divisions as house and field slaves contributed to the development of "class" differences that became divisive. (4) Religious division between black denominations.

³ Biblical scholars today realize more than ever the influence and significance of social-historical factors and the world view of the biblical

writer upon the content, focus, and interpretation of the events in Jesus' life. Contemporary biblical interpretation is influenced by the social location and world view of the interpreter or scholar. Just as Matthew, Mark, Luke, and John were each faced with the task of asking and answering the question "Who is Jesus Christ?" for their respective communities, so too contemporary theologians must answer that question in light of their particular social-cultural location. The complexity of hermeneutical method and world view becomes apparent if one reads diverse texts on biblical hermeneutics. The standard redaction; tradition; critical, literary, form, and historical criticism are not immune to the distortion of interpretations due to ideological and subjective self-interest. As such, the interpreter must be acutely aware of the horizontal values and concerns one brings to the biblical text. Some interesting texts analyzing the Bible from the perspective of social setting, culture and political social hermeneutics include the following: Norman K. Gottwald, ed., *The Bible and Liberation* (Maryknoll, N.Y.: Orbis Books, 1983); Robert McAfee Brown, *Unexpected News: Reading the Bible with Third World Eyes* (Philadelphia: Westminster Press, 1984); Carolyn Osiek, *What Are They Saying about the Social Setting of the New Testament?* (New York: Paulist Press, 1984); Itumeleng J. Mosala, *Biblical Hermeneutics and Black Theology in South Africa* (Grand Rapids: William B. Eerdmans, 1989); Cain Hope Felder, *Troubling Biblical Waters: Race, Class and Family* (Maryknoll, N.Y.: Orbis Books, 1989); Charles B. Copher, *Black Biblical Studies* (Chicago: Black Light Fellowship, 1993); Randall C. Bailey and Jacquelyn Grant, eds., *The Recovery of Black Presence: An Interdisciplinary Exploration* (Nashville: Abingdon Press, 1995).

[4] Zablon Nthamburi, "Christ as Seen by an African: A Christological Question," in *Faces of Jesus in Africa*, ed. Robert Schreiter (Maryknoll, N.Y.: Orbis Books, 1991), p. 66 (complete article, pp. 65-69). See also, Karl Rahner, "The Two Basic Types of Christology," *Theological Investigations* (New York: Seabury Press, 1961-), 13:213-23. Anthropocentric Christology, "from below," focuses on the significance of the pre-Easter life of the historical Jesus and the implications of his human-divine life for historical liberation from all that oppresses. In contrast, theocentric Christology, "from above," generally focuses on post-Easter interpretation of the divinity of Jesus the Christ and the implications of his divine-human identity for salvation or liberation from sin. Ecclesiology "from below" addresses the human mediators in the mission of the church. Ecclesiology from above focuses on the divine nature of the church, and the role of the risen Christ and the Holy Spirit's mediation of God's presence in church mission and ministry. The limits of this Rahnerian terminology is evident when one acknowledges, as Rahner does, that human life is always graced and therefore has access to the influence of the divine. According to tradition, the divine and human natures of Jesus

are integrally related in the one person of Jesus. The divine and human aspects of the church are, by contrast, integrally related by the indwelling power of the Holy Spirit.

[5] This methodology was implicit in the theological method of the oral stage of black theology found in black spirituals and black gospel music; it was later made explicit in the nascent black theology of James Cone (*God of the Oppressed* [New York: Seabury Press, 1975]), who states that the "interplay of social context, Scripture and tradition must be the starting point of an investigation of Jesus Christ's meaning for today" (p. 108). As such, black experience, the Bible, and tradition provided the three-dimensional criteria of norms of Cone's work. My own theological work maintains a similar three-dimensional mutually critiquing criteria identified as orthodoxy, orthopathy, and orthopraxy. *Orthodoxy* refers to the collective wisdom of our religious ancestors as documented in the Bible and the teachings of the magisterium (doctrine and dogma). *Orthopathy* refers to the truth that emerges from the collective, intuitive, and oral wisdom of contemporary people, that is, the *sensum fidelium*. *Orthopraxy* refers to life-giving action or ministry on behalf of justice.

[6] Marcus J. Borg, *Jesus in Contemporary Scholarship* (Valley Forge, Penn.: Trinity Press International, 1994), p. 195. Borg prefers the language of "pre-Easter" and "post-Easter" to differentiate between the historical Jesus and the Christ of faith. In his mind the later terminology gives preferential weight to the latter, while in fact the two sources of knowledge, the biblical and the post-biblical experiences, are equally important. Only knowledge born of our own and our ancestors encounters with the risen Christ and the historical Jesus is needed to ascertain a true and authentic understanding of Jesus the Christ and the significance of God's presence in the person of Jesus and in contemporary human history as we seek to fulfill authentic and distinct human meaning and purpose as followers of Christ in the world.

[7] In *What Are They Saying about the Social Setting of the New Testament* Osiek suggests that the social stratification was a fourfold one of urban elite, urban non-elite, village peasants, and beggars (p. 29). In *Jesus in Contemporary Scholarship* Borg discusses contemporary emphasis on Jesus as a social prophet who provided an alternative vision to life from that promulgated by the dominant social and religious powers (pp. 101-16).

[8] See the call of his disciples (Lk 5:11; Mk 1:16-20; Mt 4:18-22) and the Beatitudes (Lk 6:20-23; Mt 5:3-12). Elisabeth Schüssler Fiorenza, in *Discipleship of Equals: A Critical Feminist Ekklesia-logy of Liberation*, suggests that followers of Jesus were "the tax-collectors, sinners, and women, all of whom were considered to be cultically unclean . . . and did not belong to the religious establishment or the pious associations of the day" (New York: Crossroad, 1993), p. 83.

[9] See the Healing of the Paralytic (Mt 9:1-8; Mk 2:1-12; Lk 5:17-20); the Call of Levi, the Tax Collector (Lk 5:27-32; Mk 2:13-17; Mt 9:9-13); the Sending of the Twelve (Mt 9:35; 10:1, 9-11, 14; Mk 6:6b-13; Lk 9:1-6); the Menstruating Woman (Lk 8:43-48).

[10] In *What Are They Saying about the Social Setting of the New Testament?* Osiek states that "much but not all research indicates of course the disinherited, the disadvantaged of society, who have the most to gain by having the table turned. . . . The new order will provide heavenly compensation for poverty and restore the proper criteria for human dignity" (p. 40).

[11] Andrew Billingsley, "Family Community and Society," *Climbing Jacob's Ladder: The Enduring Legacy of African-American Families* (New York: Simon & Schuster, 1992), pp. 68-69. (The entire chapter is pp. 65-80.) The author must note that these conditions are not the exclusive experience of Black Americans but are rather the scourges of American society as a whole, yet their incidence and impact on the black community threaten its very existence.

[12] See William Julius Wilson, *When Work Disappears: The World of the New Urban Poor* (New York: Alfred A. Knopf, 1996); see also, Douglas S. Massey and Nancy A. Denton, *American Apartheid: Segregation and the Making of the Underclass* (Cambridge, Mass.: Harvard University Press, 1993) for extensive sociological and historical documentation of the phenomena of black economic poverty and social segregation.

[13] Wilson, *When Work Disappears*, pp. 112-15.

[14] Gerald David Jaynes and Robin M. Williams Jr., eds., *A Common Destiny: Blacks and American Society* (Washington, D.C.: National Academy Press, 1989), pp. 9-10. See the summary on pp. 1-32. This is a report of the Committee on the Status of Black Americans of the National Research Council published on the occasion of the twenty-year anniversary of the Kerner Report and forty-five years after the publication of Gunnar Myrdal's *An American Dilemma,* which had underscored the problem of race as the key problem of our century. In its introductory summary under the heading "Determinants of Black Status" the report states: "Barriers and disadvantages persist in blocking black advancement. Three such barriers to full opportunity for Black Americans are residential segregation, continuance of diffuse and often indirect discrimination, and exclusion from social networks essential for full access to economic and educational opportunities" (p. 9).

[15] bell hooks, *Killing Rage: Ending Racism* (New York: Henry Holt and Company, 1995). Four chapters of this text focus particularly on the complex integrally related dynamics of racism, sexism, and classism as these affect black women: "Challenging Sexism in Black Life"; "Integrity of Black Womanhood"; "Feminism: It's a Black Thing"; and "Revolutionary Feminism," pp. 62-107.

¹⁶ Delores S. Williams, "Social Role Surrogacy: Naming Black Women's Oppression," *Sisters in the Wilderness: The Challenge of Womanist God-Talk* (Maryknoll, N.Y.: Orbis Books, 1993), pp. 60-83.

¹⁷ Yolanda T. Moses (*Black Women in Academe: Issues and Strategies* [New York: Project on the Status and Education of Women, Association of American Colleges, 1989]) describes the dynamics and pitfalls black women in academic settings confront. Ellis Cose's work (*The Rage of a Privileged Class: Why Are Middle Class Blacks Angry? Why Should America Care?* [New York: Harper-Collins Books, 1993]) describes the barriers that persist for middle-class black men and women in corporate America.

¹⁸ Cornel West, *Race Matters* (Boston: Beacon Press, 1993), pp. 11-12. West states that the victimization theory of liberal structuralists, who advocate structural change, and the black-agency theory of conservative behaviorists, who contend that what is needed is a series of self-help programs, do not tell the whole story. Both fail to acknowledge the personal complicity of some Blacks with their own oppression.

¹⁹ Ibid., pp. 12-13.

²⁰ This self-hatred is nurtured in a context that emphasizes the negative aspects of black life with little or no acknowledgment of the positive contributions of Blacks to the church or society. At the same time we are witnessing the rise of black popular culture as a major contributor to the culture of America. In the United States the prevailing American music, dance, dress styles, aesthetics, linguistic idioms, and other cultural symbols and customs often emerge as a result of the ongoing creativity of the black community and are assimilated by many Americans who fail to recognize or acknowledge their origin in the African American community. Paradoxically, the centrality of religious belief within African American cultural tradition, with its central belief in the basic unity of the human community because of our common origin in God, is sifted out during this assimilation by the dominant and cultural groups.

²¹ One must remember that Jesus was a religious Jew living in a territory occupied by Rome. Jews were considered an inferior people who were subjected to the power and authority of Romans and the Roman government. The religious power elite, the members of the Sanhedrin, served as mediators between the Jews and the Roman rulers. Composed of Pharisees, Sadducees (including the high priest or priests), scribes— that is, the Jewish religious leaders and scholars—the Sanhedrin not only attempted to guide the Jews in the path of authentic life according to its own religious and cultural laws, but it also served as a protective body that represented the self-interests of the Jewish people in their dialogue with Roman authorities. Unfortunately, the poor and marginalized were not always protected by the social-political and religious arrangements of the day. There was need for a liberating social transformation. *Evangelii Nuntiandi*, the apostolic exhortation of Pope Paul VI on evangelization, promulgated on December 8, 1975, reminded Catholic Christians that

evangelization entails liberation and interior transformation. "Christ proclaims salvation, this great gift of God which is liberation from everything that oppresses man but which is above all liberation from sin and the Evil One" (no. 9). It further states that

the church evangelizes when she seeks to convert, solely through the divine power of the message she proclaims, both the personal and collective consciences of people, the activities in which they engage, and the lives and concrete milieu which are theirs, . . . affecting and as it were upsetting, through the power of the Gospel, mankind's criteria of judgment, determining values, points of interest, lines of thought, sources of inspiration and models of life, which are in contrast with the Word of God and the plan of salvation (nos. 18-19).

22 Donald Senior, *Jesus, A Gospel Portrait* (New York: Paulist Press, 1992), pp. 94-99. Senior suggests that Jesus was not against law as law but interpreted the law through the normative standard of love of God and love of neighbor. All else was secondary. Edward Schillebeeckx (*Jesus: An Experiment in Christology* [New York: Crossroad, 1981], pp. 249-56) explores how "Jesus liberates the individual from a narrow idea of God, by exposing the ideology as an orthodoxy that stood in a ruptured relationship to orthopraxis, and . . . had established an ethic as an independent screen between God and man, so that the relevance of the legal obligations to man's salvation had become totally obscured" (p. 256). In other words, certain interpretations of the law veiled the intent of human love and compassion by substituting the obedience to and love of law in place of love of God and neighbor.

23 James P. Mackey (*Jesus the Man and the Myth* [New York: Paulist Press, 1979]) discusses the role of the Sanhedrin and how even religious positions can be corrupted into self-aggrandizing privilege, which marginalizes rather than maintains positions of service and protection of the common good (pp. 54-61, 135-36); see also, Senior, *Jesus*, pp. 61-73.

24 Borg, *Jesus in Contemporary Scholarship*, p. 116.

25 Ibid., p. 101. Jesus' lifestyle challenged the patriarchal and other social divisions of the times.

26 James P. Mackey, *Jesus, the Man and the Myth* (New York: Paulist Press, 1979), pp. 125-42.

27 Jurgen Moltmann, *The Way of Jesus Christ* (Minneapolis: Fortress Press, 1993), p. 99.

28 Vincent L. Wimbush, "The Bible and African Americans: An Outline of an Interpretive History," in *Stony the Road We Trod: African American Biblical Interpretation*, ed. Cain Hope Felder (Minneapolis: Fortress Press, 1991), pp. 61-97. Wimbush indicates the emergence of a Black American tradition of interpreting the Bible using the social context of black life as a hermeneutical norm in the nineteenth century. The pioneer work of Howard Thurman (*Jesus and the Disinherited* [Richmond, Ind.: Friends United Press, 1949]) and James Cone (*A Black Theology of*

Liberation, 20th anniversary edition [Maryknoll, N.Y.: Orbis Books, 1990], originally published in 1970) initiated the twentieth-century critique of the ideological blindness of Christian theology to the experience of black people.

[29] See John W. Cell, *The Highest Stage of White Supremacy: The Origins of Segregation in South Africa and the American South* (Cambridge: Cambridge University Press, 1982).

[30] See Katie Geneva Cannon, "Slave Ideology and Biblical Interpretation," in *The Recovery of Black Presence: An Interdisciplinary Exploration,* ed. Randall C. Bailey and Jacquelyn Grant (Nashville: Abingdon Press, 1995), pp. 119-28. Cannon exposes the hermeneutical distortions (ideology) that led to the social, legal and religious legitimation of slavery by Christian religious and social leaders and intellectuals. See also Clarice J. Martin, "The *Haustafeln* (Household Codes) in African American Biblical Interpretation: 'Free Slaves' and 'Subordinate Women,'" in Felder, *Stony the Road We Trod,* pp. 206-31. This text examines various interpretations of the household codes as they attempted to restore the patriarchal familial arrangements that had been challenged by the notions of an inclusive community of men, women, and children called to be disciples. Subsequently these codes, reflected in Colossians, Ephesians, and 1 Peter, would be used in proslavery arguments. See also Jamie T. Phelps, "Caught between Thunder and Lightning: A Historical and Theological Critique of the Episcopal Response to Slavery," *Many Rains Ago* (Washington, D.C.: United States Catholic Conference, 1990), pp. 21-34. This article examines the proslavery, antislavery stance of American Catholic bishops in the nineteenth century and the gradual post–Civil War reversal of the former and the implications for the ethical stance of contemporary bishops in the ideological context of continued institutionalized racism.

[31] U.S. Bishops, "Economic Justice For All: Pastoral Letter on Catholic Social Teachings and the U.S. Economy" (Washington, D.C.: United States Catholic Conference, 1986).

[32] Some conspicuous examples include Jesse Jackson's development of the Rainbow Coalition; Maya Angelou's inaugural poem, *On the Pulse of Morning* (New York: Random House, 1993); and Quincey Jones's production of "We Are the World," starring Stevie Wonder. Each of these African Americans embraces the Christian humanist tradition and constantly works toward the unity of the human community understood as the overcoming of human and social division and fragmentation to reach participation in the world house of creation.

[33] Martin Luther King Jr., *Where Do We Go From Here?: Chaos or Community,* in *The Essential Writings and Speeches of Martin Luther King,* ed. James W. Washington (San Francisco: Harper Collins, 1991), p. 632.

[34] Mackey, *Jesus, the Man and the Myth,* pp. 145-54; Schillebeeckx, *Jesus,* pp. 206-13; Mackey, *Jesus, the Man and the Myth,* p. 112.

[35] See Lk 14:18; Lk 14:15-24; and Mt 22:1-14; Lk 8:4-15; Mk 4:1-20 and Mt 13:1-23.

[36] Among these organizations were Catholic organizations founded by black Catholic priests, sisters, brothers, seminarians, and laypersons: the National Black Catholic Clergy Caucus, the National Black Sister's Association, the National Office of Black Catholics, and the National Black Seminarians Association.

[37] William E. Cross, "Models of Psychological Nigrescence: A Literature Review," in *Black Psychology*, ed. Reginald L. Jones, 2d ed. (New York: Harper & Row, 1980), pp. 81-98. See page 95 for a chart of the four stages.

[38] Ibid., p. 92.

[39] Ibid., pp. 92-93. I have freely adapted Cross's interpretation in the framework of the more recent Africentric movement.

[40] The few exceptions were those organizations and communities of Catholics led by black priests or religious, including congregations of sisters, the Oblate Sisters of Providence in Baltimore, the Holy Family Sisters in New Orleans, and the Handmaids of Mary in New York. But even in this case, the model of church was often that which characterizes the pre-encounter stage.

[41] See U.S. Catholic Bishops, "Brothers and Sisters to Us," no. 46. For historical background see Jamie T. Phelps, "John R. Slattery's Missionary Strategies," *U.S. Catholic Historian: The Black Catholic Community, 1880-1987*, vol. 7, nos. 2-3 (Spring/Summer 1988), pp. 201-14; Stephen J. Ochs, *Desegregating the Altar: The Josephites and the Struggle for Black Priests 1871-1960* (Baton Rouge: Louisiana State University Press, 1990); Cyprian Davis, *The History of Black Catholics in the United States* (New York: Crossroad, 1991).

[42] Elisabeth Schüssler Fiorenza, in *Discipleship of Equals: A Critical Feminist Ekklesia-logy of Liberation*, suggests that followers of Jesus were "the tax-collectors, sinners, and women, all of whom were considered to be cultically unclean . . . and did not belong to the religious establishment or the pious associations of the day" (New York: Crossroad, 1993), p. 83.

[43] Jacquelyn Grant, "The Sin of Servanthood," in *A Troubling in My Soul: Womanist Perspectives on Evil and Suffering*, ed. Emilie M. Townes (Maryknoll, N.Y.: Orbis Books, 1993), pp. 199-218. This article grapples with teaching African American Christians that they have been called to a life of service "when they have been imprisoned by the most exploitative forms of service . . . serving is reserved for victims, while being served is the special privilege of victimizers, or at least representatives of the status quo" (pp. 209, 211). Grant concludes that it is better to use the language of discipleship rather than servanthood when teaching others to commit themselves to the way of Jesus Christ. Grant's doctoral dissertation, *White Women's Christ and Black Women's Jesus* (Atlanta: Scholars

Press, 1989) contained the prolegomena for her work as a womanist theological scholar whose major research is in the area of Christology.

⁴⁴ Howard Thurman, *Jesus and the Disinherited* (Richmond, Ind.: Friends United Press, 1981), pp. 49-57. This selection discusses extensively how the apparently simple claiming of one's identity as a child of God has profound consequences for those whose humanity and human worth has been denied.

⁴⁵ Riggins R. Earl Jr., *Dark Symbols, Obscure Signs: God, Self and Community in the Slave Mind* (Maryknoll, N.Y.: Orbis Books, 1993) documents this process through his analysis of the conversion stories found in slave biographies, slave narratives, and slave oral literary tradition. He concludes the work with a schema and interpretation of four ideal types of the narrative self revealed in his examination of the literature.

⁴⁶ Thurman, *Jesus and the Disinherited*, p. 11.

⁴⁷ James W. Washington, ed., "Suffering and Faith," in *The Essential Writings and Speeches of Martin Luther King* (San Francisco: Harper Collins, 1991), pp. 41-42; Stephen B. Oates, *Let the Trumpet Sound: The Life of Martin Luther King, Jr.* (New York: New American Library, 1982), pp. 88-89, 284-86.

⁴⁸ Gayraud S. Wilmore, *Black Religion and Black Radicalism: An Interpretation of the Religious History of Afro-American People* (Maryknoll, N.Y.: Orbis Books, 1983); Earl, *Dark Symbols, Obscure Signs*; Davis, *History of Black Catholics.*

⁴⁹ William Julius Wilson, *The Truly Disadvantaged: The Inner City, the Underclass, and Public Policy* (Chicago: University of Chicago Press, 1987), pp. 100-124. Wilson discusses the limitation of current affirmative action programs based on "the rights of minority individuals or preferential treatment of minority groups." Wilson states that while economically advantaged blacks whose participation in society was restricted by race alone experienced a change of opportunity in the Civil Rights movements of the sixties, those Blacks and whites disadvantaged primarily by economic poverty remained poor. An appeal to the liberal philosophers—such as James Fishkin, concerned with equality and social justice—who developed the principle of "equality of life chances" for those classified as disadvantaged in terms of competitive resources associated with their economic-class background would target some of the underclass. However, Wilson suggests a universal program of "economic growth and sustained full employment, not only in higher income areas but in areas where the poor are concentrated as well." Such a program would overcome the profound structural economic changes that affect the total economic picture of the nation but whose highest negative impact is felt by the black poor in the urban centers of our country. Full employment strategies addressed at the economic needs of all citizens would benefit from the support of a broad-based coalition of Americans disadvantaged

by new structural changes. Other works by Wilson worth reading on this topic are *The Declining Significance of Race: Blacks and the Changing American Institutions* (Chicago: University of Chicago Press, 1978) and *When Work Disappears*, cited above.

[50] Leon Bing, *Do or Die* (New York: Harper Collins, 1990), pp. 121-22.

[51] Ibid., pp. 123-26.

[52] Ibid., pp. 126-27.

[53] "Message to the Black Church and Community," in Gayraud Wilmore and James Cone, eds., *Black Theology: A Documentary History: 1966-1979* (Maryknoll, N.Y.: Orbis Books, 1979), p. 345. This statement was drafted and adopted by the National Conference of the Black Theology Project, of "Theology in the Americas," in session in Atlanta, Georgia, August 3-7, 1977.

[54] In the two most recent National Black Catholic Congresses (1987 and 1992) African American lay Catholics were called to assume their responsibility for the intra-ecclesial and extra-ecclesial ministries in collaboration with African American women and men religious and ordained priests and deacons and bishops and all the ministers of the Catholic church within the United States.

[55] M. Shawn Copeland, "African American Catholics and Black Theology: An Interpretation," in *African American Religious Studies*, ed. Gayraud S. Wilmore (Durham, N.C.: Duke University Press, 1989). This article gives an account of the development of the twentieth-century black Catholic movement and the contributions of selected pioneers in that movement in the fields of liturgy, pastoral ministry, and theology. Clarence Rivers was the major pioneer of black Catholic liturgical inculturation as evidenced in his publications: Clarence Joseph Rivers, *Freeing the Spirit*, 6 vols. (Washington, D.C.: National Office of Black Catholics, 1971-1974); *Soulful Worship* (Washington, D.C.: National Office of Black Catholics, 1974); and *The Spirit in Worship* (Cincinnati: Stimuli Inc., 1978).

4

And When We Speak

To Be Black, Catholic, and Womanist

DIANA L. HAYES

Historically, women have been the unheard voices calling for recognition and the freedom to speak of their lives in words of their
own choosing. Women of color have especially suffered from the
oppression of others, both male and female, of their own and other
races and ethnicities, speaking for and about them.[1]

Black liberation theology in the United States has been seen, historically, as a product of the Black Protestant church and community.
The leading scholars in the field have been Black men, most of whom
are ordained in the historically Black Methodist or Baptist churches.
It has been little more than a decade that Black women, also predominantly Protestant, have become a significant part of the
dialogue.[2] The reasons for this are both historical and social as well
as religious.

Black women, whether Protestant or Catholic, while the main-
stay, historically, of the Black church, have held few recognizable
roles of responsibility or leadership within them, especially as ordained ministers. As increasing numbers of Black Protestant women
earn doctoral degrees in theology or are ordained, their influence
has begun to grow.

This article is a condensed and revised version of Chapters 7 and 8 of
Diana L. Hayes, *And Still We Rise: An Introduction to Black Liberation
Theology* (Mahwah, N.J.: Paulist Press, 1996).

In this chapter I will address the historical reasons for the development of womanist theology as a response to and critique of Black and feminist theologies, as well as discuss the development of a Black Catholic theology that is womanist in its praxis.

WOMEN AND CHRISTIANITY

In Christianity, especially its Western (and predominant) expression, the presence and participation of women in any form of leadership roles have been systematically restricted. The image of women that emerged over the centuries has been dualistic, upholding woman as the "fount of purity," as exemplified by the Virgin Mary, and at the same time stigmatizing her as the "source of all evil," as evidenced by Eve's seduction of Adam.

Despite the historical evidence of significant participation of women in various roles in the early church, as Christianity evolved and divided, the male leadership was united in its aversion to women in ordained or other leadership roles, especially over men. This aversion crossed racial, ethnic and cultural lines, affecting, especially in the United States, the entire society.

Accompanying this, however, was the further development of the dualistic perception of women during the period of slavery in the United States, which placed white women firmly in the role of upholder of purity and Black women in the role of dehumanized temptress. These polarized definitions became firmly embodied in American society, continuing today in the almost universal depictions of Black women as "welfare queens" and single mothers, while white women are more often seen as the feminine role models of society.

This dichotomous way of viewing women became a part of the self-understanding of many in both the African American and Euro-American communities, making it difficult if not impossible for African American and white women to form any solidarity with each other.[3] Many in the early secular feminist movement were blind to the inequitable positions of Black and white women in the United States. The former usually worked out of necessity, in low-paying, often dehumanizing jobs and until recently had little formal education and little freedom of choice. They often shared this situation but little community with working-class white women. Those who were engaged in the struggle for women's rights were usually highly educated, worked often from choice more than need, and had the freedom to choose their lifestyles.[4]

FEMINIST AND BLACK THEOLOGY

As the feminist movement moved into the realm of theology, many of the same mistakes were made. Black women were more often spoken for rather than speaking themselves. White feminist theologians claimed to be inclusive of all women while speaking from and recovering only their own experiences.

At the same time that African American women were beginning to address the shortcomings, as they saw them, of the secular feminist movement, African American female theologians were critiquing the religious feminist movement and the Black liberation theology movement as well for their failure to be inclusive of the experiences and voices of women of color.

Black theology emerged in the late 1960s as an articulation of predominantly Black male voices and concerns. Early Black theologians presented a perspective on Black history, culture, and faith that often rendered Black women voiceless and invisible. Their seminal writings, in exclusive language, paid little or no attention to the strengthened courage of their Black sisters, who had managed to "mother" a new people, African Americans, into existence in union with their men.[5]

Thus, in the face of this absence of Black voices from all theological perspectives, a need was seen for Black women (and other women of color) who were rooted in their Christian faith to begin to "speak the truth" to their people and the greater United States society. Adapting the term *womanist,* as defined by Alice Walker, African American women proceeded to articulate the truth about Black women's lives in the Americas for the past five centuries.

WOMANIST THEOLOGY

According to Alice Walker, a womanist is a black feminist or feminist of color, one "wanting to know more and in greater depth than is good for [her]. . . . [She is] outrageous, audacious, courageous and [engages in] willful behavior." A womanist is universal, encompass-

ing love for men and women, as well as music, dance, food, round-
ness, the struggle, the Spirit, and herself, "regardless." She is
"committed to survival and wholeness of an entire people, male and
female" and is opposed to separation, "except for health."[6]

A womanist sees herself both individually and in community, but
that individuality, in keeping with her African heritage, arises from
the community in which she is born, shaped, and formed. It follows,
therefore, that her goal of liberation, which is both spiritual and physical, is not simply for herself but for all of her people and, beyond
that, for all who are also oppressed by reason of race, sex, and/or
class.[7] Sexism is not the only issue; rarely is it the most important
issue. Rather, it is the intertwined evils that act to restrict her and
her community that are the cause for her concern. Thus, womanism,
in an inclusive sense, can be seen as encompassing a more limited
feminism as it opens itself up to all who are oppressed. Womanist
theologians have taken this definition and broadened it in order to
invest it with a theological and spiritual interpretation, thereby going beyond Walker's own understanding in many ways.

Both Black and feminist theologies were seen as engaging in "God-
talk" from a too narrowly particular and exclusive context, erring in
seeing their own particular experiences as the norm for all theologizing. The result was theologies that saw racism or sexism as the
only issues, thereby ignoring issues of class, homophobia, and eth-
nocentrism, among others. In response to these narrow foci,
womanist theologians, however, assert that full human liberation
can be achieved only by eliminating not only one form of oppression, but all forms.

African American womanists realized that their oppression was
a triple one, of race, gender, and, too often, class, which, multiplica-
tive in its impact, had rendered the contributions of themselves and
their sisters invisible. At the same time, they recognized that they
too can, if not properly observant, become oppressors in company
with Black men and white woman, as their status in academia and
the corporate world improves.

WOMANIST VOICES

Womanist theologians present a strong rebuttal to the historical
depiction of Black women as the "mule of the world," as Hurston

herself did.[8] She simply could not depict Blacks as defeated, humiliated, degraded, or victimized, because she did not experience Black people or herself that way.

Katie G. Cannon, in her seminal work *Black Womanist Ethics*, relies on the life and works of Zora Neale Hurston to engage in an examination of the "matrix of virtues which emerge from the real-lived texture of the Black community."[9] In doing so, she goes beyond the boundaries of traditional Protestant ethics, which historically have implied "that the doing of Christian ethics in the Black community was either immoral or amoral."[10] Rather, she asserts a moral agency to be found in Black life "that may run contrary to the critical boundaries of mainline Protestantism." Because of the oppressed and discriminatory positions in which it has found itself, the Black community has been required to create and cultivate values and virtues in its own terms so that it can prevail against the odds with moral integrity.[11]

Thus, for Cannon and other womanists, neither the ethical values nor the ethical assumptions of the Black community are "identical with the body of obligations and duties that Anglo-Protestant American society requires of its membership."[12] The same holds true for Black Catholics. Nor can they be "as long as powerful whites who control the wealth, the systems and the institutions in this society continue to perpetuate brutality and criminality against Blacks.[13]

In her study of the historical context in which Black women find themselves as moral agents, Cannon analyzes the moral context of Black women in the twentieth-century situation arising out of the struggle "to survive in two contradictory worlds simultaneously, 'one white, privileged and oppressive, the other black, exploited and oppressed.'"[14] In so doing, she walks a path created by many Black women before her who sought to define the meaning of Black women's lives and to expand the boundaries of those lives beyond the limited horizons established by both white and Black patriarchal social systems.

Womanist theologians use the "stuff" of women's lives to spin a narrative of their persistent effort to rise above and beyond those persons and situations that attempt to hold them down. Their sources are social, political, anthropological, and especially literary, viewing, as Cannon does, Black women's literary traditions as a "valid source for the central rubrics of the Black woman's odyssey,"[15] for it is in her literary writings that she sets forth the documentation of the "living out" of Black lives in a world confronted daily by racism, sexism, and poverty.

The parameters for a womanist theological methodology, as first set forth by Delores Williams, consist of the following:

1. a multidialogical intent that advocates dialogue and action in many diverse communities (social, political, and religious);
2. a liturgical intent that is relevant to and reflective of the Black church but also enables womanists to challenge that institution's often discordant yet prophetic message;
3. a didactic event that provides new insights for moral life based on an ethic of justice for poor women, children, and men; and lastly,
4. a commitment both to reason and to the validity of female imagery and metaphorical language in the construction of theological statements.[16]

Other womanist theologians, both Protestant and Catholic, are raising equally critical questions and presenting them to the male- and white-dominated academic and ecclesial worlds, demanding their inclusion in the ongoing religious dialogue.

Jacquelyn Grant has become known for her incisive womanist approach to the christological question, an issue not fully explored in Black theology. Her book *White Women's Christ and Black Women's Jesus* sets forth an affirmative response to the continually raised question of white feminist theologians, "Can a male be the savior of women?" Grant goes beyond what she terms the inadequate feminist critique of historical and contemporary male theology, citing its failure to examine its own limited foundation in the Euro-American world view. Instead, she raises "racism/sexism/classism, as a conglomerate representation of oppression, [as] the most adequate point of departure for doing the kind of wholistic theology and Christology which . . . feminist theologians advocate."[17]

Womanist theology begins, therefore, not with an emphasis on the liberation of women alone, but on the liberation of an entire community, with the women's struggle seen as a focal point encompassing all other struggles along the lines of race, gender, and class. Thus, Grant contextualizes her exploration of the meaning of Jesus Christ in the context of women, particularly Black women, who are themselves grounded in and emerge from a particular community, the African American community in the United States.

It is the Black woman's experience, which goes beyond these limitations/restrictions, that serves as the context from which Grant's christology emerges. Recognizing that for Black women the Bible is considered "a major source for religious validation of their lives," she presents a twofold source for their understanding of God. The first is that of God's direct revelation to them as Black women, and the second is God's revelation as witnessed in the Bible and as received in the context of their lived-out experience, in which God is revealed as Creator, Sustainer of life, Comforter, and Liberator.[18] Jesus, therefore, is seen as the "divine co-sufferer, who empowers [Blacks] in situations of oppression."[19] He is the central frame of reference. Yet, she also makes the point that there is, for African Americans, no difference made between the persons of the Trinity.

For Grant, Black women, because of their triple oppression, are the "particular within the particular," the oppressed of the oppressed. Thus, there exists in Black women's tri-dimensional reality "an implied universality which connects them with others."[20]

Black Catholic women have also begun to develop a womanist hermeneutic in their efforts to theologize from their experience as Black, Catholic, and female. In order to understand their voices, first we must look briefly at an emerging Black Catholic theology, which serves as both source and catalyst for their theologizing.

BLACK CATHOLIC THEOLOGY

Another voice historically absent from theological debate after Christianity's first few centuries has been that of Catholics of African descent. In the aftermath of Vatican II they have begun to speak out about their often marginalized status in the Roman Catholic Church. In particular, African American Catholics have begun to find their voices both as Catholic and as Black.[21]

Despite their long history in the church—both in the Middle East and Africa, as well as in the United States (since the sixteenth century)—Black Catholics have been invisible both to those inside and outside of the Roman Catholic Church. Today they number over two million in the United States and if viewed as a separate denomination would be one of the largest in the nation.

The absence of the voice of Black Catholics from theological dialogue is a serious but in many ways understandable one. Black liberation theology, like other liberation theologies, is a contextual theology. As those who first articulated this theology in a systematic form did so from their own contextual experience—one that was primarily Protestant in nature and engaged in dialogue within the ranks of the historically Black churches—it is natural to assume that their evolving theology would be Protestant in its perspective.[22]

At the same time, ordination to the priesthood for Black men, the accepted path to leadership in the Roman Catholic Church, was not encouraged or accepted in the United States until the present century; religious vocations, for Black men and women, were also actively discouraged.[23] Thus, until the reforms of the Synod of Vatican II in the Roman Catholic Church and the Civil Rights Movement and ensuing movements leading up to the emergence of Black liberation theology in the Protestant church, the involvement of Black Catholic scholars, male or female, has been limited in number and restricted in voice. Black Catholic scholars continue to be few today[24] but their voices are beginning to be heard, coupled with and supported by a very strong and active laity involved in the Black Catholic Congress movement, with roots dating back to the latter part of the nineteenth century.[25]

As Black Catholic men and women have begun to explore their richly diverse history and to speak out of their own unique contexts, they are reshaping and reformulating our understanding of Black theology. In so doing, they are recognizing and asserting that to be Black and Catholic is not paradoxical, contradictory, or contrary to the Black liberation movement but is simply one of the many streams flowing into the mighty river of the Black experience in the United States. Their voices and experience reveal evidence of long-hidden and neglected Black experience and tradition that date back to the early church in Africa itself[26] and that have been nurtured and sustained under both slavery and freedom in the United States.[27] The Black Catholic theology that is emerging is also one decidedly womanist in its context, content, and character, due, in part, to the fact that the majority of those Black Catholic theologians working from an avowedly womanist perspective are women.

Black Catholics are engaged in the necessary process of self-definition, socially, historically, liturgically, and theologically. They are speaking out at every level of the church not only on issues of concern for themselves, most particularly their persistent and faith-filled existence in a church that is increasingly one of people of color, but also on their participation and leadership roles in that same church, which have for too long been denied them. Their questions are theological in nature: Who is God for us as Catholics? What does it mean to witness to Christ as a Black Catholic? What is our understanding of Mary the mother of God, of Jesus the Son of God, of God the Creator, and the Holy Spirit, and how are they a part of our lives? How do we express this understanding in ways that are expressive of our heritage as people of African roots yet with American branches? Thus, they are engaged in expanding the dialogue now taking place in Black theology, emphasizing the heritage that they share as people of African descent with their fellow Blacks in other churches, but doing so from a tradition that, as Catholics, is and should be different, as befitting their own unique contextual situation.[28]

Black Catholics are aware of the pitfalls in their path, especially of the dangers revealed by those who have come before them, such as Cone and others, of relying too heavily on the efforts of Euro-Catholic scholars, such as Rahner, Metz, and others, or even the efforts of those who are at work in similar fields of liberation theology, such as Gutiérrez or Segundo.[29] They recognize that the context of a Rahner or a Gutiérrez is different and cannot be universalized to fit the faith life and experience of people of other cultures. Although recognizing that they share traditions as Catholics, members of a universal church, Black Catholics acknowledge as well differences in their historical experience and their present-day existence. They realize the necessity to free themselves to critique both the Catholic church and other Catholic theologians, if and when necessary, in order to fully and freely express their own vision of Catholicism. They seek to look at the church through Black eyes, recognizing both its shortcomings, as revealed in the long, sordid history of racism, sexism, and classism in the church, and its strengths, which have enabled and encouraged them to remain, albeit too long silent, and to proclaim the life, death, and resurrection of Jesus Christ with Black voices.

Black Catholics realize that they must also look at their own failings and critique them with an eye toward strengthening their Black self-identity and self-expression. They must respond to the charges of "one-upmanship," of self-hatred and denial of their rich history and culture in order to be accepted in a church that encouraged them to deny their past and adapt to a present exclusive of their rich and diverse gifts.

What is distinctive about Black Catholicism? To be Catholic is to be aware of the two foundations upon which the church and its teachings stand: scripture and tradition. But one must recognize and assert that tradition, not as one of unchangeable heritage, but as the result of the mingled strands of traditions of all of those who name themselves Catholic and of the lived experience of their faith as it is revealed to them and lived out in the world. As Christianity was once inculturated into the Jewish, North and East African, Greek, Roman, and eventually European cultures, the peoples of Africa, Asia, and Latin America and their descendants in the United States are calling for true inculturation to take place within their cultures as well.[30] This calls for the recognition of the existence and validity of those cultures as bearers of and fertile soil for Christianity as well as for cultural retrieval and revival by the bearers of those cultures, many of whom have been alienated from them.

Over the centuries of the Black presence in this country and in the Catholic church, Black Catholics have, in many ways, been coopted and corrupted into supporting the status quo, into forsaking their own unique identities in their quest to be seen as truly Catholic. (This is not unique to African American Catholics, of course.) However, African American Catholics are now speaking out on what it means to them to be truly Black and authentically Catholic in a holistic, life-affirming and community-building way. They are articulating that meaning for themselves and others in the development of a spirituality and a theology that arise out of the context of their own lived experience in the United States.[31]

The spirituality of Black Catholics, as with all Black Christians, is biblically centered. Sacred Scripture is not rejected, but neither is it accepted uncritically. Their experience in slavery taught them to read the Bible with Black eyes and to proclaim the Word of God with Black voices and understanding. Unmoved by the efforts of masters to implant a biased and distorted Christianity, Black Christians rechristianized Christianity, opening it up to its fullest understanding as a religion of liberation proclaiming a God who created free men and women in God's own image and who gave them a liberator in Christ Jesus, the Son of God.[32]

The Black Catholic understanding of God and Christ is therefore also "colored," if you will, by that liberationist understanding. God and Jesus are not problematical; they are both immanent and transcendent in our lives. The immanent God loves us and nurtures us like a parent bending low over a child; the transcendent God is free to judge those who oppress us and to call us forth into freedom. Jesus as immanent humanity is brother and sister. He is in all ways one of us, walking and talking with us, sharing our journey and carrying our burdens, suffering the pain of our oppression and rejection; yet, as transcendent Son of God, he will come forth in glory to lead us to the Promised Land. And we rejoice in the Holy Spirit, that balm of Gilead sent to heal our sin-sick souls, to abide within us and to strengthen us on our journey while giving us the courage to fight back against our oppressors and to "keep on keepin' on."

It is in Catholicism that the transplanted Africans found a home "of sorts" that nurtured their traditional religiosity. The saints and sacramentals, feast days and fast days, processions and rituals were strikingly familiar to a people comfortable with the concept of a high God, of intercessions and special rites and rituals in their life of worship. Yet, at the same time, they were denied their more fervent expressions of faith and the music that helped them draw closer to God.[33]

Nonetheless, they remained in the church through neglect and often active opposition, and are now reaffirming that long-lost heritage, bringing it to the altar of Christ to share with all of the people of God. They are systematizing their faith and beginning to articulate it in ways that are healing and holy, yet also challenging for all.

African Americans bring to the Catholic church a long and rich tradition, in part one shared since the church's earliest beginnings, as revealed in the baptism of the Ethiopian eunuch (Acts 8:26-40). In other ways, the tradition is uniquely new, the result of the creation of a new people, both African and American. They bring a tradition that can arguably be seen as "subversive," one that is paradoxical, turning all of accepted reality upside-down to present a new reality, that of being called forth to be revealed as the bearers of a true, healing vision of Christ crucified from their experience of both racial and religious persecution. They reflect the memory of a church that preaches equality while practicing discrimination and segregation, a church that preaches a God of love while practicing racial hatred and division.[34] They also bring a healing and holy sacramentality, an extension of the "welcome table" to all of God's people, as evidenced in their gospel liturgies that invite and create new communities of Catholics from all walks of life, of all colors and classes, thus bringing about a new church that is truly representative of the entire people of God in its inclusivity.[35]

Black Catholic scholars, as evidenced in this volume, seek what is distinctive about Black Catholicism, a sharing of African roots with their Black Protestant brothers and sisters as expressed in their celebration of Christ in song and word. They also seek an appreciation of the importance of both scripture and tradition intertwined with an emphasis on a sacramentality that is Catholic in its foundation but Black in its expression. Black Catholics in the United States share the tradition of the church from its earliest beginnings, but they also bring a critique of that tradition, serving as a "subversive memory" within the church itself. They call the church to live up to its proclamation of scriptures that reveal God's consistent option for the poor and the oppressed, scriptures that have been too often submerged by a praxis that ignored the plight of those same poor and oppressed.

BLACK CATHOLIC WOMANIST THEOLOGY

An important avenue for bringing a new and Catholic perspective to Black liberation theology is through the context of Black Catholic women, who can be seen, as all women can, as the "bearers of culture,"[36] those who birth a people and a world into being. This is due, in part (as previously noted) to most of those actively engaged in research and writing on the development of a Black Catholic theology being women. As active participants in the ongoing dialogue among Black theologians, male and female, Protestant and Catholic, and having experienced for ourselves the tri- and even quadradimensional situation of being Black, Catholic, female, and poor, we are privileged, so to speak, to serve as a nexus for an emerging Black Catholic womanist theology.[37] It is here that womanist theology and Black theology converge in the voices of women who have been oppressed because of their race, their gender, their class, and their faith.

As Black Protestant women have done, we women of color in the Roman Catholic church have begun to realize that when we speak of oppression in our church, we cannot look simply at the experiences of white women nor only at the suffering of our Black men. Neither is nor can be truly reflective of what it means to be Black, Catholic, and female in the Catholic church today.[38]

It is, perhaps, in their reinterpretation of the role and presence of Mary, the mother of God, that Black Catholic women can make the most significant contribution. Too often seen as a docile, submissive woman, Black Catholic womanists, instead, see a young woman sure of her God and of her role in God's salvific plan. She is a woman who, in her song (Luke 46:1-55), proclaims her allegiance with God and with her brothers and sisters with whom she lived, as a Jew under Roman oppression, a poor and marginalized existence similar to the existence of Blacks in the church for so long. They relate to her by sharing in her experiences as women who are also oppressed but who continue to bear the burden of faith and to pass on that faith to generations to come. At a time when women were supposed to be silent and invisible, when women were considered of little importance, Mary accepted a singular call from God to stand out as "blessed among all women." As a young, pregnant, unwed woman who had many difficult questions to answer within her community, she still had the courage to say a powerful and prophetic "yes" to God that shattered all of time. She is a role model, not for passivity, but for strong, righteous, "womanish" women who spend their lives giving birth to the future. As Black Catholic women, we challenge our church to recognize the legitimacy of our presence within it and our calling as baptized in Christ to serve the church as the people of God.

The Black Catholic community stands in the unique position of serving as a subversive memory for the church, which calls it to account not only for its past and continuing sins against African American Catholics, but to listen to their prophetic voices, which, as with the Israelites and Jesus himself, have been forged in the fiery furnaces of an unrequited pain and suffering. We bring a heritage of surrogacy and yet survival, of venturing forth into new and untrodden paths, thereby paving the way for others as did Mary Magdalene at the open tomb. She was seen historically as a woman of ill repute, as Black women have often been.

In our efforts to call forth the past and herald the future, we embody our ancestors—strong, faith-filled women and men who refused to bow down to the false gods of white supremacy and who persisted in passing on that flame of hope that they nurtured eternally in their breasts. They sent their children to Mass and to Catholic schools, even when they had to build the churches and school buildings with their own hands; they sent them to novitiates and seminaries, even when they often did not recognize them upon their return. They— especially the women—were able to pass down from generation to generation the kernel of truth that they knew existed in Christianity, that Jesus Christ was the liberator who had come to set all of humanity free.

As womanists, we call upon the church and its people to recognize the human God-granted dignity of all, regardless of skin color, ethnicity, economic status, gender, sexual orientation, or language. We remind the church that without its women the church would have long ceased to exist. They are the visible, human presence of the Holy Spirit eternally breathing life into the Body of Christ.

We assert the legitimacy of our history, our heritage, our culture, and our traditions, diverse as they may be, and call for the gospel's full inculturation: singing our songs, dancing our dances, praising the risen Lord with hearts, hands, voices, feet, and our entire bodies, moving in rhythm to God's eternal Word as it has been sung from time immemorial.

As Black and Catholic, descendants of those long-ago Africans who sheltered and nurtured the gospel in their midst, providing it the time to grow stronger, we see ourselves as not just the past but the future of our church and all of its people. We are the children of Abraham and Sarah, and of Abraham and Hagar. No longer will we passively serve as surrogate sufferers for the sins of our fellow Christians, for that was never God's intent, only humanity's abuse of free will. It is time for the old, old stories to be proclaimed once more from the altars and humble tables, from the highways and byways, that we are about the serious business of proclaiming a new time, God's time, in which all will be reconciled or will perish forevermore.

Our theology is one of hope, a hope based not on ignorance or false optimism but on centuries of experience that our God is a wonder-working God who can and will "make a way out of no way" if we freely open ourselves to be created anew.

Black Catholic womanists are calling for a new hermeneutic, a new way of understanding that puts a human face on the "other," who has been faceless and nameless throughout the history of our country. They seek a new language in which to speak of their hopes and fears, their dreams and nightmares, one that is not couched solely in abstract, lifeless terms of the impersonal and dehumanized "other," a language that empowers them to become the subjects rather than the objects of their history. As women, they are the ones who bring new life into the world, life that must be taught new ways of thinking and relating to people who are different, whether racially, ethnically, sexually, or economically. They call for recognition that difference is not dangerous but can instead be enriching, empowering, and enlightening, opening all of us up to new ways of being in the world. Although we can and must continue to study and learn from European constructs of thinking and acting, we in the United States must also be engaged in the development of our own constructs that emerge from our richly diverse heritage. We must deal with the reality of those too often marginalized and invisible in our society for whom the "turn to the subject" and its subsequent failure have not been an issue but for whom the loss and/or denial of themselves as subject has been and continues to be of paramount importance. Women, especially Black women, the "mules" of the world for so long, are especially situated as articulators of a new way of being Christian and Catholic, of being faith-filled, for they have maintained their faith and passed it on against great odds. They attempt always to engage in God-talk that is liberating, not just for themselves but for all of humanity.

Black Catholic womanist theology is an embryo still in the "birthing" process. It must be nurtured and sustained with the truths of Black lives and the lives of those who have gone on before us as well as with the traditions of our faith heritage, as we have experienced and shared it, so that we can come to terms with the fullness of a new life in Christ that will, in time, sustain and nurture all of God's creation.

NOTES

[1] See Part V: "Black Theology and Black Women," in James H. Cone and Gayraud S. Wilmore, *Black Theology: A Documentary History, Volume 1: 1966-1979*, 2d ed., 2 vols. (Maryknoll, N.Y.: Orbis Books, 1993 [originally published as one volume in 1979]); and Diana L. Hayes, "Church and Culture: A Black Catholic Womanist Perspective," in *The Labor of God: An Ignatian View of Church and Culture,* ed. William J. O'Brien (Washington, D.C.: Georgetown University Press, 1991), pp. 65-87.

[2] The term *womanist* was first defined by Alice Walker in *In Search of Our Mothers' Gardens: Womanist Prose* (New York: Harcourt Brace Jovanovich, 1983), p. xi. In 1987, Delores Williams first applied the term theologically in her essay "Womanist Theology" (*Christianity and Crisis* [March 2, 1987]), developing a womanist approach to theology. This work also was undertaken by Katie Cannon in *Black Womanist Ethics* (Atlanta: Scholars Press, 1989) and Jacquelyn Grant in *White Women's Christ and Black Women's Jesus: Feminist Christology and Womanist Response* (Atlanta: Scholars Press, 1989).

[3] Many of the female leaders of the Abolitionist Movement soon revealed their racism upon realizing that Black freedmen were to receive the vote before they were. See Barbara Hilkert Andolsen, *Daughters of Jefferson, Daughters of Bootblacks* (Macon, Ga.: Mercer University Press, 1986).

[4] See Susan Brooks Thistlethwaite, *Sex, Race and God: Christian Feminism in Black and White* (New York: Crossroad, 1989), and Gloria I. Joseph and Jill Lewis, *Common Differences: Conflicts in Black and White*

Feminist Perspectives (Boston: South End Press, 1981). There are, of course, Black feminists who have been outspoken with regard to their concerns and those of their sisters of color; see, for example, Patricia Hill Collins, *Black Feminist Thought: Knowledge, Consciousness, and the Politics of Empowerment* (New York: Routledge, 1991) as well as the writings of bell hooks, Audre Lorde, and Barbara Smith, among others.

[5] Most of these works, such as James H. Cone's *A Black Theology of Liberation*, have been revised in later editions with inclusive language and the presence and significance of Black women acknowledged. The original editions are now out of print.

[6] Walker, *In Search of Our Mothers' Gardens,* p. xi.

[7] Ibid.

[8] The phrase comes from Zora Neale Hurston, *Their Eyes Were Watching God* (New York: Harper & Row, 1990), originally published in 1937.

[9] Cannon, *Black Womanist Ethics,* p. 8.

[10] Ibid.

[11] Ibid., p. 12.

[12] Ibid., pp. 3-4.

[13] Ibid.

[14] Ibid., p. 6; also see Andolsen, *Daughters of Jefferson, Daughters of Bootblacks.*

[15] Ibid., p. 7.

[16] Delores Williams, "Womanist Theology," in *Black Theology: A Documentary History, Volume 2: 1980-1992,* ed. James H. Cone and Gayraud S. Wilmore (Maryknoll, N.Y.: Orbis Books, 1993), pp. 269-71.

[17] Grant, *White Women's Christ and Black Women's Jesus,* p. 2.

[18] Ibid., p. 211.

[19] Ibid., p. 212.

[20] Ibid., p. 217.

[21] See "A Statement of the Black Catholic Clergy Caucus," in Cone and Wilmore, *Black Theology: A Documentary History, Volume 1: 1966-1979,* 230-32.

[22] However, Black Catholics have engaged in the theological discussions since their beginning, as participants in the Civil Rights Movement and as members of the Black Theology Project of Theology in the Americas (see Cone and Wilmore, *Black Theology I*). Tragically, two of the leading Black Catholic scholars died before they were able to present their theological perspectives in a systematic form. Father Bede Abrams, O.F.M.Conv., and Father Joseph Nearon, S.S.S., can be said to be the founding fathers of Black Catholic theology. They, along with Sister Thea Bowman, were the moving forces behind the establishment and staffing of the Institute for Black Catholic Studies, a summer graduate program based at Xavier University in New Orleans, the only Black Catholic university in the United States. They mentored many of those who are emerging as Black Catholic scholars today and were participants in the

first Black Catholic Theological Symposium held in 1978 (see the articles by <u>Abrams and Nearon in *Theology: A Portrait in Black,*</u> Proceedings of the Black Catholic Theological Symposium, no. 1, 1978 (Pittsburgh: National Black Catholic Clergy Caucus, 1980). A second symposium was held in 1980, but the papers were not published. The symposium has been reconstituted and now meets annually.

[23] See Cyprian Davis, *The History of Black Catholics in the United States* (New York: Crossroad, 1990), chaps. 4 and 6. Today there are still only <u>300 Black priests and religious men in the United States, 13 bishops, and 350 religious women,</u> continuing evidence of the obstacles in the path of African American religious vocations.

[24] Presently, there are only <u>six Catholic systematic theologians</u> who are African American.

[25] The first Black Catholic Congress was held in 1889, organized and led by lay Black leaders, such as Daniel Rudd, editor of the first national Black Catholic newspaper, *The American Catholic Tribune,* and others who raised their voices both to protest the exclusion of Blacks from leadership roles in the church and also to propose specific actions to be taken by the Catholic hierarchy to improve the situation of Black Catholics in the United States. See Cyprian Davis, *The History of Black Catholics in the United States,* for an in-depth presentation of the history of Black Catholics in this country, and also M. Shawn Copeland, "African American Catholics and Black Theology: An Interpretation," in Cone and Wilmore, *Black Theology* 1:99-115, for a discussion of the "pastoral and theological appropriation of Black Theology among African American Catholics."

[26] Davis, *The History of Black Catholics in the United States,* pp. 1-27.

[27] Albert J. Raboteau, *Slave Religion: The "Invisible Institution" in the Antebellum South* (New York: Oxford University Press, 1978), chap. 5, pp. 271-75; and Diana L. Hayes, "Black Catholic Revivalism," *The Journal of the Interdenominational Theological Center* 14, nos. 1-2 (Fall 1986/ Spring 1987), pp. 87-107. See also Albert J. Raboteau, *A Fire in the Bones* (Boston: Beacon, 1996).

[28] See Black Bishops of the United States, *What We Have Seen and Heard: A Pastoral Letter on Evangelization* (Cincinnati: St. Anthony Messenger Press, 1984), p. 15, where they note the "reality" of "the Black Church" that "crosses denominational boundaries and is without a formal structure," while at the same time recognizing the distinctiveness of what it means to be a Black Catholic as spelled out earlier in the document (pp. 8-9).

[29] Cone, for example, was initially severely critiqued for his seeming over-reliance on Barth, while other liberation theologians have revealed in their work the influence of their education in Eurocentric seminaries and institutions of learning both in the United States and overseas.

[30] See Diana L. Hayes, "Emerging Voices, Emerging Challenges: An American Contextual Theology," in *Theology toward the Third Millennium*, ed. David Schultenover, S.J. (Lewiston, N.Y.: E. Mellen Press, and Omaha, Neb.: Creighton University Press, 1991), pp. 41-59; and idem, "An African American Catholic Rite: Questions of Inculturation, Collegiality, and Subsidiarity," *The Living Light* (Winter 1992), pp. 35-48.

[31] See Joseph A. Brown, S.J., *To Stand on the Rock: Reflections on Black Catholic Identity* (Maryknoll, N.Y.: Orbis Books, 1998).

[32] See Jamie T. Phelps's essay on Black spirituality, chapter 8 in this volume.

[33] See Hayes, "Black Catholic Revivalism"; and Clarence Rivers, ed., *This Far by Faith: American Black Worship and Its African Roots* (Cincinnati: Stimuli, 1977).

[34] See Davis, *The History of Black Catholics in the United States.*

[35] See Bishops' Committee on the Liturgy, National Conference of Catholic Bishops, *In Spirit and in Truth: Black Catholic Reflections on the Order of Mass* (Washington, D.C.: United States Catholic Conference, 1987); and Secretariat for the Liturgy and Secretariat for Black Catholics, National Conference of Catholic Bishops, *Plenty Good Room: The Spirit and Truth of African American Catholic Worship* (Washington, D.C.: United States Catholic Conference, 1991).

[36] Gay Wilentz, *Binding Cultures: Black Women Writers in Africa and the Diaspora* (Bloomington, Ind.: Indiana University Press, 1992).

[37] See Diana L. Hayes, "To Be Black, Catholic, and Female," in *New Theology Review* (May 1993), pp. 55-62; idem, "Feminist Theology, Womanist Theology: A Black Catholic Perspective," in Cone and Wilmore, *Black Theology*, 1:325-35; and idem, "My Hope Is in the Lord: Transformation and Salvation in the African American Community," in *Embracing the Spirit: Womanist Perspectives on Hope, Transformation and Salvation,* ed. Emilie Townes (Maryknoll, N.Y.: Orbis Books, 1997); Jamie T. Phelps, O.P., "Joy Came in the Morning: Risking Death for Resurrection," pp. 48-64; and M. Shawn Copeland, "Wading through Many Sorrows: Toward a Theology of Suffering in Womanist Perspective," pp. 109-29, in *A Troubling in My Soul: Womanist Perspectives on Evil and Suffering,* ed. Emilie Townes (Maryknoll, N.Y.: Orbis Books, 1993); Toinette Eugene, "How Can We Forget," in Townes, *Embracing the Spirit,* and other writings.

[38] Ibid., all references.

5

Method in Emerging Black Catholic Theology

M. SHAWN COPELAND

Reflection on method in emerging black Catholic theology pro-
vokes several questions. On the one hand, one of the most blatant
misunderstandings about Catholic theology is that it merely repeats
what the magisterium dictates; on the other hand, one of the most
blatant misunderstandings about black theology is that it is turned-
in on itself and displays little concern for objective criteria. How is
an authentic black Catholic theology to discredit such disinformation?
How is an authentic black theology to respond to the demanding set
of traditions related to the magisterium or teaching authority of the
Roman Catholic Church? By whose or what authority does the black
Catholic theologian speak? If black theologies insist on the authoritative character of the black experience, how are we to understand
authority? How are we to understand "black experience"? To whom
or to what is the black Catholic theologian accountable? For whom
and for what is she or he responsible?

These questions, although difficult, are not necessarily antago-
nistic. Rather, they form a crucial aspect of the *locus theologicus* of
black Catholic theology. Indeed, our cultural, existential, and ecclesial
situation as African American Catholic theologians is compound-
complex. That situation obliges us to contest the imputation of the
patently false dichotomy between black and Catholic. It requires us
to excavate, critique, and reconstruct our African-derived religious,
cultural, and aesthetic wisdom, traditions, and practices. At the same
time, because our formal theological preparation constitutes both
spiritual and discursive formation, we black Catholic theologians

engage and are engaged by a liturgical, spiritual, and intellectual tradition nearly two thousand years old. Further, because our situatedness in the Americas is the result of brutal betrayal and calloused enslavement, we black Catholic theologians and scholars are challenged to critically appropriate the religions, cultures, and histories that shape our distinctive heritage.

This triangulation—religio-cultural Africanisms, Catholic faith, American history—demands that our communal and individual intellectual praxis transcend and transform boundaries imputed to us. It further discloses the importance and power of identity and identity formation. Thus, a determinative aspect of the *locus theologicus,* or the place from which we do black Catholic theology, is our despised black identity. For more than three hundred years the term *black* has been used by Europeans and European-Americans to deprecate peoples of African descent. *Black* meant dismal, dingy, dirty, defiled, filthy, soiled, polluted, base. Moreover, the work of European and European-American philosophers such as Kant, Montesquieu, Voltaire, and Jefferson lent credibility to the idea that skin pigmentation or race gave "white men" intellectual, moral, social (i.e., political, economic, technological), cultural, and spiritual supremacy. These critical philosophers of the Enlightenment uncritically surrendered their intellectual power and authority to "the domain of the naturalists, anthropologists, physiognomists, and phrenologists."[1] Their philosophical evaluation legitimated biology as human destiny: children, women, and men with black skin were said to be meant *by nature* for perpetual slavery. Within Christianity, *blackness* came to insinuate dirt and filth, evil and sin, guilt and moral degradation, death and the diabolical. Despite warnings against confusing allegorical and analogical interpretations with spiritual realities, blackness became an indispensable element of Christian cosmology.[2] These connotations were attached to peoples of African descent as a collective and as individuals, and came to function as permanent ways to describe and to explain blacks anthropologically and ontologically.

Many African peoples, both on the continent and in the diaspora, internalized these negative and, fundamentally, self-destructive meanings. Too many of us thought that our black skin rendered us base, dirty, polluted, ugly, inferior. As a community and as individuals, we underwent a deformation of identity. Only slowly, over time, in suffering, in prayer, and in struggle did we Africans and African Americans accept and espouse the notion that our black skin *is* good, *is* beautiful, that God's image *is* discerned in our black selves.

Self-definition is, above all, a human task and obligation. To name ourselves, our history, culture, intellectual and social movements, and Catholic religious praxis "black" is an act of self-determination, defiance, and courage. When we do this, we acknowledge and embrace an identity that has been shaped under duress, anxiety, and rejection in society and in our church. When we call ourselves and our enterprise "black Catholic," we are not repudiating the universal nature and mission of our church; rather, we are giving a name to our particularity, to our gift and presence within it. In conformity with our baptismal vocation, we are naming ourselves *as* church—not something to which we belong, but who *we are*.

To name ourselves "black" is, at once, *critical, commemorative,* and *celebratory*. This self-naming takes up a *critical* stance toward the thick, prickly history and meanings of the very word *black*. Naming ourselves "black" grapples creatively, courageously with the condition of having been dispossessed of land, language, and culture. At the same time, this self-identification signifies that we are a new creation, a people of faith and hope. To name ourselves "black Catholic" is to *commemorate* the daring and doings of women and men of African descent who forged a path for us in faith. When we name ourselves "black Catholic," we honor those enslaved Africans who lived the life of faith for more than two hundred years in St. Augustine, Florida; we honor those enslaved blacks of Kongo heritage and Catholic faith who led the Stono Rebellion of the eighteenth century; we honor lay evangelists like Vincent de Paul Davis and Lincoln and Julia Vallé; we honor founders of religious congregations like Elizabeth Lange, Henriette Delille, and Mathilda Beasley; we honor priests like Augustus Tolton and Charles Uncles.[3] Moreover, naming ourselves "black Catholic" acknowledges God's abiding providence, God's active involvement in our particular religious experience, culture, and history. Finally, as God's creation, naming ourselves "black" *celebrates* God's image in our black selves. While this self-naming rejoices in "blackness" as a divine gift and affirms our self-understanding as sons and daughters of God, it does so without violating the black Christian principle—that all human beings are equal before the Author of life.

This chapter investigates the method of emerging black Catholic theology. The first section briefly outlines the origin and priorities of black theology and then takes up in more detail the origin of black Catholic theology. However, this section can only suggest the intellectual and pastoral ferment that sets the backdrop for the emergence of black Catholic theology. Much more work needs to be done in recovering this recent past. The second section examines elements particular to method in black Catholic theology. Like many of our colleagues, most of us black Catholic theologians use method of correlation. The difficulties with this method are examined here along with black Catholic responses to them. This section also considers other key dimensions of method in black Catholic theology. The third section focuses on some of the priorities that black Catholic theology shares with other expressions of black and liberation theology as well as some of the differences that distinguish it from these. This section also raises some ongoing issues that press on and challenge the development of black Catholic theology.

BLACK THEOLOGY AS A CATHOLIC THEOLOGY

The term *black theology* irrupted in the United States in the mid-1960s, during the waning days of the Civil Rights Movement, to account for black people's social ferment, spiritual urgency, and unyielding gritty 350-year-old struggle to win and realize their freedom, to create for themselves before God a future full of hope. Its life-world was not some aloof armchair musing, but the social and psychic rage of black people enduring nearly a century of legal and customary segregation and discrimination. Black theology proposed a critical reading of the U. S. religious, cultural, and social condition in light of God's revelation in the life and ministry, passion and death, and resurrection of Jesus of Nazareth. Black theology distinguished Sacred Scripture as the word of God from Sacred Scripture as an ideology wielded for the religious, cultural, and social benefit of white Protestant and Catholic churches and their membership. It directly linked the struggle of black people for freedom and liberation to the message of the gospel.

From its inception, black theology manifested a concern for the welfare of the whole person; thus, it went beyond conventional Western dualisms of soul and body, spirit and matter, reason and emotion, sacred and profane. Even as black theology explicitly focused on historical and social liberation, it did not deprecate the necessity and importance of the Christian demand for holiness of life, for spiritual health. It underscored the continuity between the essential freedom of human persons as such, and the effective or social freedom that makes fully human living possible. At the same time, black theology grasped the universal aspect of the gospel in meeting the creative tension between the particular and universal. Indeed, black theology carries within it the seed of universal concern that extends most particularly to all marginalized and oppressed persons and that advocates for the liberation of *all*—oppressed as well as the oppressor.

It has been rather convenient to date the formal emergence of black Catholic theology with the first meeting of the Black Catholic Theological Symposium (BCTS) in October 1978. This event was organized and chaired by Thaddeus Posey under the auspices of the National Black Catholic Clergy Caucus.[4] It provided an opportunity for the few theologically credentialed clergy along with those religious women and men who had been reading and studying black and Latin American liberation theologies collaboratively to evaluate the meaningfulness of these efforts for African American Catholic experience. However, this meeting was preceded by other black Catholic attempts, in the early 1970s, to articulate a theology adequate for our particular pastoral and social needs. Among the more conspicuous of these efforts are essays by Edwin Cabey, Theresa Perry, Edward Braxton, Toinette Eugene, Clarence Rivers, and lectures by Patricia Grey Tyree, Cyprian Davis, Elizabeth Harris, Jamie T. Phelps, and me.[5]

Yet, even as we black Catholics opened our pastoral and scholarly questions to the insights of black theology, most U.S. Catholic theologians ignored it. There were, thankfully, exceptions. John Carey published two interpretative essays in *Theological Studies,*[6] and, in 1973, the Catholic Theological Society of America (CTSA) invited black social ethicist Preston N. Williams of Harvard Divinity School to address the annual convention.[7] In speaking to the members of the CTSA, Williams focused on the absolutizing character of race in the U.S. cultural and social context. He called upon the Catholic church "to become more universal and more pluralistic" by taking black experience and culture more seriously—encouraging black clergy to design new cultural and religious forms, recruiting and nourishing black vocations, and educating black Catholics as theologians and scholars.[8] Richard McBrien, at that time president-elect of the CTSA, took up Williams's challenge. He asked Joseph Nearon, a black priest and Roman-trained scripture scholar who was teaching at John Carroll University, to form a research committee to study black theology "as it affects Roman Catholic theology."[9] Nearon's own educational and teaching situations were such that he had not been preoccupied at all with black theology; he took the request as a catalyst for a program of careful reading and reflection.

At the 1974 CTSA meeting, Nearon postponed both the research committee and substantive report in favor of what he called a "pre-preliminary" paper in which he explored three questions: To what extent is Roman Catholic theology racist? To what degree can reflection upon the black experience enrich Catholic theology? and What has the Roman Catholic tradition to offer the quest for black identity?[10] In response to the first question, Nearon observed that Catholic theology had treated the black experience as if it were "irrelevant." Catholic theology was racist, and its racism was one of omission; the social and cultural experience of blacks was outside the scope of Catholic theological reflection. In response to the second question, Nearon resumed the critique of classicist culture. In other words, Catholic theology was a product of the Western (European) cultural tradition; it understood that culture as culture and, thus, the singular medium for transmitting the message of the gospel. Nearon argued that black culture and traditions, both in the United States and in Africa, had much to teach Catholic theology. In response to the third question, Nearon agreed that in black theology, black identity and black liberation were of uppermost concern; but, he went on to say, "a black theologian working in the Roman Catholic tradition would find new and important insights in the search for reconciliation." Finally, Nearon repeated Williams's call for the formal training and preparation of black Catholic theologians. This ought to be "the first priority for the CTSA . . . a concerted effort to raise up a generation of black Catholic theologians."[11]

At the next annual CTSA meeting, Nearon delivered a substantive report. This analysis interpreted black theology as a paradigm shift in theology and, as such, could not be confined to any one confessional, denominational, or ecclesial context. Thus, the hermeneutical, theoretical, moral, practical, emancipatory, and pastoral priorities of black theology were not foreign or alien to the experience of black Catholics. This report reiterated the need for "a corps of competent black Catholic theologians [as] an absolute necessity," if the continuing challenge of black theology is to receive an adequate Catholic response.[12]

Three years later the Black Catholic Theological Symposium met for the first time. The four-day meeting steered a course between rigid apologetics and romanticized rhetoric. The purpose was not simply to absolve the church of its inadequate pastoral treatment of blacks nor rancorously to heap scorn upon it. The posture of the symposium was (and remains) constructive: evaluating the historical, cultural, psychic, and social situation of black people and proposing ways to initiate a dialogue between black history and culture and Catholic doctrine and theology. The 1978 meeting anticipated a theological agenda to contest the imputed dichotomy between black and Catholic, which dishonored not only our intellectual potential, but the committed faith of our black Catholic ancestors, indeed, our very being.

METHOD IN BLACK CATHOLIC THEOLOGY

It is rather ambiguous to speak about "black Catholic theology." The triangulation of the religio-cultural Africanisms, Catholic faith, and American history specifies content or data for black Catholic theology, but not method. Black Catholic theology is still in its formative stage, yet it is possible to comment on how black Catholic theologians have adapted method of correlation and to offer a general, tentative description of four increasingly key interactive elements of black Catholic theological reflection. These are critique, retrieval, construction, and social analysis.

METHOD OF CORRELATION

Many black Catholic theologians, like many of our contemporaries, use method of correlation, which has become fairly common among Roman Catholic theologians. Even as this method presents several difficulties, it represents a shift away from the revelational positivism, the manual-style Catholic theology so prevalent prior to the Second Vatican Council. Method of correlation entails formulating questions from contemporary human experience, then showing how the Christian message of revelation provides adequate answers.[13] At its best, method of correlation aims to establish the universal (transhistorical, transcultural) relevance of the Christian message. Method of correlation as *apologetic* explains the meanings of Christian claims in a language understandable to a given age; it makes the truth of Christian revelation manifest. Method of correlation as *dialogic* brings traditional Christian symbols into conversation with contemporary culture, so that as the symbols make sense out of present-day issues, the issues make sense out of the symbols.

Yet method of correlation is not value-free, not innocent. Because method of correlation does not acknowledge the possibilities of mutual conditioning between the Christian message and the cultural situation, it presents a risk for black theologies. This mutual conditioning can leave the scriptures and the situation vulnerable to uncritical, self-serving interpretations by the dominant culture. Method of correlation also lacks criteria for its correlation. It offers no grounds for the criteria for appropriating the tradition, for the choice of analysis of the present situation, or for the criteria for bringing the two into correlation, leaving each theologian free to adopt her or his own criteria. The result is an uncritical, theological pluralism, which may conceal moral or philosophic stances that have never been submitted to critical reflection.[14]

Black Catholic social ethicist Toinette Eugene (in her early work) and systematic theologian Jamie Phelps have tried to meet this difficulty by proposing that theology in an African American Catholic perspective hold itself accountable to the threefold interrelated criteria of orthodoxy, orthopathy, and orthopraxis.[15] With these criteria Eugene rejected any artificial separation between orthodoxy or "right teaching" and orthopraxis or "righteous action" by focusing on their relation through the middle term, orthopathy, or "righteous heart or feeling."[16] Although Eugene seems to have moved away from this explicit formulation, she remains committed to the integration of mind, heart, and action. Phelps, on the other hand, continues to use these criteria in her theological praxis. She insists on the intrinsic connection among theology, life, and ministry: cognitive learning should transform the heart as well as lead to morally and ethically appropriate social and personal action.

Another way of addressing difficulties in method of correlation is to focus on foundations. Systematic theologian Edward Braxton and I have introduced Bernard Lonergan's notion of foundations into black Catholic theology.[17] This notion of foundations emphasizes the importance of critical understanding and judgment in theological interpretation. It appeals to the theologian's unrestricted commitment to the invitation to *be attentive! be intelligent! be rational! be responsible!* These transcendental precepts summon the theologian to attend to, to distinguish, and to appropriate her or his religious, moral, and intellectual activities. On this account, theological foundations are grounded, not in religious propositions or the tradition or the culture or the social situation, but in the religiously, morally, intellectually converted persons, theologians who are responsible for the selection, articulation, and control of meaning in theologizing. Although the emphasis is on the individual, the theologian is never isolated but is a person-in-community. Finally, the stress on foundations also concurs with the discernment of our colleagues that a commitment to seek truth, to embrace self-sacrifice and genuine humility, to strive for holiness has a bearing on our theology.

CRITIQUE AND RETRIEVAL

Like other black theologies, black Catholic theology critiques not only the cultural and social situation, but the Christian scriptures, Catholic tradition, symbols, and ecclesial structures. Doing so allows black Catholic theology to expose cover stories of repression in cultural, historical, social, and ecclesial situations; to debunk the assumptions that undergird those stories as well as the way in which those assumptions impede our ability to grasp the reality of those situations. Moreover, this critique recognizes that the Christian tradition and the cultural and social situation are neither as separate nor as pure as method of correlation would have it. Even as the Christian tradition has had a powerful impact in shaping the culture and social structures of the world in which we live, that same tradition has been shaped by cultural forces and social structures.

In black Catholic theology, retrieval relies on critical historical method. This is a two-pronged archeological process directed toward overlooked sources of black culture and history and sources of lived Roman Catholic faith. On the one hand, because religious consciousness has been the crucial mediation of African American personal and communal transformation, black Catholic theology must critically appropriate the African-derived religio-cultural traditions of the enslaved peoples. This appropriation entails a form of "archaic critique" or "crawling back through [black] history" to understand the cultural and social experiences that evoked such religious consciousness and response, and to offer a form of a critique.[18] My own work has tried to meet this challenge by posing a notion of base-line religious consciousness expressed in black religion, a phenomenological rather than denominational heuristic in which Africa and African fragments hold a more or less normative status, while Christianity furnishes language, images, and symbols through which the enslaved peoples interpreted their condition and mediated transformed meanings.[19] On the other hand, the neglected story of the black Catholic life of faith must be excavated. Historian Cyprian Davis has made a major contribution to this task with *The History of Black Catholics in the United States.*[20] In this work Davis challenges two prevailing notions about American religious history—that the religious history of African Americans is chiefly Protestant and that the religious history of Catholics is chiefly immigrant European. Davis's research reveals a portrait of African American loyalty and creativity in the practice of our Catholic faith, despite institutional discrimination and rejection.

Other black scholars use historical method in the recovery of the active and creative participation of black lay women and men in Catholic ministry. Jamie Phelps has incorporated historical research in her ecclesiological studies. Focusing on the nineteenth-century evangelizing ministry of Josephite priest John R. Slattery, Phelps has cleared the ground for critical reflections on current Catholic efforts at evangelization and inculturation by and among African Americans.[21] Historian Thaddeus Posey has added to our understanding of the struggle and spiritual traditions of the Oblate Sisters of Providence, the oldest of three black congregations of vowed black women religious.[22] The efforts of historian Cecilia Moore have brought to light the work of black Catholic laity to establish and sustain centers of Catholic academic and vocational education.[23] And, in a study of religious education among nineteenth-century African American Catholics, religious educator Addie Walker has shown that pastoral neglect literally forced us black Catholics to catechize ourselves.[24] In addition, anthropologist and historian Giles Conwill has drawn out African retentions in African American culture and demonstrated their viability for black Catholic liturgical and pastoral life. African American Studies specialist Eva Regina Martin, in locating West African symbols in the artistry of enslaved ironworkers in antebellum New Orleans, shows how the descendants and apprentices of Mende blacksmiths covertly infused and ornamented Catholic parishes and cemeteries with the devotional symbols of their culture.[25]

Social Analysis and Social Science

Since black Catholic theology takes the actual situation in which black people live as its point of departure, a comprehensive understanding of that situation is necessary. To this end, black Catholic theologians emphasize social analysis and social science, including political theory, political philosophy, and social science. Through appropriation of social theories and employing social analysis, black Catholic theology seeks critical understanding of the material or social, cultural, and religious (including the structural, symbolic, and doctrinal) incongruities that impinge upon the black human condition.

Toinette Eugene's work bears the mark of her doctoral preparation in sociology of religion. Her theological ethical essays on the African American family, moral values, moral development, AIDS, sexuality, violence, and sexual abuse are informed by the work of sociologists, political philosophers, and psychologists. Her starting point is the actual condition of marginalized and oppressed women and men.[26]

Drawing on formal degrees in sociology and psychiatric social work, ecclesiologist Jamie Phelps dialogues with sociologists, political philosophers, and psychologists in reading the social matrix in which the church is incarnated. Writing in passionate language about social sin, social justice, violence, and racism, Phelps employs social analysis to gain a more comprehensive and critical understanding of acute political, economic, and technological situations, while uncovering their historical and structural basis. This allows Phelps to make concrete the social situation in which the church is inserted and to uncover how the church, constituted in the supernatural communion of believers, participates in and is subject to this sinful situation.

As systematic theologians, Diana Hayes and I both use social analysis as a tool to make concrete the U.S. social and cultural matrix and to clarify the ambiguous interdependence of the "first" and "two-thirds" worlds; we also accentuate the notion of the common good as a way of pursuing this investigation. Hayes proposes a "contextual theology" for the United States that, while acknowledging the racial, cultural-ethnic diversity of its people, is grounded in the faith and suffering of those whose "American experience" has been one of protracted oppression and marginalization. Those who have been considered "nonpersons" or "objects" of history are restored to personhood, are subjects of their own history and theology.[27] My work is directed toward developing a politically responsible methodical theology of social transformation, utilizing Bernard Lonergan's "structure of the human good" in formulating, asking, and answering questions that get at the meaning of development and progress (or devolution and decline) of the common human good in the U. S. context.[28]

CONSTRUCTION

While *all* black Catholic social ethicists and moral and systematic theologians are engaged in constructive work, what follows is a brief review of a few theological projects in progress.

Jamie Phelps has begun to work out a *christological reflection* that makes a serious response to the denial of the full humanity of black peoples and that examines how black women and men have understood Jesus in the struggle to survive slavery, lynching, segregation, and discrimination in society; that elaborates the black community's apprehension of Jesus as sustainer, liberator, and prophet of a new social order; that interprets the gospel so as to reveal "how black women, men, and children encounter, embody, and manifest the living presence of the risen Christ in the Gospel and in their life experience."[29] Her contribution to this volume is a good example of making these concerns explicit in the contemporary social context.

As a moral theologian, Bryan Massingale has set himself the two-fold task of critically appropriating and bringing into dialogue the *black social experience* and the *Catholic moral and social tradition*. He presents a critique of the moral tradition's silence on such issues as anti-black racism and affirmative action, but he has begun creative formulation. Massingale is working out moral norms that draw out the social tradition's commitment to the inviolability of the human person, while respecting individual uniqueness and historical and cultural particularity; that emphasize historically conditioned responsibility and ethical action, but reject situational determinism, making no pretense to absolutism, and humbly leaving room for revision. Massingale, further, has begun to make thematic the grave difficulty of formation of conscience in the morally compromised situation of the modern world.[30]

In its early stages, black theology centered its critique on racism but overlooked sexism in the black community; the presence and suffering of black women were erased in the articulation and praxis of black liberation theology. Feminist theology leveled a critique against the normativity of maleness and the subordination of women to men in patriarchy; the critique of sexism overlooked white women's racial privilege and their participation in white supremacy. Black—and red, brown, yellow—women were erased in the articulation and praxis of (white middle-class) feminist theology. Womanist perspective calls these erasures into question and projects black women's experience into Christian theology. While Eugene, Hayes,

Phelps, and I have each written essays and lectured from a womanist perspective, Eugene and Hayes have done so more extensively.[31]

Eugene's work addresses the ways in which a womanist perspective makes explicit how black women come to know and to think about oppression. Gender, race, and class are grasped as interlocking, mutually conditioning systems of oppression that shape, but do not determine, black women's social experience.[32] Hayes argues that a Catholic womanist perspective must resist the dominance of Eurocentricism in Catholic theology and its corresponding lack of criticism of racism and racialized sexism. Hayes has mined black women's literature as a source for reflecting on and writing about black spirituality. She has proposed also to reinterpret the role and presence of Mary of Nazareth as "womanish." Drawing on contemporary womanist hermeneutics, Hayes pushes Catholic devotion beyond a Madonna of romantic piety to a woman transformatively cooperating with God in history.[33]

SOME QUESTIONS FOR BLACK CATHOLIC THEOLOGY

Like other black theologies, black Catholic theology explicitly addresses the historical, cultural, and social subordination of black peoples within contexts dominated by white supremacist rule. It affirms concrete Christian social praxis and seeks to collaborate actively with the social sciences in efforts to apprehend, understand, diagnose, and transform society. Yet, black Catholic theology neither is nor understands itself to be a substitute for social science, social analysis, or social activism. Through critical biblical, historical, and doctrinal interpretation, black Catholic theology has begun to uncover liberating aspects of some key Christian understandings. By uncovering the intelligibility, truth, and relevance of Catholic Christian faith to meet the exigencies of the black human condition, black Catholic theology supports black Catholic identity and engages black experience as an authentic source of theology. However, if the continued and authentic development of black Catholic theology is not to be jeopardized, there are several unsettling questions with which my colleagues and I must grapple—and soon. Here, I name five of these and suggest their contours.

First, let me recall the rather crude misconceptions about Catholic theology and black theology with which this chapter began: that Catholic theology merely repeats what the magisterium dictates and that black theology is turned in on itself and has little, if any, interest in objective criteria. How is an authentic black Catholic theology to discredit these stereotypes? How is it to engage and relate to the church's magisterium? By what authority does the black Catholic theologian speak? How are we to understand authority? To whom or what is the black Catholic theologian accountable? In what does the black Catholic theologian's responsibility consist?

The difficulty of these questions arises from the tension between the older notion of theology as a practice or *habitus* and the more recent notion that theological teaching authority belongs strictly to bishops by virtue of their ecclesial charism.[34] We black Catholic moral and systematic theologians commit ourselves to fidelity to the authority of tradition, and this fidelity includes the responsible exercise of creative and critical mediation. In other words, the practice of black Catholic theology is an act of "creative fidelity" and, as such, it entails intellectual, moral, and religious "responsibility to God, to the traditional sources of God's revelation, and to the historical medium in which they are appropriated by the believing church."[35]

A second issue is closely interwoven with these questions. If systematic theology has a principal responsibility for doctrinal continuity, what is the status of the dogmatic tradition in black Catholic theology? How does black Catholic theology meet this responsibility? For the most part, we black Catholic theologians have not entered into rigorous constructive or analytical engagement with the doctrinal tradition. Our work has focused mainly on social sins—racism, sexism, heterosexism, and class exploitation; in this, Catholic social teaching has served as the primary dialogue partner. Although black Catholic theology has been alert to those doctrines (for example, theological anthropology and ecclesiology) that undergird this teaching, it has not pushed beyond the edges of Catholic doctrinal teaching.

Black Catholic theology is conservative—critically and intentionally so. By this, I mean, black Catholic theology locates, appropriates, and preserves black religio-culture and history; it engages, appropriates, and mediates traditions of Catholic faith. This conservative posture has profound implications for the *one* socially transformative and supernatural end of human living. To clarify this point, let us consider, briefly, black Catholic theology's critique of black (Protestant) theology's attitude toward the normative status of christological statements in the Nicene/Chalcedonian Creed. Some black theologians have contended metaphysical questions pertaining to the divine and human natures of Christ have little, if any, normative significance for a theology directed toward the urgent needs of the African American community.[36] Black Catholic theology situates this issue in light of our explicit *locus theologicus*, that is, our despised black identity. Thus, black Catholic theology grasps "Chalcedon as a condition for a hermeneutic of liberation." In other words, black Catholic theology affirms the unity of the word and the world, "the humanity of human beings in the incarnation of God."[37] For, in Jesus of Nazareth "the unity of the reality of God and of the world . . . has been accomplished [and] is realized, ever afresh" in the lives of women and men of every race and nation and tongue.[38] The very grounds of our critique of the dehumanization, denigration, and alienation of the "human other" are at stake in a critically conservative interpretation of the Nicene/Chalcedonian Creed.

Third, the "color-line" continues to press on our ecclesial situation. In principle, African American Christianity, whether Catholic or Protestant, has always opposed segregation. For African Americans who are members of predominantly white Christian churches, this has been ambiguous terrain. The Catholic church in the United States, unlike the Presbyterian, Baptist, and Methodist churches, did not split over slavery. However, most of the Catholic hierarchy considered slavery a political rather than a moral issue. In practice, the church swallowed the culture and custom of racism; with rare exceptions, ignorance, benign neglect, and segregation obtained. Certainly, since the late-nineteenth century, black Catholics consistently have challenged the establishment of segregated parishes; but our appeals for authentic inclusion and pastoral care were sidelined, often conveniently, by the establishment of ethnic-language parishes that flourished in response to European immigration.[39]

Our struggle "to be church," not merely "to belong," has placed us black Catholics and black Catholic theology on the horns of a dilemma. On the one hand, the moral integrity of black Catholicism and the theology that would mediate it requires an unequivocal rejection of segregation in any form. As members of the Body of Christ, we too desire to live as Jesus lived, to put our communal and personal, cultural and social decisions at the service of the coming Reign of God. On the other hand, pastoral neglect and disregard by white clergy and hierarchy have forced black Catholics to seek out separate sites for the development of our own spiritual life. Must we, as full baptized members of the church, as members of the Body of

Christ, relinquish our desire and attempt to live a life worthy of our Christian calling? This struggle to be church, to be authentically black and truly Catholic, is most poignant, for our tendencies toward authentic integration, inclusion, and participation historically have proved dangerous for black Catholic initiatives. The thwarted work of the black Catholic congresses of the nineteenth century, the collapse of the Federated Colored Catholics in the early twentieth century, the demise of Catholic schools in so many cities, along with the mergers and closures of so many parishes that nurtured black Catholics challenge our current Black Catholic Congress movement to reflect more deeply on our situation. In this endeavor the work of black Catholic theologians and scholars will be crucial.

Because racism remains a brutal fact of life in the United States, black Catholic theology must grapple with the postmodern analysis of race. Critical race theory presents black Catholic theology with a fourth consideration. Critical race theory is a recent form of inquiry into the origin and effects of racism from the field of contemporary legal studies. It confronts the historical centrality and complicity of law in upholding white supremacy.[40] On the one hand, critical race theory contests both spurious and positive theories of race and racial identity. Drawing on postmodern strategies, African American culture critics bell hooks and Victor Anderson, in particular, expose the crippling limitations of treating racial identity as essentialist.[41] Their arguments push for a move beyond ontological blackness— that is, experiencing black life as bound by truncated, "unresolved binary dialectics of slavery and freedom, Negro and citizen, insider and outsider, black and white, struggle and survival," with no possibility of transcending or mediating these fruitfully.[42] Yet, the daily lives of many black people remain dominated and directed by this very polarity. Cornel West's account of the refusal of ten mid-town Manhattan taxi cab drivers "to see" him as a "human being," a "person" (a potential, well-dressed fare), not a threat (black), is insulting—even passively racist. Although West's experience does not register as a matter of life and death (that is, a matter of being killed or assaulted because of skin color), it does underscore the humiliation of stigmatized visibility.[43] The discomfort and anger that many of us feel at this anecdotal notation of racism is, I would wager, due more to Cornel West's public stature and our esteem for him than to trained readings of the volatile U.S. racial landscape. For Emmett Till and Medgar Evers, for Willie Horton and Rodney King, race and racism were real, viciously real.

In its analysis of the racial situation, black Catholic theology can benefit from a critical race theory, but one that would take into account the complexity of contemporary social (that is, political, economic, and technological) relationships; that would be global in scope; and that would be grounded in historical analysis. Such a theory would support a critical notion of black identity in which relationships with "others" shape the self without fixing it under oppressive forces. Such a theory ought to dissolve the black-white polarity of race relations, without either purchasing the hazardous fiction that racism is dead or uncritically reviving the essentialist position. Moreover, such a theory would assist black Catholic theology to promote cultural, social, theoretical, practical dialogue and collaboration among the so-called U.S. minority groups, not from the vantage of competing self-interests, but from a renewed vision of a common human good.

Fifth, since black culture is a source for its reflection, black Catholic theology must attend to the current results and debates around Afrocentric method and Afrocentricity. Afrocentric method is a controversial intellectual and cultural praxis that "places Africans and the interests of Africa at the center of . . . approach[es] to problem solving" and study.[44] Afrocentric method contests the hegemony of European and European-American history, which, rooted in "otherizing" colonial expansion and exploitation, denied the culture-making capacities and products of Africans and indigenous peoples of the Americas. So, in narrating various relations between Africa and Europe, European and European-American history conclude that Europeans and European-Americans are active subjects and Africans are passive objects. Afrocentric method calls into question the reliability and veracity of these judgments; it re-envisions and de-centers the deeds and achievements of European and European-American peoples and cultures. To enact this critique, Afrocentric method relies upon such tools as historical analysis, archeology, aesthetic theory, cultural and literary analysis, geography, linguistics, musicology, and philosophy. Because the aim of this critique is decolonization or freedom of the black mind, Afrocentric theory tries to explain and demonstrate how peoples of African descent can "disidentify" with the control exerted by cultural and social structures.[45]

In the summer of 1996, the faculty of the Institute for Black Catholic Studies sponsored a forum on Afrocentricity—its difficulties, excesses, contributions, and utility in academic and pastoral preparation for Catholic ministry in the black community. Participants dealt with the sharpest criticisms of Afrocentricity—that it is, itself, ideological. In the effort to contest ideological Eurocentrism, Afrocentricity mounts an analysis of the cultural, intellectual, and social importance of Egypt that situates Egypt as the fount and center of *all* Africa, thus uncritically claiming the legacy of Egypt for the descendants of the enslaved peoples in the diaspora. With this move, critics assert, Afrocentricity turns itself inside out and becomes as ideological as the ideology it seeks to combat.

The IBCS discussion included a range of evaluations, but here I mention only the comments of historian Cyprian Davis and African Americanist Eva Regina Martin. Their remarks elucidate some of the best and the worst possibilities of Afrocentric method.[46]

Davis argued that dispassionate study of the history of Africa was of utmost importance to the integrity of African and African American or Black Studies. However, he argued that any attempt to romanticize Africa or to adopt unexamined, even biased, positions violates the canons of historical method and cheapens not only history but Black Studies as a discipline. Wary of Afrocentricity's possible slide into ideology, Davis cautioned black Catholic theologians against indiscriminate appropriation of Afrocentric-derived content. He advocated careful attention to the historically conditioned perspectives of texts as well as of interpreters and called for the nuanced distinction between a working hypothesis in history and verified judgments grounded in data.

Eva Regina Martin shared Davis's concern for rigorous scholarly commitment in historical and interpretative understanding. However, Martin outlined some of the features of an Afrocentric worldview, which, when manifest in literature, the fine and plastic arts, discursive analysis and creation, distinguish and differentiate that worldview from a Eurocentric one. These features include polycentricity, polyrhythm, holism, dimensionality, repetitiveness, curvilinearity, and epic memory.

At its best, Afrocentric method refers to a critical discursive effort that effects a shift in religious, cultural, social, and psychological worldview. This shift differs in its intellectual priorities and values (moral and aesthetic) orientation from those of the West. In this African-centered worldview ambiguity is not merely tolerated but appreciated; the sacred and secular, being and doing, are not separated but united; the individual person is not set over against the community but becomes a person-in-community. This shift affirms "blackness" as more than a biological fact of skin pigmentation. Black-

ness *is* color, but it is more than color; it signifies critical consciousness and functions as a commitment to a historical project that honors
the history and experiences of the ancestors—the enslaved Africans.
Afrocentric method affords black Catholic theology an enriched reading of African American material culture and cultural practices, but
black Catholic theology must resist temptations, from any sector, to
cheap, quick scholarship.

CONCLUSION

This chapter has examined method in emerging black Catholic
theology. It began with brief accounts of the origins of black theology and black Catholic theology. The second section considered
method. It furnished a brief account of the method of correlation,
sketched some of the difficulties which that method presents to black
Catholic theology, and commented on adaptations or correctives to
that method by black Catholic theologians. Then the section reviewed
the elements of critique, retrieval, and social analysis in the construction of black Catholic theology. The third section raised some
ongoing questions and challenges for the future of black Catholic
theology.

James Cone once voiced his concern about the conditions for the
possibility of a black Catholic theology: "The white power structure
in the Catholic Church is so restrictive on what blacks can do or say
that it is almost impossible to think creatively."[47] Of course, by now,
this charge has been met substantively and certainly. But Cone had
a point—and a good one. If all that Catholicism could mean for its
black theologians is restriction, limitation, and censorship, then a
black Catholic theology would only be an exercise in uncritical imitation, fundamentalist apologetics, and revelational positivism. But
a theology authentically *black* and *truly* Catholic opposes imitation
and uncriticality with an authentic, if halting and provisional, search
for voice. For, indeed, a *theologos* with no *logos*, no word of its own,
is mute; it is no *theologos* at all.

In its radical turn to the "other," the "black," as "human person,"
and theological subject; in its focus on the material and spiritual concerns of marginalized U.S. peoples, including Native Americans,
Hispanic/Latinos, and poor marginalized people—especially children
and women—of all races; in its protest of the flaccid evangelization

and pastoral care that the Catholic church historically, with but few exceptions, has rendered to its black members; in its challenge to our church's self-understanding as "an immigrant church"; in its distinction of Catholic and African-derived values and sensibilities from consumerist, materialist, and individualistic ones; in its engagement of the historical, religious, cultural, and social horizon of the United States; in the humble commitment of its theologians and scholars to the demands for intellectual, moral, and religious conversion: black Catholic theology finds its voice and asserts its word.

NOTES

[1] Cornel West, *Prophesy Deliverance! An Afro-American Revolutionary Christianity* (Philadelphia: Westminster Press, 1982), p. 61. See Immanuel Kant, *Observations on the Feeling of the Beautiful and Sublime* [1764], trans. John T. Goldthwait (Berkeley: University of California Press, 1960), p. 111; see also David Hume, *Essays and Treatises on Several Subjects*, 2 vols. (Edinburgh, 1825), esp. 1:521-22.

[2] Robert E. Hood, *Begrimed and Black: Christian Traditions on Blacks and Blackness* (Minneapolis: Fortress Press, 1990).

[3] John K. Thornton, "African Dimensions of the Stono Rebellion," *American Historical Review* 96, no. 4 (October 1991): pp. 1101-13; Cyprian Davis, *The History of Black Catholics in the United States* (New York: Crossroad, 1990).

[4] For the proceedings of this conference, see Thaddeus J. Posey, O.F.M.Cap., ed., *Theology: A Portrait in Black* (Pittsburgh: The Capuchin Press, 1980).

[5] This list is in no way exhaustive. It names some black Catholics who had begun to explore this theological shift prior to the first meeting of the Black Catholic Theological Symposium: Edwin Cabey, "God and Liberation," *Signs of Soul* 3, no. 1 (January 1971): 11, 13; Theresa Perry, "Towards the Development of a Methodology for a Black Theology," *Signs of Soul* 3, no. 2 (May 1971): 3-4; Edward Braxton, "Reflections from a Theological Perspective," in *This Far by Faith: American Black Worship and Its African Roots* (National Office for Black Catholics: Washington, D.C. and the Liturgical Conference: Washington, D.C., 1977), pp. 58-75; and "What Is 'Black Theology' Anyway?," *The Critic* (Winter 1977), pp. 64-70; Toinette Eugene, "Training Religious Leaders for a New Black Generation," *Catechist* 6, no. 2 (October 1972), pp. 6-11, and "Reflections of a Black Sistuh," *Freeing the Spirit* 3, no. 2 (1974), pp. 11-15; Clarence Rivers, "The African Diaspora: The Continuity of African Culture in the Western Hemisphere," A Background Paper, 1973, typescript, pp. 1-24; idem, *Soulful Worship* (Cincinnati: Stimuli, 1974); idem, "The

Oral Tradition Versus the Ocular Western Tradition," in *This Far by Faith*, pp. 39-49; and idem, *The Spirit in Worship* (Cincinnati: Stimuli, 1978).

In the late 1960s and early 1970s, Tyree (then a religious Sister of Mercy, Mary Martin de Porres Grey), Executive Director of the National Black Sisters' Conference (NBSC), wrote and lectured on vowed religious life for black women in the language of a black theology of liberation. A series of NBSC-sponsored "Institutes in Black Sister Formation," which I directed during my tenure on the national staff, provided a venue that benefited from and encouraged the historical research of Cyprian Davis and the articulation of a theology of religious life by Elizabeth Harris and me in the light of a black theological reading of the U. S. social context.

Between 1974 and 1975, in preparation for Catholic participation in the bicentennial of the United States, the National Conference of Catholic Bishops (NCCB), through the United States Catholic Conference (USCC), formed a Committee for the U.S. Bicentennial. Using the model of "congressional hearings," the bishops heard testimony in several cities around the country. Jamie T. Phelps was invited to give testimony at the Newark, New Jersey hearing, which focused on "ethnicity and race," December 4-6, 1975. Phelps was asked specifically to reflect theologically on the mission of the church from the perspective of African Americans.

[6] John Carey, "Black Theology: An Appraisal of the Internal and External Issues," *Theological Studies* 33, no. 4 (December 1972): 684-97, and also "What Can We Learn from Black Theology?" *Theological Studies* 35, no. 3 (September 1974): 518-28.

[7] Preston N. Williams, "Religious and Social Aspects of Roman Catholic and Black American Relationships," *CTSA Proceedings* 28 (1973): 15-30.

[8] Ibid., 24.

[9] Joseph R. Nearon, "Preliminary Report: Research Committee for Black Theology," *CTSA Proceedings* 29 (1974): 413.

[10] Ibid., p. 414.

[11] Ibid., p. 417.

[12] Joseph R. Nearon, "A Challenge to Theology: The Situation of American Blacks," *CTSA Proceedings* 30 (June 1975): 201.

[13] Paul Tillich, *Systematic Theology*, vol. 1 (Chicago: University of Chicago Press, 1951), pp. 59-66.

[14] Robert Doran, *Theology and the Dialectics of History* (Toronto: University of Toronto Press, 1990), p. 454; Neil Ormerod, "Quarrels with the Method of Correlation," *Theological Studies* 57, no. 4 (December 1996): 712.

[15] Toinette Eugene, "Whatchumean, Jellybean? Or Integration in Black Catholic Ministry," in *Making a Way Out of No Way: Proceedings: Joint Conference of the National Black Sisters' Conference, the National Black*

Catholic Clergy Caucus, the National Black Catholic Seminarians (August 1982), pp. 1-12; Jamie T. Phelps, Appendix 2: "The Sources of Theology: African-American Catholic Experience in the United States," *Black and Catholic: The Challenge and Gift of Black Folk: Contributions of African American Experience and World View to Catholic Theology*, ed. Jamie T. Phelps (Milwaukee: Marquette University Press, 1998), pp. 159-73.

[16] Eugene, "Whatchumean, Jellybean? Or Integration in Black Catholic Ministry," pp. 7-8.

[17] Edward K. Braxton, *The Wisdom Community* (New York: Paulist Press, 1980); M. Shawn Copeland, "Foundations for Catholic Theology in an African American Context," in Phelps, *Black and Catholic*, pp. 107-47.

[18] Charles H. Long, *Significations: Signs, Symbols, and Images in the Interpretation of Religion* (Philadelphia: Fortress Press, 1986), p. 9.

[19] Copeland, "Foundations for Catholic Theology in an African American Context."

[20] Cyprian Davis, *The History of Black Catholics in the United States*; idem, "The Holy See and American Black Catholics: A Forgotten Chapter in the History of the American Church," *U.S. Catholic Historian* 7 (Spring/Summer 1988): 157-81; idem, "God's Image in Black: The Black Community in Slavery and Freedom," in *Perspectives on the American Catholic Church, 1789-1989*, ed. Stephen J. Vicchio and Virginia Geiger (Westminster, Md.: Christian Classics, 1989), pp. 105-22.

[21] Jamie T. Phelps, "John R. Slattery's Mission Strategies," *U.S. Catholic Historian* 7, nos. 2-3 (Spring/Summer 1988): 201-14; idem, "The Mission Ecclesiology of John R. Slattery: A Study of an African-American Mission of the Catholic Church in the Nineteenth Century," Ph.D. diss., The Catholic University of America, 1989; idem, "Caught between Thunder and Lightning: An Historical and Theological Analysis of the American Bishops and Slavery," in *Many Rains Ago: A Historical and Theological Reflection on the Role of the Episcopate in the Evangelization of African American Catholics* (Washington, D.C.: United States Catholic Conference, 1990), pp. 21-34; idem, "Catholic Evangelization among Southern Peoples," in *Mission 2000*, ed. John S. Rausch (Atlanta: Glenmary Research Center, 1990), pp. 105-14.

[22] Thaddeus J. Posey, "An Unwanted Commitment: The Spirituality of the Early Oblate Sisters of Providence," Ph.D. diss., St. Louis University, 1993; idem, "Praying in the Shadows: The Oblate Sisters of Providence, A Look at Nineteenth-Century Black Catholic Spirituality," in *This Far by Faith: Readings in African-American Women's Religious Biography*, ed. Judith Weisenfeld and Richard Newman (New York: Routledge, 1995).

[23] Cecilia Moore, "A Brilliant Possibility: The Cardinal Gibbons Institute, 1924-1934," Ph.D. diss., University of Virginia, 1996.

[24] Addie Lorraine Walker, "Religious Education for the Regeneration of a People: The Religious Education of African-American Catholics in the Nineteenth Century," Ph.D. diss., Boston College, 1996.

[25] Giles Conwill, "Culture: A Unique People," in *Tell It Like It Is: A Black Catholic Perspective on Christian Education* (Oakland, Calif.: National Black Sisters' Conference, 1982), pp. 25-34; Eva Regina Martin, "Forging from Sun-up to Sun-down: African Symbols in the Works of Black Ironworkers in New Orleans," Ph.D. diss., Temple University, 1995.

[26] Toinette Eugene, "Black Catholic Belonging: A Critical Assessment of Socialization and Achievement Patterns for Families Black and Catholic," Ph.D. diss., Graduate Theological Union, 1983; idem, "African American Family Life: An Agenda for Ministry within the Catholic Church," *New Theology Review* 5, no. 2 (May 1992): 33-47; idem, "Moral Values and Black Womanists," in *Feminist Theological Ethics*, ed. Lois K. Daly (Louisville, Ky.: Westminster/John Knox, 1994), pp. 160-71; idem, "'Swing Low, Sweet Chariot!': A Womanist Ethical Response to Sexual Violence and Abuse," in *Violence against Women and Children: A Christian Theological Sourcebook*, ed. Carol J. Adams and Marie M. Fortune (New York: Continuum Books, 1995), pp. 183-200.

[27] Diana L. Hayes, "Tracings of an American Theology of Liberation: From Political Theology to a Theology of the Two-Thirds World," S.T.D. diss., Catholic University of Louvain (Belgium), 1988; idem, "Tracings of an American Theology," *Louvain Studies* 14, no. 4 (Winter 1989): 365-76.

[28] M. Shawn Copeland, "A Genetic Study of the Idea of the Human Good in the Thought of Bernard Lonergan," Ph.D. diss., Boston College, 1991; idem, "Reconsidering the Idea of the Common Good," in *Catholic Social Thought and the New World Order: Building on One Hundred Years*, ed. Oliver F. Williams and John W. Houck (Notre Dame: University of Notre Dame Press, 1993), pp. 309-27; idem, "The Exercise of Black Theology in the United States," *Journal of Hispanic/Latino Theology* 3, no. 3 (February 1996): 5-15.

[29] Jamie T. Phelps, "A Critical Response to Mary Rose D'Angelo's Biblical Feminist Christology with a Prolegomenon to Womanist Christological Construction," *CTSA Proceedings* 49 (1994): 155.

[30] Bryan Massingale, "The Social Dimensions of Sin and Reconciliation in the Theologies of James H. Cone and Gustavo Gutiérrez," S.T.D. diss., Academia Alphonsiana, 1991; idem, "Catholics Should Stand Firm on Affirmative Action," *Salt of the Earth* 16, no. 5 (September/October 1996): 10-15; idem, "Ethical Reflection upon Environmental Racism in the Light of Catholic Social Teaching," in *The Challenge of Global Stewardship: Roman Catholic Response*, ed. Todd David Whitmore and Maura Ryan (Notre Dame: University of Notre Dame Press, 1997); and idem, "African American Experience and U.S. Roman Catholic Ethics: 'Strangers and Aliens No Longer,'" in Phelps, *Black and Catholic*, pp. 79-101.

[31] See Jamie T. Phelps, "Women and Power in the Church: A Black Catholic Perspective," *CTSA Proceedings* 37 (1982): 119-23; idem, "Joy Came in the Morning, Risking Death for Resurrection: Confronting the Evil of Social Sin and Socially Sinful Structures," in *A Troubling in My Soul: Womanist Reflections on Evil and Suffering*, ed. Emilie M. Townes (Maryknoll, N.Y.: Orbis Books, 1993), pp. 48-64; M. Shawn Copeland, "'Wading through Many Sorrows': Towards a Theology of Suffering in Womanist Perspective," in Townes, *A Troubling in My Soul*, pp. 109-29; idem, "Difference as a Category in Critical Theologies for the Liberation of Women," in *Concilium: Feminist Theologies in Different Contexts* (1996/ 1), ed. Elisabeth Schüssler Fiorenza and M. Shawn Copeland, pp. 141-51; idem, "Towards a Critical Christian Feminist Theology of Solidarity," in *Women and Theology: The Annual Publication of the College Theology Society*, ed. Mary Ann Hinsdale and Phyllis H. Kaminiski (Maryknoll, N.Y.: Orbis Books, 1995), pp. 3-38.

[32] Toinette Eugene, "Womanist Theology," in *New Handbook of Christian Theology*, ed. Donald Musser and Joseph Price (Nashville: Abingdon Press, 1992); idem, "Appropriation and Reciprocity in Womanist/ Mujerista/Feminist Work," in *Feminist Theological Ethics*, ed. Lois K. Daly (Louisville: Westminster/John Knox Press, 1994), pp. 88-94; idem, "No Defect Here: A Black Roman Catholic Womanist Reflection on a Spirituality of Survival," in *Defecting in Place: Women Claiming Responsibility for Their Own Spiritual Lives*, ed. Miriam Therese Winter, et al. (New York: Crossroad, 1994), pp. 217-20.

[33] Diana L. Hayes, "To Be Black, Catholic, and Female," *New Theology Review* 6, no. 2 (May 1993): 55-62; idem, *Hagar's Daughters: Womanist Ways of Being in the World* (Mahwah, N.J.: Paulist Press, 1995).

[34] John E. Thiel, *Imagination and Authority: Theological Authorship in the Modern Tradition* (Minneapolis: Fortress Press, 1991), p. 133.

[35] Ibid.

[36] For example, see Kelly Brown Douglass, *The Black Christ* (Maryknoll, N.Y.: Orbis Books, 1994), pp. 110-13.

[37] Theo Wvietliet, *The Way of the Black Messiah: The Hermeneutical Challenge of Black Theology as a Liberation Theology* (Oak Park, Ill.: Meyer-Stone Books, 1987), pp. 61, 62.

[38] Dietrich Bonhoeffer, *Ethics* (New York: Macmillan, 1965 [1949]), pp. 198-99.

[39] See John T. McGreevy, *Parish Boundaries: The Catholic Encounter with Race in the Twentieth-Century Urban North* (Chicago: University of Chicago Press, 1996).

[40] Cornel West, "Forward," in *Critical Race Theory: The Key Writings That Formed the Movement*, ed. Kimberle Crenshaw, et al. (New York: The New Press, 1995), p. xi.

[41] bell hooks, *Yearning: Race, Gender, and Cultural Politics* (Boston: South End Press, 1990), esp. pp. 23-31; idem, *Outlaw Culture: Resisting*

Representations (New York: Routledge, 1994); Victor Anderson, *Beyond Ontological Blackness: An Essay on African American Religious and Cultural Criticism* (New York: Continuum Books, 1995).

⁴² Anderson, *Beyond Ontological Blackness*, p. 14.

⁴³ See Cornel West, *Race Matters* (Boston: Beacon Press, 1993), pp. x-xi.

⁴⁴ Molefi Kete Asante, trained as a psychologist, is the foremost proponent of Afrocentrism; see his *The Afrocentric Idea* (Philadelphia: Temple University, 1987), p. 198; idem, *Afrocentricity* (Trenton, N.J.: African Third World Press, 1988). Professor Leonard Jeffries is an ideological advocate of Afrocentrism. At the July 1991 Empire State Black Arts and Cultural Festival, Jeffries gave a speech, tainted by anti-Semitism, which led to his censure and removal from the chairmanship of the Black Studies Department at the City University of New York. Jeffries sued the university and was subsequently reinstated as chair and awarded damages.

⁴⁵ Asante, *Afrocentric Idea*, p. 25.

⁴⁶ Discussants were BCTS members Cyprian Davis, Leon Henderson, Eva Regina Martin, and Jamie Phelps, along with our Baptist colleague and scholar of Hebrew Bible, Randall C. Bailey; I served as moderator. I am working here from my notes.

⁴⁷ James Cone, *For My People* (Maryknoll, N.Y.: Orbis Books, 1984), pp. 50-51; see also his "A Theological Challenge to the American Catholic Church," in his *Speaking the Truth: Ecumenism, Liberation, and Black Theology* (Grand Rapids, Mich.: William B. Eerdmans Publishing Co., 1986), pp. 50-60.

PART III

ETHICAL IMPLICATIONS

6

The Case for Catholic Support

*Catholic Social Ethics
and Environmental Justice*

BRYAN N. MASSINGALE

Until recently, concern about the environment has focused upon issues such as natural resources conservation, wilderness and wildlife protection, and population distribution. Now increasing attention is being given to matters of so-called human welfare ecology, that is, to the harm visited upon the human residents of environmentally compromised or threatened areas.[1] For ground, air, and water pollution, accumulations of toxic chemicals and pesticides, and improper management of radioactive wastes are not only damaging to the environment but also entail significant— even life-threatening— consequences for human survival and well-being.

With this shift in perspective, there is now mounting, indeed one could say indisputable, evidence that environmental hazards are not randomly or evenly distributed across population groups but rather are borne disproportionately by people of color and the poor.[2] In fact, the Environmental Protection Agency itself has concluded, "The evidence indicates that racial minority and low-income populations are disproportionately exposed to lead, selected air pollutants, hazardous waste facilities, contaminated fish tissue and agricultural pesticides in the workplace."[3] Many see this as an issue of environmental justice, or indeed "environmental racism,"[4] charging that this disparate impact results from the intentional or unintentional exploitation of groups that are politically powerless and socially

vulnerable. Yet despite a widespread conviction that such disproportionate burdening is unjust, there is still little explicitly ethical
analysis and reflection found in the environmental-justice literature
to support such beliefs.[5]

This essay, then, will offer an ethical reflection upon the disproportionate impact of environmental hazards upon communities of
color and the poor in the United States in the light of Catholic social
teaching. I want to develop a solid and reasoned case/basis for the
church's support of communities addressing the issue of environmental justice. More concretely, I hope to provide some answer, or
at least perspective, to questions such as: What does any of this have
to do with faith in the God of Jesus Christ? Why should Christians,
and Catholics in particular, take environmental justice seriously?
And how are we to reflect upon the fact that people of color and the
poor bear a disproportionate share of the harms occasioned by the
environmental hazards present in our communities, our country,
and the world?

I will not rehearse for you the various studies that have demonstrated the existence of disproportionate environmental harm; one
can read these elsewhere.[6] Rather, I will structure my remarks around
the following points: the dignity of the human person; the linkage
between environmental and human well-being; the right to a safe
environment as a basic human right; the concept and demands of
distributive justice; the moral responsibility of "standing with the
least" of society in an option for the poor; the principle of participation; an ethical analysis of racism; concern for "the city" as an
"environment" in Catholic social teaching; and finally, the importance of hope in the struggle for justice.

THE FUNDAMENTAL DIGNITY OF THE HUMAN PERSON

It is important to realize at the outset that Catholic social thought
is not a secular or humanistic ethic; Catholic concern for social justice is not simply a humanitarian matter. Rather, the fundamental
perspective and orientation of Catholic social thinking are profoundly
religious, that is, the core motivation and inspiration stem from belief in a transcendent Creator God who has endowed human creatures
with intrinsic dignity, value, and worth. Thus the starting point of
Catholic ethical reflection is "God's essential respect and concern
for each person"; the proper human response to this divine concern

is the protection and promotion of the welfare of human persons so that they may come to enjoy the fullness of life that God intends.[7]

Thus, fundamental to Catholic social reflection is a belief in the sacredness of all persons—without exception—as reflections of the image of God. The dignity of each individual human person comes from God; it is not a human achievement or conferral; nor is it dependent upon "nationality, race, sex, economic status, or any human accomplishment."[8] This core conviction and its radical implications have been poetically articulated by the Catholic bishops of Guatemala:

> The human being—every human being—is
> —God's beloved creature,
> —made to his image and likeness,
> —endowed with intelligence and will
> and therefore called to be free and live in community.
>
> Moreover, every human being is called by Christ to grow, so as to become a sharer in the divine nature, and thus reach full realization in God. This is the source of the immense dignity of the human person. Therefore, every human being should have the very same opportunities for his or her development, and likewise be responsible for the same duties and obligations.
>
> Hence,
> —the most humble of all Guatemalans,
> —the most exploited and outcast,
> —the sickest and the most unschooled,
> is worth more than all the wealth of the country, and is sacred and untouchable.[9]

This conviction and understanding of the dignity of the human person as created in the image of God —especially the infinite worth of the poor, the destitute, and the outcast—is a basic presupposition for Catholic social reflection.

THE INTERCONNECTION OF HUMAN BEINGS AND THE ENVIRONMENT

In the eighth psalm we have a profound meditation on the mutuality that exists between human creatures and the natural environment:

> O LORD, our Sovereign,
>> how majestic is your name in all the earth! . . .
>
> When I look at your heavens, the work of your
>> fingers,
>> the moon and the stars that you have established;
> what are human beings that you are mindful of them,
>> mortals that you care for them?
>
> Yet you have made them a little lower than God,
>> and crowned them with glory and honor.
> You have given them dominion over the works of
>> your hands;
>> you have put all things under their feet,
> all sheep and oxen,
>> and also the beasts of the field,
> the birds of the air, and the fish of the sea,
>> whatever passes along the paths of the sea.
>
> O LORD, our Sovereign,
>> how majestic is your name in all the earth! *(NRSV)*

Note how the Psalmist moves in one breath from wonder and awe at the majesty of creation and the beauty of the natural environment to wonder and amazement at the dignity of the human being. Indeed, there is a sense of humility at our smallness as compared with the grandeur of the cosmos—and yet a realization of our essential, God-given role as part of creation. Thus there is no dichotomy, no separation, between humanity and nature; rather, human beings are seen as one with nature, as part of the created order. Mortals have a unique role within creation, for its welfare is entrusted to our care. Yet, the psalm proclaims that we, too, are part of creation; we are part of the "environment."

Psalm 8 thus shows in an intuitive, mystical, religious fashion an obvious yet profound truth: the profound linkage and interconnection between care for the earth and care for human beings. Human dominion cannot be understood in an "over against" manner relative to the environment. Because of the profound connection between human beings and nature—the fact that we do not exist outside of "nature"—human well-being cannot flourish in a compromised environment. Environmental despoliation invariably negatively affects human beings; human exploitation is often a symptom or result of environmental irresponsibility. Environmental well-being and human well-being are not mutually exclusive; one cannot exist without the other. Nature depends upon responsible stewards; we depend upon the natural environment for health, beauty, and renewal.

Psalm 8, then, provides the backdrop for understanding, in the light of faith, the interrelationship between social justice (that is, human well-being and flourishing) and the natural environment. Leonardo Boff, famous for his advancement of a theology that liberates humans from social injustice, describes this interconnectedness as a social-environmental ethic:

> The environment does not exist alone. Within it are human beings, socialized in unequal and unjust ways of living, working, distributing goods, acting and reacting to it. In this social context there is violence and there are those who are condemned to a deplorable quality of life, breathing polluted air, drinking infested water, living on poisoned soil. This is a new type of aggression.
>
> Our ethic must therefore be social and environmental, since our environment is affected by social elements and society by the environment. We discern two types of injustice: social-economic-political injustice . . . and environmental injustice. . . . Social injustice affects people directly; environmental injustice indirectly and perversely attacks human life, producing disease, malnutrition and death not only for the biosphere, but also for the entire planet.[10]

Thus concern for the dignity of the human person demands a social-environmental ethic that struggles against this "new type of aggression"—the environmental assault upon human well-being—through education, public policy, and empowerment.

FUNDAMENTAL HUMAN RIGHTS
AND THE RIGHT TO A SAFE ENVIRONMENT

In Catholic social thought, human rights refer to those minimum conditions that are essential in order to live a life befitting a human person; they establish a protective fence around the well-being of human persons. The absence or denial of these essential needs compromises the intrinsic value of human beings and makes "human dignity" a hollow phrase. Although he was speaking of totalitarianism, the words of John Paul II apply as well to social justice:

> The root of modern [social injustice] is to be found in the denial of the transcendent dignity of the human person who, as the visible image of the invisible God, is therefore by his very nature the subject of rights which no one may violate—no individual, group, class, nation, or State.[11]

In the heritage of Catholic social teaching one finds an ever-developing articulation of these essential human rights as this tradition achieves deeper insight into the minimum requirements and conditions for a fully human life. What is especially noteworthy is the recent expression in Catholic social thought that the right to a safe environment is an essential human right, one that must be "ever more insistently presented today."[12] This right to a safe environment finds its grounding in a respect for human life; for human life is threatened when persons are exposed to dangerous pollutants or toxic wastes.[13] Indeed, the pope declares that environmental despoliation and exploitation are symptoms of, and lead to, "a genuine contempt for man."[14]

What one finds, then, in Catholic social teaching is a declaration that respect for creation is not simply a concern for natural resources, but also a matter of social justice having immediate ramifications for the value and worth of persons. Note also that a safe environment is a right to which all human persons are entitled, regardless of nationality, class, or race. In fact, the pope explicitly states that in the matter of environmental justice "special attention" must be given "to the most vulnerable sectors of society."[15] At the very least, Catholic reflection upon the right to a safe environment leads one to a prima facie suspicion and negative moral evaluation of race- or class-based disparity in the bearing of environmental risks.[16]

THE CONCEPT AND DEMANDS
OF "DISTRIBUTIVE JUSTICE"

At the heart of the debate over disparate levels of environmental harms being visited upon the poor and people of color is the conviction that such differential disadvantage is unjust and unfair. Such a conviction finds great resonance and support in Catholic social ethics. In Catholic social teaching distributive justice is that form of justice which obliges the State to ensure a fair distribution of the benefits and burdens of social life among the members of a society. In fact, distributive justice maintains that a primary responsibility of government is to develop and implement social policies that "protect social groups which suffer from the malfunctioning of the social system."[17] In line with this tradition, the U.S. bishops declare: "Distributive justice requires that the allocation of income, wealth, and power in society be evaluated in light of its effects on persons whose basic material needs are unmet."[18] Thus distributive justice imposes a duty upon all public entities—and especially upon the government as the primary agent of the common good—to ensure that all the members of a society have access to basic social goods, especially the poor, vulnerable, and socially at risk. At any rate, what is absolutely excluded and prohibited is a preferential allocation of benefits and avoidance of harms on account of greater social rank, standing, or privilege—the primary offense against distributive justice.[19]

This reflection upon distributive justice calls into severe question the practice, whether intentional or unintentional, of imposing disparate environmental risks upon those segments of our society least able to bear them. Even if one grants (for the sake of argument) that environmental hazards are an unavoidable and costly byproduct of the lifestyle desired by the American people, then distributive justice demands either that these burdens be fairly apportioned across all segments of society, or that a rational justification be offered as to why certain populations are uniquely suited to bear a disproportionate share of these burdens.

In my research the principal justification offered is the contention that these risks are freely assumed by poor and minority communities in light of the economic compensation or benefits they receive from hosting a hazardous waste site.[20] In other words, the argument is that these communities freely enter into a contractual agreement to endure health and environmental risks in return for direly needed financial assistance.

However, distributive justice requires that we question and examine the broader social context in which such a "free" contract is negotiated. Specifically, distributive justice demands that advantage not be taken of an economically vulnerable population whose basic needs are already compromised because of a deficit of social power and economic resources; in fact, such social and economic disparity may well be a reason to establish a social policy of avoiding the location of environmentally compromising facilities in these communities.

Moreover, according to Catholic social teaching, fundamental human rights are held to be "universal, inviolable, and inalienable"[21] because of their importance in protecting the dignity of the human person. Since the right to a safe environment is a fundamental human right necessary for life, one must question the level of financial compensation that could be adequate for the compromise of this "inalienable" right that "cannot in any way be surrendered."[22] Catholic social teaching thus challenges the rationale of "negotiated compensation" in exchange for environmental risk; indeed, this ethical tradition specifically holds that "market forces" can never be allowed to set the limits of, or be the principal determinants of, fundamental human rights. In the words of John Paul II:

> There are many human needs which find no place on the market. It is a strict duty of justice and truth not to allow fundamental human needs to remain unsatisfied, and not to allow those burdened by such needs to perish. . . . Even prior to the logic of a fair exchange of goods and the forms of justice appropriate to it, there exists something which is due to man because he is man, by reason of his lofty dignity. Inseparable from that required "something" is the possibility to survive and . . . make an active contribution to the common good of humanity.[23]

In other words, a safe and healthy environment is not a commodity to be provided according to the conditions of the marketplace. It is something that is due to all human persons, irrespective of their economic condition. Market forces alone cannot ensure care for the environment and justice for the poor. Just as the Catholic tradition has insisted that a just wage cannot be determined solely by the market conditions of labor supply and demand,[24] so also an unsafe and compromised environment cannot be justified solely by appealing to negotiated contractual agreements.

On the basis of Catholic social teaching, then, the existence of race-based and class-based environmental inequity is morally unacceptable. It violates the dignity and worth of vulnerable human persons and offends against the dictates of distributive justice.

THE OPTION FOR THE POOR/"STANDING
WITH THE LEAST"

Another recent and ever more important theme in Catholic ethical reflection is the idea that Christians have a moral obligation to be in solidarity with the poor. It should go without saying that the "option for the poor" is neither a partisan stance nor a political slogan. Rather, it comes from a core conviction of our faith; namely, Christ is truly present in the least of our brothers and sisters, so much so that the measure of our response to the poor is the measure of our response to Christ (cf. Mt 25:31-46).

Thus the "option for the poor" expresses a profound religious conviction about the inherent dignity and worth of all persons, including the socially rejected, politically powerless, and economically destitute. "Solidarity with the poor" connotes a faith-inspired commitment to identify oneself with the plight of the neglected, despised, and insignificant of society—and a consequent resolution to advocate on their behalf for a more just social order. Moreover, it entails a decision to view social reality from the perspective of the victims of injustice. The U.S. bishops express this understanding of solidarity when they declare that public policies and economic decisions "must be judged in light of what they do *for* the poor, what they do *to* the poor, and what they enable the poor to do *for themselves.*"[25]

The relevance of our conviction that the treatment of the poor is the "litmus test" of the justice or injustice of a society[26] to the issue of environmental justice is obvious. It is the poor and powerless who most directly bear the burden of environmental irresponsibility. "Their lands and neighborhoods are more likely to be polluted or to host toxic waste sites, their water to be undrinkable, their homes contaminated with lead, their children to be harmed."[27] They are likely to have less access to structures of power in order to protect their interests— and the structures of power are more likely to handle their environment with callousness or indifference. Thus, in today's world, "standing with the least" entails a concern for their ecological well-being and a willingness to be the voices for the voiceless—or more accurately, those who are rendered voiceless and absent in the zoning commissions and other entities whose decisions affect the ecology of the poor.

THE PRINCIPLE OF PARTICIPATION

The right to participate in the public life of one's society (and to be truthfully informed about public affairs) was recognized as a fundamental requirement of human dignity by Pope John XXIII in *Pacem in Terris* (nos. 12, 26). In harmony with this tradition, the U.S. bishops declare: "Basic justice demands the establishment of minimum levels of participation in the life of the human community for all persons."[28] The bishops thus reject all forms of marginalization or exclusion from social, political, and economic life as being incompatible with the fundamental dignity of persons. Indeed, the document notes the existence of "patterns of exclusion" and asserts: "The task of overcoming these patterns of exclusion and powerlessness [is] a most basic demand of justice. . . . Justice demands that social institutions be ordered in a way that guarantees all persons the ability to participate actively in the economic, political, and cultural life of society."[29]

The disparate environmental harms experienced by people of color and the poor are often abetted by "patterns of exclusion" in that these groups are the least represented, if present at all, on the boards, commissions, and agencies charged with zoning, planning, and regulatory responsibilities. Their absence from positions of social and political power increases the vulnerability of these groups to abuse and exploitation. Thus a commitment to environmental justice entails, and is reflective of a commitment to overcoming "patterns of exclusion" by promoting the principle of participation (that is, bringing the poor to the table), which is an essential part of the work for justice.

THE SIN OF RACISM

"Racism is not merely one sin among many; it is a radical evil that divides the human family."[30] In Catholic social ethics, racism encompasses not only the personal actions and attitudes of prejudiced individuals but also the covert, anonymous forms of institutional and structural racial animus, which are embedded in the normal functioning of social agencies: "The structures of our society are subtly racist, for these structures reflect the values which society upholds. They are geared to the success of the majority and the failure of the minority. Members of both groups give unwitting approval by accepting things as they are."[31] Thus racism can be properly ascribed to not only conscious, intentional acts of discrimination but also to unintended, structural forms of racial marginalization and exclusion as well.

Many environmental-justice studies point out that race is a more reliable predictor than class concerning the disproportionate presence of environmentally based health disorders and location of toxic waste sites. At any rate, no study regards race as a neutral or insignificant variable. Thus the struggle for racial justice needs to include also a concern about the disproportionate ecological harms suffered by peoples of color. For environmental racism reflects and exacerbates existing racial inequities. Conversely, it is highly unlikely that substantial progress in dealing with environmental problems can be achieved without attending to the race-based and class-based disparity of power that permits communities to be the forced recipients of disproportionate environmental costs and risks. Simply put, the environmental crisis cannot be resolved in the absence of social—indeed racial—justice.

"THE CITY" AS AN "ENVIRONMENT"

In an insightful article, University of North Carolina professor Bill Lawson posits a connection between negative views of urban life and the environmental hazards visited upon its residents.[32] He develops the historic and widespread view in the United States that cities are "hotbeds of crime, corruption and moral decay" and thus are dangerous and predatory areas. In media, literature, film, and television, the image conveyed is that cities are "threatening places filled with people who are out to do you harm."

But not only do Americans tend to view cities as dangerous and threatening places, they also are "racialized" places. That is, because cities are increasingly viewed as black enclaves, discussions of urban life have taken on racial overtones. Indeed the word "urban" has become almost synonymous for "black" as in "urban education" "urban transportation," even "urban contemporary music." And "black," for all too many Americans, is negatively associated with dangerous, violent, predatory, lazy, and immoral persons.

Hence, Lawson argues that when the negative image of urban life is matched with the historic negative attitudes toward blacks and other persons of color, one has a recipe for social neglect, abandonment, and exploitation. This has severe environmental consequences:

> When cities are seen as black homelands, urban residents claim that policy makers minimize the impact of dumping and other hazardous forms of pollution. . . . "Why should we care what happens to cities?" The blacks have taken them over. . . . Why not put waste dumps in poor black neighborhoods? We are not hurting anyone by dumping here, if we put housing and parks in [their] neighborhoods, they will only destroy them. . . . If a place is thought to be already polluted by racial identifiers, we need to contain the pollution by keeping it in that area.[33]

Catholic social teaching offers a different, more nuanced interpretation of "the city."[34] Cities are seen as places where people live, express, and discover their humanity. This is not to say that urban living does not pose difficult challenges to human persons and their well-being. Yet, as Pope Paul VI pointed out, cities are not only places of "sin and pride" but also places "where God is encountered."[35] Thus implicit in Catholic social thinking is the insight that "cities," as well as vacation wilderness areas, are "environments" that must be cultivated and protected for human flourishing to occur.

This insight of Paul VI needs further development and reflection on the part of theologians and ethicists. What is clear, however, is that the concern of environmental-justice advocates over the ecology of urban life finds resonance and support in Catholic social thought.

THE IMPORTANCE OF HOPE

Whenever I address audiences on social-justice concerns, sooner or later someone raises the question (often in anguish), "Where's the hope?" This question engages, haunts, and challenges me both professionally, as a Christian ethicist, and personally, as an African American man.

Hope has suffered from a kind of "benign neglect" in Christian theology and ethics. Yet a Catholic social ethics cannot long evade the question: Upon what grounds does one stay engaged in and committed to the frustrating, costly, and perhaps never-ending struggle for a justice that constantly eludes us?

Perhaps the most important contribution the church can make to the struggle for justice is instilling and sustaining a sense of hope. For hope—that inner orientation of the human spirit that motivates and sustains one to work for a non-guaranteed future in the face of formidable obstacles—is always, to some degree, a move beyond or despite the empirical evidence. As Jim Wallis is fond of saying, "Hope is believing in spite of the evidence, and watching the evidence change."[36]

Religious hope places human hope in an ultimate perspective, rooting it in the Transcendent, in the Divine. In a paradoxical way religious hope "assures" the future by grounding it in the reality and promises of God. In the Christian perspective Jesus' resurrection grounds our hope that the evil of human exclusion and marginalization, despite its stubborn tenacity, is not ultimately victorious.

Thus, in the cause of environmental justice, Christians as individuals and as groups need to be intrepid and fearless witnesses and agents of hope to a weary, calloused, alienated, and indifferent world. We need to believe, and then proclaim, that the work of justice, because it is the work of God, cannot end in ultimate failure. In the words of the Brazilian theologian João Batista Libânio, "The last word on history has already been said. No human power, no dictator, no ruling power will decide the final destiny of the poor."[37] For while human beings can hinder and delay its arrival, they cannot definitively block the coming of the reign of God.

NOTES

[1] Dorceta E. Taylor, "Environmentalism and the Politics of Inclusion," in *Confronting Environmental Racism: Voices from the Grassroots*, ed. Robert D. Bullard (Boston: South End Press, 1993), p. 53.

[2] The literature on environmental equity/environmental racism/ecoracism is voluminous and growing. For a relatively comprehensive bibliography, see Robert D. Bullard, ed., *Unequal Protection: Environmental Justice and Communities of Color* (San Francisco: Sierra Club Books, 1994), pp. 362-75

[3] U.S. Environmental Protection Agency (EPA), *Environmental Equity: Reducing Risk for All Communities* (Washington, D.C.: U.S. EPA), cover letter.

[4] Readers should be aware that there are a variety of terms used in the literature to describe the disparate impact of environmental hazards upon people of color and the poor. Community activists and academic advocates speak principally in terms of "environmental racism" or

"ecoracism," especially when making specific reference to communities of color or geographical areas with a high concentration of racial and ethnic "minority" residents. When the focus is expanded to include the poor, "environmental justice" seems to be the preferred term. Government officials and agencies, however, prefer the term "environmental equity" when speaking of the distribution of environmental risks, stating that "'environmental equity,' in contrast to 'environmental racism,' includes the disproportionate risk burden placed on any population group, as defined by gender, age, income, as well as race" (EPA, *Environmental Equity*, p. 10). It should also be noted that many activists and advocates criticize the term "environmental equity" out of a belief that it blunts or denies the reality of a racially based disparity in environmental risk (cf. Robert D. Bullard, "Conclusion: Environmentalism with Justice," in Bullard, *Confronting Environmental Racism*, pp. 195-201).

[5] Several reasons might be advanced for this lack of explicitly ethical reflection. One is that much of the literature and activity in this field is the work of grassroots activists and organizers, for whom "the discussion of environmental justice is not a philosophical debate . . . but an issue of life and death" (Benjamin F. Chavis, "Preface," in Bullard, *Unequal Protection*, p. xii). Hence the urgency of the cause and the practical demands of community organizing relegate the development of ethical argumentation to a secondary place. Also, the fact that the scholars writing in this area are principally from such disciplines as sociology, political science, and law might explain the paucity of sustained ethical analysis. Moreover, one should note that most professional ethicists, being members of the middle class and living in comfortable neighborhoods, are not likely to be directly affected by the issue of environmental justice. Finally, Catholic scholars, for the most part based in university settings, are not rewarded for grassroots reflection and involvement with community groups, as such activity counts for little in the tenure-and-promotion process of most universities.

[6] For collections of theoretical perspectives on and case studies of disproportionate environmental harms, see Bullard, *Unequal Protection*; Bullard, *Confronting Environmental Racism*; and Laws Westra and Peter S. Went, eds., *Faces of Environmental Racism: Confronting Issues of Global Justice* (Lanham, Md.: Rowman and Littlefield, 1995).

[7] Gerald Darring, *A Catechism of Catholic Social Teaching* (Kansas City, Mo.: Sheed and Ward, 1987), p. 1.

[8] National Conference of Catholic Bishops, "Economic Justice for All," no. 12. It is customary to cite the official documents of the Catholic church by author, title, and paragraph number. A comprehensive collection of the documents that constitute the official corpus of Catholic social teaching can be found in David J. O'Brien and Thomas A. Shannon, eds., *Catholic Social Thought* (Maryknoll, N.Y.: Orbis Books, 1992). Thus the full text

of the cited document can be found in O'Brien and Shannon, *Catholic Social Thought,* pp. 572-78.

[9] Bishops of Guatemala, "Unidos en la Esperanza," in *Los Obispos Latinoamericanos Entre Medellin y Puebla: Documentos Episcopales 1968-1979* (San Salvador: UCA Editores, 1978), p. 183. Cited in Philip Berryman, *Liberation Theology* (New York: Pantheon Books, 1987), p. 112.

[10] Leonardo Boff, "Social Ecology: Poverty and Misery," in *Ecotheology: Voices From South and North,* ed. David G. Hallman (Maryknoll, N.Y.: Orbis Books, 1994), p. 243.

[11] John Paul II, *Centesimus Annus,* no. 44. The full text of this document can be found in O'Brien and Shannon, *Catholic Social Thought,* pp. 439-88.

[12] John Paul II, *The Ecological Crisis: A Common Responsibility* (Washington, D.C.: United States Catholic Conference, 1989), no. 9.

[13] Ibid.

[14] John Paul II, *The Ecological Crisis,* no. 7.

[15] Ibid., no. 9.

[16] In this context it is important to note the distinction between a civil right and a human right. Civil rights are those social entitlements and/or public immunities that the law recognizes, grants, allows, or protects. Human rights are those entitlements and/or immunities that, being essential to a life of dignity, one is entitled to by virtue of being human—regardless of what the law recognizes or protects. (In making this distinction, I am indebted to the thought of Malcolm X as expressed in his text *By Any Means Necessary* [New York: Pathfinder Press, 1970], pp. 56-57.) Hence, it is important to note that in Catholic social teaching the right to a safe environment is a human right, a basic human right, and not simply a civil right. Thus the question that community groups and activists must wrestle with is how to make this human right a civil right, which is recognized and protected by law.

[17] Johannes Messner, *Social Ethics: Natural Law in the Western World* (St. Louis: B. Herder Books, 1965), p. 322.

[18] National Conference of Catholic Bishops, "Economic Justice for All," no. 70.

[19] Messner, *Social Ethics,* p. 322.

[20] Cf. Christopher Boerner and Thomas Lambert, "Negotiated Compensation," in *Environmental Justice,* ed. Jonathan S. Petrikin (San Diego, Calif.: Greenhaven Press, 1995), pp. 85-99.

[21] Darring, *A Catechism of Catholic Social Teaching,* p. 2; citing John XXIII, *Pacem in Terris,* no. 9. The complete text of *Pacem in Terris* can be found in O'Brien and Shannon, *Catholic Social Thought,* pp. 131-62.

[22] John XXIII, *Pacem in Terris,* no. 9.

[23] John Paul II, *Centesimus Annus,* no. 34.

[24] Cf. *Rerum Novarum*, no. 34; *Quadragesimo Anno*, nos. 70-75; and *Laborem Exercens*, no. 19. These documents also can be found in O'Brien and Shannon, *Catholic Social Thought.*

[25] National Conference of Catholic Bishops, "Economic Justice for All," no. 24; emphasis in original.

[26] Cf. "Economic Justice for All," nos. 24, 86, 90, 123; and John Paul II, *Sollicitudo Rei Socialis,* nos. 42-43. The complete text of *Sollicitudo Rei Socialis* can be found in O'Brien and Shannon, *Catholic Social Thought,* pp. 395-436.

[27] United States Catholic Conference, *Renewing the Earth: An Invitation to Reflection and Action on Environment in Light of Catholic Social Teaching* (Washington, D.C.: United States Catholic Conference, 1991), p. 2.

[28] National Conference of Catholic Bishops, "Economic Justice for All," no. 77.

[29] Ibid., no. 78.

[30] National Conference of Catholic Bishops, "Brothers and Sisters to Us" (Washington, D.C.: United States Catholic Conference, 1979), p. 10.

[31] Ibid., p. 3.

[32] Bill Lawson, "Living for the City: Urban United States and Environmental Justice," in Westra and Went, *Faces of Environmental Racism,* pp. 41-55.

[33] Lawson, "Living for the City," p. 49.

[34] Paul VI, *Octogesima Adveniens,* nos. 10-11. This document can be found in O'Brien and Shannon, *Catholic Social Thought,* pp. 265-86.

[35] Ibid., no. 12.

[36] Jim Wallis, *The Soul of Politics* (Maryknoll, N.Y.: Orbis Books, 1994), p. 240.

[37] João Batista Libânio, "Hope, Utopia, Resurrection," in *Mysterium Liberationis: Fundamental Concepts of Liberation Theology,* ed. Ignacio Ellacuría and Jon Sobrino, (Maryknoll, N.Y.: Orbis Books, 1993), p. 727.

7

Between "Lord, Have Mercy!" and "Thank You, Jesus!"

Liturgical Renewal and African American Catholic Assemblies

TOINETTE M. EUGENE

PROLEGOMENA

Liturgical renewal since Vatican II has been a gift that has immensely benefited the cultural identity of African American Catholic assemblies in numerous ways. The seminal liturgical and musical innovations and inspiration of Father Clarence Rivers and others[1] established a legacy beginning in the early 1970s that has been sustained within the ongoing work of renewal. Post-conciliar renewal has permitted and encouraged the adaptation of the liturgy to accommodate the style and eloquence of African American communal prayer[2] while adroitly resisting the recommendations of some to develop a separate canonical rite.[3] The Black Liturgy Subcommittee, formed by the Bishops' Committee on the Liturgy in 1984 has been working collegially to address the liturgical issues and concerns of African American Catholic communities of faith.[4]

This essay is a commentary on the response to liturgical renewal taking place within African American Catholic assemblies as we maintain a cutting edge on our own ebonized adaptations in this broader ecclesial movement. It is an essay with an ethical edge in that the role of social justice in relation to the reform of the sacred liturgy is a key element of this composition. It is as well an experiential essay on renewal in that it focuses on the meaningfulness of liturgical changes as they are lived out in the context of the daily lives of many black Catholics.

As we seek to ensure that social justice is always a constitutive element of evangelization and liturgical expression, we are well aware that religious tradition and cultural transition sometimes bump heads. One cause for this "collision" is that, since the turn of the century, changes within ritual worship traditions have been closely linked with issues of social change. Two general approaches have predominated; they model broadly a concern for maintaining "tradition" in ritual worship, on the one hand, while sustaining a movement for change or "transition," on the other. Both approaches have application within African American Catholic communities of faith.

The first approach, rooted in W. Robertson Smith's study of Semitic sacrifice,[5] has been developed with great sophistication by cultural anthropologists Victor Turner and Mary Douglas, among others.[6] This approach has focused on the role of ritual worship in the maintenance of social groups. A second approach has focused on how groups change and grow through ritual worship. Within this perspective, liturgical ritual action is seen as integral to the way in which the ideas and cultural traditions of a worshiping assembly are adapted to changing circumstances. This sociological approach is (probably?) rooted in Durkheim's analysis of cult but is articulated in the work of Clifford Geertz.[7]

According to this perspective, liturgical or ritual worship is seen to facilitate meaningful social change by fusing a community's "general conceptions of the order of existence" with the actual circumstances of its daily life.[8] Thus liturgical ritual action would invite the social group to confront the present, disallow it from living in an ideal and non-confrontational world, challenge the reconciliation with which we are comfortably living, and bring us to a new tradition in a future that is realistic yet full of hope.

Both approaches have relevance for liturgical renewal within active African American Catholic assemblies as the roles of tradition and transition are attended to and honored. The place of both tradition and transition must remain operative as ebonized expressions of spirituality, pastoral theology, and social justice are symbolized and celebrated within a eucharistic community that is rooted in an authentic African American culture that is vibrant and thus always in the midst of social change and religious renewal.

The pressure to change, which is visited upon our culture, our church, and even our worship, increases each year. But the resistance to change increases as well. How do we hold tradition and transition in balance? There is the inherent challenge of being both authentically black (a particular cultural given) and authentically Catholic (a participation in a universal or global religious reality). What cultural adaptations are inevitable or desirable in liturgical renewal for active African American Catholic assemblies? What social forces and factors are affecting the face of our culture, our church, and our worship?

CONFESSION

These endemic touch points that focus on the tensions inevitable in renewal processes remind me of an experience that I have regularly in my home parish. Like a good, lifelong Catholic who loves and appreciates at least selected aspects of our tradition, I have chosen to begin my reflection on liturgical renewal and Black Catholics by starting with a confession. I begin my confession as a recollection of the memories of the cultural community from which I have sprung. As we struggle with the tension of traditions and transitions, I choose to begin by first reflecting on a proverb from the prophetic book of "Mama Said"—a book from which many womanist theologians and ethicists obtain their lessons on the practicalities of ministry situations that call for prophetic/pastoral care that is both loving and liberating in miraculous ways.

Whenever I am invited to participate in a ministry of leadership at a Sunday eucharistic assembly at my "home church," I am automatically also engaged in an African American religious and cultural ritual of greeting the Mothers of the Church. The elders in the assembly are embodied as those wizened and wise older women who have become smaller yet stronger with the passing of the years be cause they have survived, with some success, the heat and the burden of racism, sexism, poverty, and so many other social ills.

One of the ever-present Mothers always offers me this ritual expression of a "Mama Said." This particular "Mama" always says to me when I enter the liturgical assembly, "Why, Chil', Girl, how you all doin'?" and I say, "Well—I'm just fine, Mother Rebecca. And how 'bout you?" She always looks me straight in the eye, and says with a straight face, *"Why Baby, I'm somewhere between 'Lord, Have Mercy!' and 'Thank You, Jesus!'"*

This Mama then says to me, as I am processing up the aisle to proclaim the good news, "Girl, you go now!" [*a message of commission to do justice, to act like a womanist*]. Then she winks and hands me a wadded-up dollar bill—the widow's mite—and she says again, tongue in cheek—"Now, girl, don't you give this to Father, he don't need it!" [*a message of autonomy for me*]. Finally, she says, "Now don't you embarrass us!" [*a paradoxical message for me containing both admonition and tender affection as I represent the assembly through leadership*].

I will use this bit of African American folk wisdom of "being somewhere between 'Lord, have mercy' and 'Thank you, Jesus'" in order to develop a commentary on the kinds of cultural conditions that sustain and maintain both tradition and change in liturgical renewal within active African American Catholic assemblies who take seriously their responsibility to make justice a constitutive element of renewal.

True confessions are good for the soul and vitally important for active African American Catholic assemblies intent on maintaining their cultural identity and integrity in an era when liturgical renewal has sometimes come to mean mainstream and middle-class modernization. In order to highlight the tensions that occur in balancing cultural traditions and transitions in life and liturgy, I have chosen an example from my own life to personify the struggle to move from "'Lord, have mercy,' to 'Thank you, Jesus'" as a modus operandi and strategy for renewal.

I confess that even though I am black by birth, I am also, by academic training and theological tradition, a Western Catholic Christian. Because of that latter designation, I have inherited and sometimes even handed on, like bread gone stale, the pernicious dualism that our dichotomous Western Christianity has long held sacred. We have held up and handed on the notion that there is between God, the church, and the "world," a theological, social, pastoral, and liturgical split that has made a big difference between that which is sacred and profane, between sexuality and spirituality, between justice and peace. This ideological world view has historically served to broaden the gap between human and divine experience. And so I am compelled to cry out with Mother Rebecca and with the countless others who suffer most from this dichotomy, "Lord, have mercy!" *Kyrie, eleison.*

The gap causes me to confess that I am longing to stand more closely in communion with all those "others" whose radical vision, politics, and spirituality I have come to trust: those who know, through the experience of suffering and struggle, that we can only really meet the Sacred in relation to one another, and who understand that any authority or power that we or others use in ways that are not mutually empowering is abusive.[9]

I look to such prophetic people, of whatever color, religion, class, sexual preference or orientation, to confirm in me a joyful commitment to live responsibly in this one, holy, catholic, and apostolic church as well as within our diverse, pluralistic, ecologically and ecumenically fragile world. And so I am empowered to cry out with Mother Rebecca and those many nameless but fortunate others who actually and regularly live in the interstices where I would like to remain. As Mother Rebecca would say, "Thank you, Jesus!" *Deo Gratias.*

Dealing with ethical and experiential issues involving theological, liturgical, and social renewal obviously means more than just welcoming or recruiting more African American Catholics to ministerial and liturgical leadership in the prayer of the assembly. Dealing with liturgical renewal includes honoring our cultural differences, while confronting racism, sexism, classism, and the liturgical literalism that limit our well-being and effective worship within the universal ecclesia. Dealing with ethical and experiential issues involving ongoing metanoia in liturgical renewal requires the confession: "It's the church, the church, the church, O Lord, standing in the need of prayer!" As Mother Rebecca would say, "Lord, have mercy on us!" *Kyrie, eleison.*

CONVICTIONS

We have already observed that the pressure upon our culture, our church, and on our liturgical lives to implement social change in our world increases as we pray to live more justly. Thus, our confessions must lead to convictions about what has to follow if we are truly to hold together and not split the presence of Roman Catholic tradition and black cultural expressions that foster the purpose of liturgical renewal as it is related to social transformation.

It is this conviction that I choose to investigate more thoroughly by reflecting briefly on a black folk parable offered by Alice Walker, and by alluding to a litany of African American Catholic liturgical pioneers who have challenged us to ongoing renewal of both our Catholic and our cultural traditions.

We know that confessions traditionally lead to convictions, literally and figuratively. This was certainly the case for the African Catholic bishop of Hippo, Augustine, whose personal conversion, captured in his classic work *The Confessions*, led him to articulate ecclesial reform and renewal in a universal way. His legacy as an African and as a Catholic who combined tradition and transition is one we can hope to emulate.

We also need to know of and share the pastoral and prophetic convictions of Augustine's cultural and religious descendants. We are indebted to Father Augustus Tolton, the first African American Catholic priest, and to Blessed Pierre Toussaint, beloved Haitian immigrant hairdresser and healer in eighteenth century Harlem, both of whom worked for social justice as lived expressions of the *leiturgia* of the active African American Catholic assemblies with which they were associated. We need to celebrate and emulate the prophetic convictions of Holy Thea Bowman and of Archbishop James Patterson Lyke, both now of happy and sacred memory, who struggled mightily and publicly lobbied for much needed cultural and liturgical renewal within African American Catholic circles as well as within the larger ecclesia.

Thea Bowman and James Patterson Lyke predicted and prefigured renewal for us in their own unique Black Catholic way through remodeling styles of ordained and lay leadership within the assembly and by initiating and molding innovative forms of social justice as expressed in their public, prophetic lifestyles.[10]

Pulitzer-prize-winning author Alice Walker provides yet another model of this same approach, wherein black prophetic models effect social as well as liturgical renewal. She offers a story that lends itself to the kind of moral imagination needed in order to envision and model the kinds of extended parabolic expression the church might make use of as we continue to journey and to claim the beauty of African American cultural traditions and to employ the ministries that will best encourage, empower, and embody our liturgical assemblies. Alice Walker provides this witness through a recording in her journal:

April 17, 1984

The universe sends me fabulous dreams! Early this morning I dreamed of a two-headed woman. Literally. A wise woman. Stout, graying, caramel-colored, with blue-grey eyes, wearing a blue flowered dress. Who was giving advice to people. Some white people, too, I think. Her knowledge was for everyone and it was all striking. While one head talked, the other seemed to doze. I was so astonished!

For what I realized in the dream is that two-headedness was at one time an actual physical condition and that two-headed people were considered wise. Perhaps this accounts for the adage "Two heads are better than one." What I think this means is that two-headed people, like blacks, lesbians, Indians, "witches," have been suppressed, and in their case, suppressed out of existence. Their very appearance had made them "abnormal" and therefore subject to extermination. For surely two-headed people have existed. And it is only among blacks (to my knowledge) that a trace of their existence is left in the language. Rootworkers, healers, wise people with "second sight" are called "two-headed" people.

This two-headed woman was amazing. I asked whether the world would survive, and she said No; and her expression seemed to say, The way it is going there's no need for it to. When I asked her what I/we could/should do, she took up her walking stick and walked expressively and purposefully across the room. Dipping a bit from side to side.

She said: "Live by the Word and keep walking."[11]

In this brief pericope, a combination of a deeply religious folktale and an ethical exegesis, Alice Walker captures the essence of what our own African American Catholic convictions might mean and contain. For African American Catholic assemblies seeking to maintain a balance between religious tradition and cultural adaptation, this story and its concomitant hermeneutic can offer considerable sagacity for all who are making strong efforts to address issues of change and renewal. "Living by the Word" offers both a summary of Roman Catholic scriptural tradition as well as a type of African American liberational action. This story and others like it can bring transformation into our church's theological, pastoral, and liturgical life in the midst of what we claim and celebrate as cultural and religious diversity. In the ingenuous cultural world and belief system of Alice Walker, we are enjoined to "live by the Word and keep walking." She incorporates into her culturally contextualized fable a biblical reply to the ethically constructed question of "what I/we could/should do" in a world that will only survive if our absolute attention is given to theological, liturgical, cultural, and spiritual transformation.

Liturgical renewal and, by extension, liturgical education within African American Catholic assemblies provide a location from which we are empowered to challenge the status quo. Liturgical renewal and, by extension, liturgical education provide the members of the assembly a moral authority and a moral imagination that has the ethical power to dispel a dominant "culture of disbelief."[12]

I am arguing that in the midst of a dominant societal culture of disbelief, epitomized by ennui and apathy, indigenized liturgical renewal within African American Catholic assemblies holds the potential and the power to transform life in liberating and justice-orienting ways through the process of contextualization.[13] As Alice Walker contends, I argue that active African American Catholic assemblies are enjoined and empowered as wise persons, as provocative providers and pastoral purveyors of liturgical renewal, "to live by the Word and keep walking." That is, we are responsible and accountable publicly to articulate the content and context of our black Catholic traditions on behalf of the universal church as well as for the civic, racial-ethnic, and socially diverse forms of community in which we are rooted and in which we live our daily lives.

Here the invitation of Pope Paul VI to African Catholics is revitalized in the context of African American experience. The pope, speaking to a synod of bishops in Kampala, declared:

> An adaptation of the Christian life in the fields of pastoral, ritual, didactic, and spiritual activities is not only possible, it is even favored by the Church. The liturgical renewal is a living example of this. . . . You will be capable of bringing to the Catholic Church the precious and original contribution of "Blackness" which she particularly needs in this historic hour.[14]

I hold the conviction that in order to honor both tradition and transition within liturgical renewal, members of African American Catholic communities must be empowered as liturgical leaders and evangelizing educators. We are enjoined to move from "Lord, have mercy!" to "Thank you, Jesus!" by intentionally addressing and re-dressing particularly those liturgical and social realities that previously may have kept us ineffective and unenthusiastic for the faith that does justice.[15]

We are likewise enjoined to find authentic, culturally relevant liturgical expressions and ritual actions that allow us more fully to "live by the Word and keep walking" in the face and in the form of a contrary "culture of disbelief." This includes excising old and obsti-nate routinization of outmoded rituals which have served to privatize and to depoliticize ways in which we as a faithful and believing black people are called. We must begin to exercise anew the rights, re-sponsibilities, and forms of liturgical renewal and change, which ought to extend a transforming praxis of liberation and justice for all. This is the extension of Mother Rebecca's commission to move from "Lord, have mercy!" to "Thank you, Jesus!" This is the way by which we are able to "live by the Word and keep walking!"

COMMITMENTS

Having made my confession, and named my convictions, as a con-clusion this essay recommends some commitments that may effect renewal at both the level of liturgical adaptation and the level of cultural retention. This final section on commitments that foster transformative liturgical change examines the concept and metaphor of "cultural worker" as a category that might be useful to conceptu-alize the work of liturgical leaders who would wish to engage active African American Catholic assemblies more practically in the pro-cess of contextualization.[16] I am arguing that contextualization is the liturgical successor in the global dialogue on the place and role of indigenization and inculturation within the liturgy.[17]

Henry Giroux, a Harvard educational theorist, has published ex-tensively on issues of contextualization and education in recent years.[18] His work is extremely relevant, in much the same way as that of Paulo Freire, to the task of incorporating the lived experi-ences of oppressed peoples into theological, social, and spiritual revivals. Giroux addresses contextualization and education by draw-ing upon the paradigm and metaphor of the "cultural worker"[19] in order to better effect the acceptance of cultural differences. I con-tend that the category of cultural worker has important implications for active African American Catholic communities of faith who would foster positive forms of renewal, not only in their assemblies, but also in our other places where life is lived out "somewhere between 'Lord, have mercy' and 'Thank you, Jesus.'"

The concept of "cultural worker" has evolved from a category that originally was used to refer to artists, writers, worker-priests, media producers, and other liminal individuals. In Giroux's framework the description of the cultural worker is extended to those people working in professions such as liturgy, law, social work, architecture, medicine, theology, education, and literature. His intention is to rewrite the concept and practice of cultural workers by inserting the primacy of political, pedagogical, ritual, and therapeutic activities as strategies that can transform social injustices.

The understanding and adaptation of Giroux's notion of cultural worker and the application of it to the ministries of liturgical leadership in African American Catholic assemblies may extend the possibilities for creating new spheres of worship. The understanding and adaptation of the notion of an African American Catholic [liturgical] cultural worker may lead to the acquisition and engagement of a larger moral imagination within the African American Catholic community as it engages in works of justice as an expression of the purpose of the liturgy.

Indeed, such a task of renewal is ultimately the liturgical "work of *all* the people," which demands both a rethinking and a rewriting of the meaning of religious ritual and rite itself. It requires renewed cultural reflection on the ways in which Black Catholic people understand ourselves and the ways in which we engage not only our ecclesial community, but also our relationship with the historic Black Protestant churches and communities to which we are also related.

Of primary importance for those cultural workers who seek to utilize the benefits of liturgical renewal in active African American Catholic assemblies through the means of contextualization, indigenization, and transformative liturgical education is the need to recall traditions and memories that provide a new way of reading our religious and secular history and of reclaiming or rejuvenating our cultural identity. This requires that we must constantly remember and reverence who and *Whose* we really are: proud, black, and catholic people made in the image of God. Within the recovery of this memory, which is always resident within the liturgy, there is the reformation of the "great anamnesis." The "great anamnesis" or the practice of the "great remembrance" is the section of the liturgy so called by early Greek Christians, which was and is now a time at worship wherein we are to recall the acts of redemption that renew us, reconcile us, and put us in solidarity with all of God's people in all times and everywhere. We know that those who do not remember the past are doomed to repeat it in the future. The call to "anamnesis" or "to remember" our cultural and racial history as we celebrate the liturgy in the context of an active African American Catholic assembly is quintessential. As we employ our "great anamnesis," there is the distinct possibility of creating new social and religious practices that connect rather than separate liturgical renewal from other forms of cultural work entailed in living out faithfully and prophetically our everyday life.

It is the prophetic and pastoral witness of those irreplaceable cultural workers working for liturgical renewal that is able to bridge the painful interstices experienced by Mother Rebecca and so many others who find themselves somewhere struggling between the wide gaps of "'Lord, have mercy!' and 'Thank you, Jesus!'" To this end and by this means of revolutionary cultural work, I am committed to the renewal of all liturgical traditions and transitions that reinforce the work and witness of the universal faith community that does Justice/Love.

As members of active African American Catholic assemblies, we are invited, and indeed required to gather and to celebrate together as God's people, willing to risk everything to be present around the table of the One who invites us to live in holiness and wholeness and to be finally at peace in the breaking of the bread and the sharing of the cup. Thus we are enjoined and invited to participate in the ancient yet ever new liturgical call and refrain so readily available every Sunday in active African American Catholic assemblies that identify themselves as "the church." That call and refrain is the resounding, ever ancient and ever new song sung by black and believing Catholic peoples everywhere—"Lord, have mercy"—*Kyrie Eleison,* and it is expressed always and everywhere within the words, actions, and the "great remembrance" of our eucharistic thanksgiving—"Thank you, Jesus!"

NOTES

[1] See Clarence Joseph Rivers, *Soulful Worship* (Washington, D.C.: The National Office for Black Catholics, 1974), and *The Spirit in Worship* (Cincinnati, Ohio: Stimuli, 1978); Robert Hovda, ed., *This Far by Faith: American Black Worship and Its African Roots* (Washington, D.C.: The National Office for Black Catholics and the Liturgical Conference, 1977).

[2] Secretariat for the Liturgy and Secretariat for Black Catholics, *Plenty Good Room: The Spirit and Truth of African American Catholic Worship* (Washington, D.C.: National Conference of Catholic Bishops, 1991).

[3] The National Black Catholic Congress commissioned a sociological and statistical study to determine the desirability and feasibility of establishing an African American Catholic rite. While the study showed little enthusiasm for a separate canonical rite, it did indicate the desire for greater use of more African customs at the Sunday eucharist and other sacramental celebrations. See Msgr. Leonard Scott, "Canonical Reflections on the Study Conducted by the National Black Catholic Congress Regarding the Establishment of an African American Rite," in *A Study of Opinions of African American Catholics* (Baltimore, Md.: The National Black Catholic Congress, 1995), pp. 43-50.

[4] Bishops' Committee on the Liturgy, *In Spirit and Truth: Black Catholic Reflections on the Order of Mass* (Washington, D.C.: National Conference of Catholic Bishops, 1987).

[5] W. Robertson Smith, *The Religion of the Semites* (New York: Meridian, 1956; originally published in 1889).

[6] Mary Douglas presents a more historically nuanced critique of recent liturgical changes in general in *Natural Symbols* (New York: Random House/Vintage, 1973), pp. 19ff. David Martin has also published several critiques of changes in the Anglican *Book of Common Prayer*, speaking both as a sociologist of religion and as a deacon in the Church of England.

[7] See Emile Durkheim, *The Elementary Structures of the Religious Life,* trans. J. W. Swain (New York: Free Press, 1965; originally published in 1912).

[8] See Clifford Geertz, *The Interpretation of Cultures* (New York: Basic Books, 1973).

[9] See James N. Poling, *The Abuse of Power: A Theological Problem* (Nashville: Abingdon Press, 1991); also, Joanne Carlson Brown and Carol R. Bohn, eds., *Christianity, Patriarchy, and Abuse: A Feminist Critique* (New York: The Pilgrim Press, 1989).

[10] For additional models and examples of Black Catholic change agents whose lives have renewed their eucharistic assemblies, see Cyprian Davis, O.S.B., *The History of Black Catholics in the United States* (New York: Crossroad, 1990).

[11] Alice Walker, "Journal," *Living By the Word* (San Diego: Harcourt Brace Jovanovich, 1988), p. 2.

[12] See Stephen Carter, *The Culture of Disbelief: How American Law and Politics Trivialize Religious Devotion* (New York: Basic Books, 1993).

[13] See Robert J. Schreiter, "Contextualization from a World Perspective," *Theological Education* 30, supplement 1 (Autumn 1993), pp. 63-86, for further development of this theme and prescriptive definition of

contextualization as it relates to theological education and religious education.

[14] Paul VI, "Address at the Closing of the Symposium of African Bishops Given at Kampala," excerpt on the Liturgy and Different Cultures (July 31, 1969), as cited in *Plenty Good Room*, p. 22.

[15] See John C. Haughey, ed., *The Faith That Does Justice: Examining the Christian Sources for Social Change* (New York: Paulist Press, 1977).

[16] See Schreiter, "Contextualization from a World Perspective."

[17] Jamie T. Phelps, O.P., has articulated a finely honed summary of the theology of inculturation that gathers in conciliar and post-conciliar documents with reference to African American Catholicism in her "Ecclesiological Implications of 'The Study of Opinions of African American Catholics,'" in *A Study of Opinions of African American Catholics*, previously cited. See also "African American Catholicism: A New Day," *New Theological Review* 7:1 (February 1994) for additional articles by African American Catholics relative to inculturation and evangelization in the United States Catholic Church.

[18] See Henry A. Giroux, *Living Dangerously: Multiculturalism and the Politics of Difference* (New York: Peter Lang, 1993); Henry Giroux and David Purple, eds., *The Hidden Curriculum and Moral Education: Deception or Discovery?* (Berkeley, Calif.: McCutchan Publishing Corporation, 1983).

[19] I strongly recommend the analogy of the "cultural worker" as a concept that describes pedagogues and other proponents of the teaching/learning process within liturgical education and renewal. The term "cultural worker" is introduced by Giroux and explicated in his work *Border Crossings: Cultural Workers and the Politics of Education* (New York: Routledge, 1992). With this work Giroux names his desire to meet across boundaries, declaring his political solidarity with postmodern feminist thought, anti-racist theory, and all who think critically about pedagogy. With clarity and insight he writes about the points of connection, expanding the scope of critical pedagogy and inviting us to engage in a broad political project that is fundamentally non-hierarchical and non-autocratic in the forms and styles of leadership for change and transformation.

PART IV

PASTORAL AND LITURGICAL IMPLICATIONS

8

Black Spirituality

JAMIE T. PHELPS, O.P.

There is neither Jew nor Greek ... slave nor free ... male nor female; for you are all one in Christ Jesus.

—Galatians 3:28

While it is common practice to describe the spiritual life within the context of a particular historical period (early church or medieval), a commanding figure in religious history (Ignatius Loyola or John Wesley), or a specific theological tradition (Reformed or Roman Catholic), it is also possible to speak of culturally or racially determined spiritualities (French, Spanish, Hispanic, African, Native American). Yet the essence of spirituality—the attempt to encounter the Divine Other—is fundamentally the same for every human being, despite the particularities of gender, race, culture, class, or national heritage.

Black spirituality is a vital and distinctive spirituality forged in the crucible of the lives of various African peoples. Black Africans and those members of the African Diaspora whose ancestors were brutalized by enslavement in the New World all share a common racial heritage, a common relationship to the dominant Western culture, and a common spirit. This common spirit found in people of African descent is an attitude that sees all of life in the context of the

This essay was originally published in *Spiritual Traditions for the Contemporary Church*, ed. Robin Maas and Gabriel O'Donnell, O.P. (Nashville: Abingdon Press, 1990). Quoted material has not been adjusted to incorporate inclusive language.

encounter with the Divine, and the all-embracing vision of the Divine-human encounter—which is really the essential clue to understanding the nature of black spirituality—is rooted in a distinctive and ancient world view.

THE AFRICAN WORLD VIEW

No matter where or when they live, black people are fundamentally *African* people, whose perspective and way of life have been conditioned by their roots in Mother Africa. Therefore, the study of black spirituality properly begins with a look at the African world view and African traditional religions.

As African and African American philosophers identify experiences that are uniquely African, they note a distinctive world view in traditional religions' proverbs, oral traditions, social ethics, and moral codes.[1] A foundational aspect of the traditional African world view is the primacy of the group as the basis for identity and survival. This attitude is directly reflected in the communal character of traditional African religions:

> Traditional religions are not primarily for the individual, but for his community of which he is part. Chapters of African religion are written everywhere in the life of the community, and in traditional society there are no irreligious people. To be human is to belong to the whole community, and to do so involves participating in the beliefs, ceremonies, rituals and festivals of that community. A person cannot detach himself from the religion of his group, for to do so is to be severed from his roots, his foundations, his context of security, his kinships and the entire group of those who make him aware of his own existence. To be without religion amounts to a self-excommunication from the entire life of the society, and African peoples do not know how to exist without religion.[2]

Thus Africans and African Americans tend to both communicate and organize by a process of human and spiritual networks or groups. Work is done more efficiently by groups, and the community is supported by the networks of groups that are, in turn, sustained by community worship. The communal understanding of religion gives rise to a community anthropology whereby the "I" signifies "we."

A second fundamental element of the African world view, which differs significantly from that of the dominant Western culture, is its concept of time and reality. Time, for the traditional African, is the eternal present; that is, the past and present are *now*, and *now* is the most important concern of one's religious activities and beliefs. The concept of the future is absent from traditional African thought. Since the future has not occurred, it does not exist within the context of "actual time." Yet through the influence of Western culture and Christianity, Africans are discovering the future under the rubric of "potential time." This concept of time influences the African understanding of human life, death, and immortality.[3]

Edwin Nichols's research into the African world view yielded what he considers to be a distinct axiology (theory of value), epistemology, logic, and way of processing information.[4] His description of the African philosophical perspective identifies interpersonal relationships as the highest value in African society, making community the center of and foundation for all of African life. Further, Africans and African Americans both see all of life as an organized whole, with each thing or being integrally related to every other. Thus the sacred and secular categories typical of traditional Eurocentric Christianity do not exist in the African world view. Because African-rooted logic is a diunital process by which the mind tends to seek the unity of opposites, the African typically does not use categories of "either-or" but rather those of "both-and." God speaks through the roar of the mighty wind or lion as well as through the quietness of a gentle breeze or rabbit. God is found in the midst of community activity as well as in quiet moments of solitude. Life is not complete without the unity of the male and female. The rhythm of life requires activity and rest, laughter and mourning, thought and emotion. In this way, the African way of life tends to unite that which seems to be mutually exclusive.

Africans and African Americans process thought through the use of symbolic imagery and rhythm. African linguistic expression uses analogy and metaphor extensively to reflect concrete experience and the environment, and information is relayed through descriptive images. For example, in my childhood I heard people describe someone inebriated by alcohol as being "as high as a Georgia pine!" Or a child who was fidgety might be described as having "ants in his pants." In a similar vein, blacks rely on the use of rhythm aids for learning. While teaching black first-graders, I found that singing numerical facts aided their retention of mathematics. In the same way, clapping the rhythm of a word improved their pronunciation.

The philosophical distinctiveness of the African world view gives rise to equally distinct understandings of religion, spiritual expression, and spiritual development. The remainder of this chapter will survey the development and chief characteristics of black spirituality, with its roots in African religions, slave religion, and the black church.

AFRICAN RELIGIONS

Since African religions are tribal and national, theoretically one cannot speak of African religion in the singular. However, a review of the religions of several West African tribes—the Fon of Dahomey, the Yoruba of Nigeria, and the Akan of Ghana—does reveal similarities in patterns of behavior and belief, and given that most American blacks trace their origins to West Africa, it is appropriate to look briefly at one of these religions in a representative way in order to understand what kind of a God—or gods—Africans typically worship.

The Fon understanding of God is of a Supreme Being who creates all things and participates in a cosmic harmony with human beings and inanimate things. In some tribes the supreme Creator God is assisted by lesser deities who interact in the daily affairs of human life to bring them into conformity with the will of the Supreme God— the all-powerful, ever-present, and all-knowing Creator, Begetter, Originator, Sustainer—the One who orders all things.

This Supreme Creator God is assisted by his two descendants, Mawu, the male god who represents coolness, wisdom, and mystery, and Lisa, the female god who represents the strength and energy of the dialectical rhythm of life. Mawu and Lisa act together as a universal complementary force in nature and are symbolized by the snake. Below Mawu and Lisa, the Fon pantheon contains two levels of deities known collectively as "vodu." These greater and lesser vodu, offspring of Mawu and Lisa, guard land and sea or are involved in everyday human pursuits. In the religious system of Dahomey, "the gods meet man at every point of life."[5]

Besides belief in a Supreme Being, the African religious traditions emphasize belief in the ancestors, the practice of sacrifice, belief in spirits and powers (both good and evil), and, finally, belief in the fullness of the present life. Reverence for ancestors, in particular, is a universally important feature of African religions. These ancestors are the "living dead" who continue to influence the present as long as they are remembered by their kinfolk. Ancestors are not worshiped but are held in respect and reverence similar to that given to the older living members of the family or tribe. The spirit of the ancestors is a vital part of the African concept of community, in which the collective power of all members of the community—the living and the "living dead"—energizes and pervades the daily life of everyone. Those ancestors who exhibited special moral virtue and strength in life are held up as spiritual guides for the living.[6]

Sacrificial ritual was the centerpiece of traditional African worship. Priests and priestesses offered sacrifice on behalf of the people for purposes of "propitiation, substitution, prevention, or purification" and in conjunction with the key events and rites of passage of human life: birth, puberty, marriage, and so on. A second component of African ritual, spirit possession, was a prized experience. The singing and drumming characteristic of African worship were used to invoke the presence of the lesser deities among the assembly, and as possession occurred, the devotees danced. The essential element of African religious expression, spirit possession—with its accompanying music and dance—was maintained in the transfer of African religion to the black church.[7]

The organizing principle of all African religion is the preservation and strengthening of life-force or power. Life is to be lived with great enthusiasm and energy and, simultaneously, protected from evil spirits and human malice. Various kinds of intercessory prayer—chants and invocations—are used to assuage the evil spirits, and medicine men or traditional healers are called upon to cure sickness with incantations as well as with medications.[8]

The power of the gods and spirits, for good or evil, is a central aspect of African life and belief. While African tribes do not share all such beliefs, Albert Raboteau portrays, in general terms, a picture of the interpersonal and relational character of African religions:

> The gods and men related to one another through the mediation of sacrifice, the mechanism of divination, and through the phenomenon of spirit possessions. Widely shared by diverse West African societies were several fundamental beliefs concerning the relationship of the divine and the human: belief in a transcendent and benevolent God, creator and ultimate source

of providence; belief in a number of immanent gods, to whom people must sacrifice in order to make life propitious; belief in the power of the spirits animating things in nature to affect the welfare of people; belief in priests and others who were expert in practical knowledge of the gods and spirits; belief in spirit possession, in which gods, through their devotees, spoke to men.[9]

Although most Christian missionaries to Africa summarily dismissed these traditional religious beliefs and practices as pagan and idolatrous, one may argue that some points of African belief could have provided a basis for religious dialogue between African religions and Western Christianity. African belief in a supreme, all-powerful, omniscient, and immutable God is suggestive of the Christian understanding of the one true God. "Who is God?" asks the catechism. "God is the Supreme Being who made all things" is the reply. A Christian raised in the Catholic scholastic tradition must also hear in the African definition of the divine echoes of Aquinas's description of God's attributes in the *Summa Theologica*.

Some aspects of the African ancestor traditions seem to correlate with the Christian doctrine of the "communion of saints," in which the living and the dead maintain a spiritual unity before the Lord, and what Catholic Christian worship has traditionally called the "sacrifice of the Mass" was seen not only as a community celebration of God's presence in our lives but also as an actual reenactment and memorial of the sacrifice of Jesus, who, in our place, died to atone for our sins and to redeem us from the condemnation of original sin. Even the concept of a spirit taking possession of an individual is not totally foreign to Christian concepts of the divine indwelling and the strengthening of one's faith by the celebration of the sacraments. In confirmation, the Holy Spirit is called upon to strengthen the faith and direct the ministry of the recipient of the sacrament. Sacramental rituals are celebrated to effect the presence and strength of God: Father, Son, and Holy Spirit are asked to protect—"take possession"—of the person in the sacrament of baptism, to forgive the person in the sacrament of reconciliation or penance, and to heal the person in the sacrament of anointing of the sick.

This is not to say that traditional African and Christian beliefs are identical, only that there are inherent in both sets of beliefs some shared meanings that provide a basis for understanding between two religious communities rooted in cultures with distinct world views. Such similarities account for the development of religious syncretism when African religious traditions encountered Christianity in the New World.

SLAVE RELIGION

Along with the beliefs and practices of African religions, both medicine men and sorcerers were transported to the New World as slaves. The continued presence of these religious leaders could not, however, ensure that African religions would survive the Atlantic crossing intact, for the very important communal bases of African religious perspectives and practices were more often than not destroyed by slave traders, who separated members of clans and tribes to ensure against insurrection and create dependence on the slave master. Some sources argue that these practices, along with the trauma of the "middle passage" from Africa to the American shores, totally eradicated the slaves' cultural and religious traditions by destroying their community. Other scholars suggest that new bonds were forged during the middle passage, allowing a creative integration of the common elements of the tribal rituals and religious perspectives to emerge.[10]

Raboteau suggests that both sides of the argument possess some truth, depending on the receptiveness of the receiving cultures. While African beliefs and rituals endured in the Latin cultures of Cuba, Haiti, Brazil, and the Caribbean Islands, they generally did not survive in the United States, though some residuals of the African pantheons and rituals are evident in the isolated Sea Islands of the Carolinas and in Louisiana. Two factors account for this difference: the cultural systems of the receiving countries and the density of the African population in the New World.[11] For example, in Cuba, Haiti, Brazil, Trinidad, and the Virgin Islands, where the African population is dense, religious cults exhibit recognizable elements of African rituals and ancestor cults.[12]

The new and hostile environment of the slaves inevitably required some transformation of African religious beliefs and practices. The question that dominated the slaves' world was one of survival, seen—as it traditionally had been—in terms of a struggle against evil forces. But these evil forces were (consistently) much more evident now in the day-to-day conditions of slavery than they had ever been in life on the African continent. The medicine man and conjurer now had to focus on conquering the illness and evil that accompanied slavery. The situation was a matter of life and death, and the life-force was to be preserved and strengthened by any means possible. Yet even in slavery, Africans knew that God had not abandoned the community but was in their midst, and the slave was grateful that God had provided means of survival. Thus the rituals of slave religion were a joyous affirmation of God's presence and providence. As the drums beat, slaves opened themselves to receive the Spirit, to become united with that spirit which strengthened their life-force and restored their wounded bodies. Amazingly, in the midst of the violence of slavery, the major theme of slave religion was joy!

> Even carnal pleasure had its prominent place. Such a religion bound men and women to the organic vitalistic powers of creation—to powers that they believed could provide for and sustain those who joyfully acknowledged and served the Creator. Behind the recognition that in existence there is some radically opposing force, some intrinsic mischief that we must somehow overcome or learn to control, was an even greater recognition that life is good and is to be savored and enjoyed while it lasts.[13]

As slave religion encountered Christianity, the slaves integrated those aspects of Christianity that eased "the burden of their captivity and gave little attention to the rest."[14] In Latin America and the Islands, Catholic piety, with its use of sacramentals, veneration of saints, and religious societies, combined with the African propensity for survival and harmony, resulted in the development of an African-Catholic syncretism in which the slaves' popular piety identified the attributes of the lesser gods with the intercession of the saints. This African-Catholic syncretism thrived in the cults of Latin America, where Catholicism and the Latin cultural system were dominant. It was not so well preserved where the dominant cultural system was English Protestantism.[15]

Despite the hostile circumstances of slavery in the New World, the African world view, which affirms the presence of the spirit world in the daily affairs of the community and the individual, was not destroyed. The African slave continued to see all of life as permeated with the Spirit. All of life was sacred. The individual and community were obligated to affirm this divine presence in ritual, prayer, and other forms of worship. Such rituals strengthened the life-force of the community and each of its members. Africans creatively indigenized their new environment through religious syncretism and, in some instances, secret cults. Where African life was harshly restricted and religious expression suppressed, religion became the basis of the struggle for liberation. For example, the vodun cult of Haiti, a syncretistic practice combining the African religion of Dahomey and Catholic Christianity, was the source of spiritual strength for Haitian nationalists who revolted in 1791.[16]

THE BLACK CHURCH

The primary locus for and nurturer of black spirituality has been the traditional black church. The term "black church" designates both those black Christian churches that originated as a consequence of the rejection and second-class citizenship blacks experienced in the mainline Protestant denominations and those independent churches that have roots in the religion of the slave quarters and fields (e.g., Baptist and Pentecostal).[17]

The forms of Christianity the African slaves encountered in captivity had already degenerated by their accommodation to the immoral enslavement of other human beings. These Protestant and Catholic Christians had anesthetized themselves to the immorality of slavery by philosophical and theological rationalizations that "justified" the economic and personal exploitation of their estranged African brothers and sisters. Indeed, few of these Christians would ever concede that Africans were fully human and therefore their equals in the eyes of God. To the contrary, in the eyes of most slave traders and missionaries, Africans were uncivilized barbarians who were being saved and elevated by their mere association with Christian civilization.[18]

In the United States, where English Protestantism was the dominant religious culture, few efforts were made to convert the slaves to Christianity until the eighteenth century, and these efforts increased only when it was guaranteed that baptism would not alter the "property" status of the slave.[19] That these baptisms were often attempts to pacify the enslaved Africans is indicated by one slave catechism from the mid-nineteenth century: The question "What did God make you for?" is followed by the answer "To make a crop." Another question, "What is the meaning of 'Thou shalt not commit adultery'?" is answered "To serve our heavenly Father, and our earthly master, obey our overseer, and not steal anything."[20]

In general, the Christian churches remained indifferent to the spiritual welfare of their African slaves, who were viewed primarily as property. Blacks were thought to be the cursed descendants of Ham. In reality, they were not cursed by God but by the indifference of those Christians who used "their bodies but denied their souls, and . . . turned them away from their churches."[21] Even when the doors of the church were opened, blacks were relegated to the back pews and balconies of the assemblies to prevent social contact. Yet it was in these back pews and balconies that the slaves heard the liberating words of the gospel. While the white preacher attempted to use the gospel to justify the current social and economic relations between the races, the slaves heard the liberating themes of the gospel and integrated them with their traditional African beliefs of a loving, ever-present, and provident God. When their interpretation of the biblical message and its implication for blacks clashed with denominational stances and boundaries, some blacks left their parent churches and formed independent African churches.

Black Christian preachers realized that God's provident love requires that human beings be free to develop their humanity to its fullest potential. If God is free, then human beings, created in the divine image and likeness, were meant to be free. Thus Christian responsibility requires those who have been enslaved to recover their God-given freedom so their *force-vitale*, or inner spirit, can be free. Such was the meaning and message of the liberating actions of Henry Highland Garnett, Thomas Fortune, David Walker (who followed in the footsteps of Nat Turner), and Denmark Vessey.[22]

It was not unusual for the early black Christian slaves who assembled in the balconies and back pews of the white Christian churches to reassemble in the backwoods and swamps, where they could express their common experience and common spirituality in more congenial forms of rhythm, song, and prayer. With the emergence of the independent African churches in the eighteenth and nineteenth centuries, the invisible black church of the backwoods became the visible black church in the United States.[23] These churches generally maintained the structures and central doctrines of their originating denominations; nevertheless, they developed a unique black American religious culture—a blend of both African religion and Euro-American Christianity. This distinctive religious culture, like the African religious cultures that preceded it, sought and still seeks to interpret the meaning of black life in relationship to both God and its environment. The preaching and worship styles of the black church echo and reflect the African world view and understanding of God's love and active presence in the daily affairs of human beings. In varying degrees, the liberating spirit that gave birth to the black church is evident in the content and style of its preaching and song, as well as in the involvement of its members in evangelization and action for social justice.

Although some traditional black Christian churches have maintained a faithfulness to the essential meaning and message of Jesus Christ as apprehended from an African or black perspective, others have become accommodated to a dualistic view that divides the world into the sacred and the secular, thus contradicting their African origin. This culturally alien dualism can give rise to a variety of problems. On the one hand, black churches can be solely havens of emotional security from the world's racial hostility. On the other hand, they can be both comforting and challenging sources of spiritual regeneration, empowering their members to struggle to liberate their families, their community, and the world from moral compromise with personal and social sins such as narcissism, materialism, racism, sexism, imperialism, and militarism. Then again, the black church can be corrupted into an institution that functions solely as a political-economic base for a racially isolated community.[24] The authentic black church must have a holistic approach to its members. It must comfort as well as challenge, and it must address the spiritual as well as the social and political needs of its members.

THE CHARACTERISTICS OF BLACK SPIRITUALITY

Black spirituality is characterized by a number of specific emphases and attitudes, none of which is exclusive to it but all of which, taken together, combine to produce a unique vision and practice of the spiritual life.

First, black spirituality, like the African religions in which it is rooted, is community centered. It shapes the community and, in turn, is shaped by the community, which defines itself and its history as being integrally connected with God. It is in the context of the worshiping community that the God-awareness of black spirituality is nurtured. What was true of slave religion of the past is equally true of the black church today: In common worship the community is called by song to be conscious of the Spirit who comes to join the assembly. Just as the drums of the African ritual opened the door for the spirit to enter the assembly, gospel song invites the Holy Spirit to be manifest in the midst of the worshiping community.

Another fundamental element of black spirituality is its strong biblical character. The worship services of the traditional black church are dominated by the dynamic and evocative preaching of the minister, and the starting point of the sermon is always the Word of God. The preacher begins by retelling an entire biblical story or dramatically announcing a few lines from a text taken from the Old or New Testament. After this vivid proclamation of the Scripture, the preacher brings the biblical text to life by indicating how the story has meaning in the lives of the congregation. Often the preaching is a dialogical experience, with the congregation affirming the preacher's truth-telling by nods of the head, applause, amens, and the like. When the Spirit of Truth envelops the assembly, some of the worshipers respond in a manner similar to their African ancestors, who experienced spirit possession. The preaching and singing are necessarily emotional, because the worshipers have been touched at the core of their being, moved by the presence of the Spirit deep in their soul.

In African-American culture the emotional is not the opposite of the spiritual, nor is there any separation between the emotional and the intellectual. Both the mind and the heart are needed to grasp the truth. If the preacher does not preach the truth, it will not be long before the congregation calls him to task.[25]

The point of the black church's biblically centered worship is to hear God's word from the past as it is evidenced in the present. This "immediate" interpretive principle or hermeneutic is a reflection of the African concept of time, in which past and present are one and continuous. Thus black spirituality is always concerned to situate itself firmly in the present, in the midst of concrete daily experience. By the same token, the biblical characters are not simply heroes and heroines of long ago; they have joined the ranks of the ancestors, and their lives, like those of the biological ancestors of African Americans, influence the lives of the living community.

In some worship services, members of the congregation testify to God's action in their lives and those of their extended family during the week. Increasingly, black Catholic liturgies are incorporating this testimonial aspect through spontaneous prayers of the people during the penitential rite and in the general intercessions during the Liturgy of the Word. In communal worship the assembly gathers up the experiences of its individual members and transforms them into the experience and concerns of the entire community. The suffering caused by unemployment, poverty, hunger, homelessness, rejection, and the human degradation of racism is all brought to the church to be transformed; and all of it *is* transformed by offering the entire community to God for healing, relief, and strengthening.

Most Africans and members of the African Diaspora have an experience of God that is both transcendent and immanent—God who is beyond us but dwells within us. Black believers know experientially ("deep down in my soul") that the Spirit of God dwells within their inner selves, directing their memory, imagination, intellect, feelings, and body. Any person born into the religious tradition of African or African Diaspora cultures is nurtured from birth into a style of life that witnesses to the belief that God is manifest everywhere and in every person, thing, or event. This attitude corresponds to the traditional religions of Dahomey, in which God meets the human being at every point of life; but the involvement of God in human life by way of "the gods" has been replaced, in the black church, by the concept of God being present by means of the Spirit sent by Jesus after his ascension. Thus a person steeped in the black spiritual tradition is trained, so to speak, in a particular kind of mystical tradition. One sees God's hands in every human encounter and event in life and is conditioned by environmental nurturing to abandon oneself, in obedience to God's will, to the movements of the Holy Spirit.

It is not unusual for a black child reared in a religious home to hear family members, especially the mother, talking to Jesus as they mull over family concerns. Not is it unusual to hear in family and community conversations testimony that a person has been led by God to use his or her talents in a specific way or to do this or that thing, even when the individual involved was initially resistant to such a course of action. The impulse in black spirituality to abandon oneself to the divine will and the indwelling Spirit lends itself to a particularly intimate experience of God.

Yet the kind of abandonment black worship invites is not a somber resignation to or hopeless acceptance of a life over which one has no control. The mystical union to which black spirituality predisposes one is the source of an emotional, energetic, and joyful approach to life and worship. The life experiences of African Americans attest that God is reliable and benevolent, involved in the daily life of individuals and the community. Blacks in touch with their spiritual traditions are confident about their ultimate well-being, because our God is a loving God who, in the last analysis, can be counted upon to give joy, power, and liberation from the debilitating oppressions of sin, racism, or any form of evil. This deep sense of joy finds expression in a correspondingly deep and pervasive sense of peace, even in the midst of great adversity or trial, and it is the same deep joy that overflows in quiet tears, loud shouts, exuberant or emotional songs, dancing, and clapping by choir and congregation gathered in worship.

While the joy of the Spirit's presence manifests itself in vivid and diverse ways in the worshiping community, such expression alone does not authenticate black spirituality. The absolute criterion of authentic black spirituality is its impact on the quality of the believer's life. It assumes that the true nature of our faith is reflected in the way in which we relate to other human beings and the created order, and that our concern for others will naturally generate witness and actions directed toward the realization of freedom for all human beings to live a liberated and joyful life, energized by the power of the Spirit. For example, does the person possessed by the Spirit of God treat family, neighbor, friends, and enemies with a sense of respect for the presence of God within each and every person? Does this person struggle to establish right relationships with others, regardless of race, gender, or creed? Does this person act right and call others to be right? Does this person struggle for the liberation of oppressed persons, races, nations?

Since the center and organizing principle of all African religion is the preservation and strengthening of the life-force or power of the community, in black spirituality, too, the central focus is the preservation and strengthening of the life-force or power that dwells within each individual and in the community. This life-force is the Spirit of God.

Individuals oppressed by reason of gender, race, class, or nationality have had their authentic freedom, their unique expression of the God-force, suppressed. Thus they are denied their role as co-creators of God's kingdom. Authentic black spirituality leads to prophetic action on behalf of justice, a justice that requires liberation from sin and its effects. This understanding of justice entails a reordering of the false and unjust structures of institutions, nations, and even ecclesial bodies that have become stumbling blocks rather than facilitators of an individual's or community's right relationship between God and one another. A person imbued with the life-force at the center of black spirituality—with the Spirit of God—is willing to struggle for this liberation, knowing that even death is not too high a price to pay for the establishment of those right relationships that characterize the kingdom of God.

In their commitment to the liberation and justice of the poor, the marginalized, and the oppressed, adherents of the prophetic tradition so prominent in authentic black spirituality recognize that they must stand for the truth. The Christian person must walk the path of Jesus Christ, who is the Way, the Truth, and the Life. A man of love who announced the gospel to the poor, the oppressed, and the marginalized of his society (Lk 4:14ff.), Jesus not only spoke the good news, he *was* the Good News.

The gospel writers portray a Jesus who, in his love, invited and challenged all he encountered to a way of being and acting that reflected their true dignity and identity as members of the one family of God. Pharisee, Sadducee, Samaritan woman, disciple, Roman governor, tax collector—any and all persons encountered were invited or challenged. No one was (or is) beyond God's call to conversion in Jesus. Thus black spirituality challenges any exclusive interpretation of those invited to the wedding feast of the kingdom. Christ's message of love, justice, and liberation was good news for some and a fear-inducing challenge to others. Those who heard his message as good news became disciples and apostles. Those who heard his message as demanding a change that threatened their security—the rich, the powerful, and the pious—responded by calling for his crucifixion. This Jesus is love. Out of this love he died and rose from the dead to free humankind from its sin and oppression. His death and resurrection have freed us from fear and empowered us to live for and with God.

Not all black Christians embrace this universal and community-centered understanding of the meaning of Jesus. They, like some other Christians, believe that the life and death of Christ have nothing at all to do with the ecclesial and social structures of human society, even when these structures oppress the spirit of love, truth, and liberation given to each person and community for building up and preparing for God's kingdom.

BLACK SPIRITUALITY AND THE CHURCHES

It should be apparent that black spirituality transcends and crosses denominational and ecclesial boundaries. Its characteristic cultural expressions are more evident in some congregations and denominations than in others; consequently, it is more or less empirically evident in the lives of individual black Christians.

Many African American Catholics and other blacks nurtured in predominantly white Christian congregations have become estranged from their cultural religious heritage because they were introduced to missionaries who were not conscious of the cultural wrapping with which they presented the gift of Christianity to the children of the African Diaspora. The spiritual traditions of the Catholic church, for example, were transmitted to the sons and daughters of Africa without any consciousness of the culture-specific ways—Spanish, Irish, German, English, French, or Italian—in which they were being transmitted. In addition, these ministers of God's good news sometimes maintained a disdain for the natural religious expression of blacks. For them, blacks needed to be elevated and rescued from their immorality by their participation in what was perceived to be a universal spirituality that was, in fact, a particular cultural-ecclesial spirituality and way of life. White missionaries assumed that blacks had no culture worth preserving, and that their religiosity was a natural disposition based primarily on fear and ignorance. Christianity would provide them both with culture and the true faith.[26]

In contrast to the missionary endeavors of the nineteenth century, the writings of St. Paul suggest that the early church approached Gentile cultures with an implicit sense of the need for cultural adaptation. Unfortunately, this sense of cultural adaptation was absent from the method of evangelization used by many missionaries encountering non-European peoples, whether they were Asians, Africans, Native Americans, or black Americans. Universality was narrowly defined as uniformity, rather than as unity in diversity.[27]

Today, the picture is changing. The twentieth-century shift to a historical consciousness in biblical studies and theological interpretation and the church's attempt to address the role of God in the modern world call for a shift in evaluating the religious, racial, cultural, economic, and social-political diversity evident within the world and the church. This shift is obvious in recent Roman Catholic documents relating to liturgy, mission, evangelization, and non-Christian religions, which urge respect for and utilization of cultural expressions, symbols, and practices that are not fundamentally at odds with Christian orthodoxy.[28]

Most significant for our discussion is the emerging theological understanding of the relationship between the natural and the supernatural spheres of reality. Traditionally the church has taught that "grace builds on nature." Many modern theologians, notably Karl Rahner, would assert that nature itself is "graced." This graced human nature is a reality that is unified and organically interrelated yet manifests itself in diversity of all kinds, and this diversity does not eliminate any person or group from participating in the universal salvific will of God. Everything created by God manifests God's creative Spirit, indeed, *embodies* that Spirit in one form or another. Positions such as Rahner's are in harmony with the African world view, in which the world is not dichotomized into sacred and secular realms.

Taken seriously, these philosophical and theological shifts would lead those engaged in ministry and mission to first seek the manifestation of the Spirit in cultural diversity rather than always thinking in terms of "bringing Jesus" to non-Christian nations and cultures. Further, respect for God-given cultural diversity in the human community requires pastoral ministers to develop religious educational materials that reflect such diversity. Congregational worship or liturgies serving distinct cultural or multicultural constituencies should attempt to integrate the music, symbolic expressions, and theological interpretations of God and Christ so as to nurture the spiritual consciousness of worshipers. At the same time, the church needs to challenge culturally different populations to deepen their spiritual awareness by prayer and a study of the Scriptures directed toward discerning the authentic meaning/message of Jesus as it affirms and critiques their present way of relating to God and others.

Christian churches engaged in the spiritual nurturing of African Americans must take seriously the particular culture and context of black life in America. In this regard, they would be wise to take account of the challenges presented in the work of contemporary black theologians, historians, anthropologists, religious leaders, and scholars, who are reexamining the Scriptures and black religious traditions in order to discern how God is being revealed in today's black community and what the black church's mission is in relation to the world and the world church.[29]

Pope Paul VI, in a historic visit to Kampala, Uganda, urged African Catholics to enrich the church with their "gift of Blackness," and increasingly, African and black Christians in the United States and throughout the world are ready and willing to share with their black and white brothers and sisters the rich gift of black spirituality given to them by God. They, in turn, will continue to integrate and enrich their African religious heritage and spirituality with the gifts of other Christian traditions and world religions.

NOTES

[1] John S. Mbiti, *African Religions and Philosophy* (New York: Doubleday Anchor Books, 1970), pp. 1-2.

[2] Ibid., p. 3.

[3] Ibid., pp. 19-36.

[4] Edwin J. Nichols, Ph.D., a black Catholic philosophical psychologist, is the chief of Service Systems Technology Transfer Branch at the National Institute of Mental Health. After teaching briefly at the University of Ibadan, Nigeria, he developed a comparative schema that he presented at the World Psychiatric Association and Association of Psychiatrists at the University of Ibadan on November 10, 1976. Nichols consults in the area of cross-cultural management and decision making and has worked with missionaries engaged in cross-cultural interactions to interpret the philosophical aspects of cultural differences between ethnic and racial groups.

[5] Leonard E. Barrett, *Soul Force* (New York: Doubleday Anchor Books, 1974), pp. 17-20.

[6] Ibid., pp. 22-24; and Albert Raboteau, *Slave Religion* (New York: Oxford University Press, 1978), pp. 12-13.

[7] Barrett, *Soul Force*, pp. 24-26; and Raboteau, *Slave Religion*, pp. 10-11, 15.

[8] Medicine men are carefully selected and must undergo a minimum of ten years of apprenticeship and training, then pass a test administered by their peers. The Western mind has looked upon these practices as "magic" and nonscientific, yet this does not seem to be the reality. Increasing numbers of scientifically trained doctors have acknowledged the psychosomatic component of much physical illness and are exploring the relationship between diet and disease in what is now termed "holistic medicine." The distinction should be noted that whereas the medicine man seeks to protect the life-force of human beings, the sorcerer or conjurer employs witchcraft to diminish the life-force of persons and thereby hurt or kill them. See Barrett, *Soul Force*, pp. 27-31, 60; and Raboteau, *Slave Religion*, pp. 13-14.

[9] Raboteau, *Slave Religion*, pp. 11-12.

[10] For a review of this classic discussion, see E. Franklin Frazier, *The Negro Family in the United States*, rev. and abr. ed. (New York: Dryden Press, 1948); and Melville J. Herskovits, *The Myth of the Negro Past* (New York: Harper & Bros., 1941). Frazier suggests that African American religious practices owe little to African influence, while Herskovits argues for essential continuity evidenced both in African American culture and religious practices.

[11] Raboteau, *Slave Religion*, p. 86.

[12] Barrett, *Soul Force*, p. 69.

[13] Gayraud Wilmore, *Black Religion and Black Radicalism* (Maryknoll, N.Y.: Orbis Books, 1983), pp. 12-13.

[14] Ibid., p. 11.

[15] For a detailed look at the parallels made, see Raboteau, *Slave Religion*, pp. 22-23. Raboteau discusses the issue of syncretism on pp. 15-42.

[16] Wilmore, *Black Religion*, p. 23. Vodun and its "vodu" rituals have been grossly misunderstood in Western religious traditions as satanic evil. Wilmore gives a more positive view of this tradition; see pp. 20-23.

[17] Only recently have blacks in predominantly white churches been included in this designation. As blacks in predominantly white churches begin to identify, embrace, and nurture the spiritual aspect of their African cultural heritage, some are rediscovering the spiritual expressions and experiences characteristic of African peoples. Previously these blacks had adopted the spiritual understandings and expressions of their denominations, as they were expressed in a European or Euro-American mode.

[18] See C. Eric Lincoln, *Race, Religion, and the Continuing American Dilemma* (New York: Hill & Wang, 1984).

[19] Raboteau, *Slave Religion*, p. 88; Lincoln, *Race, Religion and the Continuing American Dilemma*, pp. 44-49.

[20] Wilmore, *Black Religion*, p. 24, quoting Anson West, *A History of Methodism in Alabama* (Nashville: Publishing House, Methodist Episcopal Church South, 1893).

[21] Lincoln, *Race, Religion and the Continuing American Dilemma*, p. 39.

[22] Ibid., p. 63.

[23] Ibid., pp. 33, 64ff. The major independent African churches—the African Methodist Episcopal, the African Methodist Episcopal Zion, the Christian Methodist, the National Baptist Convention, the National Baptist Convention of America, the Progressive Baptist Convention, and the Church of God in Christ—collectively account for 95 percent of the black Christians in our country. Ibid., p. 69.

[24] See Joseph Washington, *Black Religion: The Negro and Christian in the United States* (Boston: Beacon Press, 1964).

[25] Clarence Joseph Rivers, *The Spirit in Worship* (Cincinnati: Stimuli, 1978), p. 5; see also Henry Mitchell, "Black Preaching," in *The Black*

Christian Experience, ed. Emmanuel L. McCall (Nashville: Broadman Press, 1972), pp. 43-62; and Giles A. Conwill, "Black Preaching and Catholicism," in McCall, *The Black Christian Experience,* pp. 31-43.

²⁶ Jamie Phelps, "The Mission Ecclesiology of John R. Slattery," dissertation in progress at the Catholic University of America. The dissertation examines Slattery's missiology and his cross-cultural evangelization in the American Catholic church in the late nineteenth century.

²⁷ See James Dunn, *Unity and Diversity in the New Testament* (Philadelphia: Westminster Press, 1977); also, Marcel Dumais, "La Rencontre de Foi et des Cultures," *Lumière et Vie* 153/154 (July-Sept. 1981): 72-86.

²⁸ See the respective documents in Austin Flannery, ed., *The Documents of Vatican II* (New York: Costello Publishing Co., 1981-1982): "Evangelii Nuntiandi," nos. 40-58; "Ad Gentes," nos. 10-12, 13-18; "Sacrosantum Concillium," nos. 21-40; "Gaudium et Spes," nos. 23-32, 53-62; "Unitatis Redintegratio," nos. 5-12.

²⁹ For example, C. Eric Lincoln, Vincent Harding, James Cone, Gayraud Wilmore, Joseph Washington, Deotis Roberts, Jackie Grant, Albert Raboteau, Cyprian Davis, Albert Pero, Shawn Copeland, Toinette Eugene, and Thea Bowman, to name only a few.

9

Black Catechesis

Catching the Flame and Passing It On

GILES CONWILL

I caught the fire from those who went before,
The bearers of the torch who could not see
The goal to which they strained. I caught their fire,
And carried it only a little way beyond;
But there are those who wait for it, I know,
Those who will carry it on to victory.
> —Alfred Noyes

CATECHESIS IN THE EARLY CHURCH: THE CATECHUMENATE

The early church considered the New Testament itself as catechesis—the oral teaching of the Christian faith passed on to those who would willingly hear and accept it.[1] By the third century, Christianity had grown beyond the mere "movement" stage and was on the way to developing organizational structure and at least a seminal sophistication in the formulation of theological concepts. Creedal definitions and meanings were evolving and becoming more technical. Such was also the case with the term *catechesis*. The technical use of the word restricted its meaning to the instruction given to those who were being prepared for baptism (baptismal catechesis) within the structure of the catechumenate, or the stages immediately following baptism, namely, "the mystagogical catechesis of the neophytes."[2] Catechesis is a major aspect of evangelization.

Initially, the catechumenate was established as a period of pre-baptismal instruction for adults. But by the sixth century it was being used less and less for that purpose. By then the focus was on the baptism of children rather than adults.

The church's concept and practice of catechesis were also affected, according to M. E. Jegen, by the huge numbers belonging to Germanic tribes who were being incorporated into the church's fold:

> With mass conversions, entire tribes were baptized after only a few weeks, or with little or no instruction. From this time the Church had to take into account the problem of educating in the faith large groups of rude, unlettered people.[3]

Careful and diligent pre-baptismal preparation and continued instruction of neophytes declined to such an extent that by the eighth and ninth centuries the catechumenate itself was abandoned as a formal structure. Non-use of the term *catechesis* accompanied the demise of the catechumenate.

From this period up to the Reformation, the content of religious instruction was mainly determined by missionary monks and the pastoral treatises of bishops and popes. One example of the treatises used was Pope Gregory I's (d. 604) *Libri Dialogorum*, a hagiographical work that promoted Christian principles through the exemplary lives of the saints. Another example, the discourses of St. Boniface (d. 754) as he evangelized Germany, demonstrated a Christocentric focus and a reliance on Sacred Scripture and the Fathers of the church.

The fundamental basics of catechesis entailed at least the memorization of the Creed, the Our Father, and acceptance of the essential doctrines, such as the Trinity. Liturgical celebrations themselves were also great didactic experiences.

From the twelfth to the fifteenth centuries, the establishment of religious orders, such as the Dominicans and the Franciscans, was a great boon to the catechetical enterprise. The teaching and preaching of these friars were effectively able to touch many souls. The High Middle Ages saw catechesis and catechetical methodology positively affected by the rise of universities and the application of systematic theology. Then too, the Reformation must be given proper credit for the part it played in the development of Catholic catechesis. In 1528 Luther circulated a catechism whose short question-and-answer format proved very popular. The Catholic church reacted to this catechism and to Protestantism in general by devoting even greater diligence to the articulation of Catholic theology and doctrine. In fact, the Council of Trent (1545-63) could be credited with, among other things, bearing "catechetical fruit" with the *Roman Catechism* of 1566.

The outstanding catechism authors who should be mentioned in cursory review are St. Robert Bellarmine (†1621) and St. Peter Canisius (†1597). Both men produced works of lasting value. Bellarmine's work was of such importance that it was translated into sixty languages, including editions in Arabic, Hindustani, Chinese, Congolese, Ethiopian, Hebrew, and Quechua.[4] Sts. Vincent de Paul (†1660) and Francis de Sales (†1622) were also outstanding catechists and missionaries who served the church in the post-Reformation era.

CATECHETICAL EVANGELIZATION OF NORTH AMERICA

THE BALTIMORE CATECHISM (1885)—
FIRST OFFICIAL AMERICAN CATECHISM

North America has had its own significant history of catechetical evangelization. Just as the country had depended initially upon priests and religious from abroad for its sacramental and ministerial needs, so likewise there was an initial dependence on Europe for catechetical resources. Spanish and French missionaries had catechized the Indians, using materials that accommodated the Christian message to the languages of these native Americans.

Colonial America saw the importation of catechetical materials from abroad supplemented by those published in this country. Priests and religious who accompanied the huge numbers of European immigrants to this country made one of their priorities the development, use, and dissemination of catechetical materials written in the language of their respective ethnic groups.

Although the Catholic bishops had unsuccessfully tried to establish a national catechism for this country, it was not until 1885 that the first official American catechism was approved. Having been promulgated by the Third Council of Baltimore, it was popularly known as *The Baltimore Catechism*. Revised in 1941, this text served as the staple for religious education in many an American school, church, and home. This was the text my own teachers used in elementary school. My parents and grandparents also used it. For those Catholics attending non-Catholic schools, the Confraternity of Christian Doctrine developed, during the 1930s, a program specifically geared to those not having the benefit of daily contact with Catholic education and educators.

STAGES, PHASES, AND APPROACHES IN CATECHETICS

If one examines closely the various formats that catechetics has employed over the last fifty years, it is possible to distinguish several different stages and approaches. R. M. Rummery has identified five stages in the development of catechetics from about 1930 to the present: (1) the traditional; (2) the pedagogical; (3) the kerygmatic; (4) the life-centered and situational; and (5) the group-centered. It serves our purpose well to review his analysis of these five stages because his observations are quite accurate.

The Traditional Approach

The first stage identified by Rummery is what he calls the traditional approach. It held dominance from around the post-Reformation era well into modern times. Memorization of questions and answers, with a syllabus based on the Creed, commandments, sacraments, and prayer, characterized this approach. The relationship between catechist and students was very authoritarian in style, namely, that of master and pupils. The dimension of religion (the person's relationship with God) emphasized was doctrinal and moral. The Bible was seldom dealt with directly. Rummery maintains that this traditional approach, used for so many centuries by the church, was seriously deficient:

> It not only had a limited view of religion and of what was involved in passing on the truths of faith to other believers . . . but it also failed to distinguish sufficiently between this faith of the Church and the development of the personal faith of the believer and sometimes tended to confuse conformity and acceptance of a prevalent pattern of church attendance with personal faith and free response.[5]

The traditional approach was employed by both Protestants and Catholics. This question-and-answer format was apparently also used in catechizing the slaves. Charles Colcock Jones, one of the outstanding Protestant preachers of the South during the 1800s, wrote *A Catechism for Colored Persons*, a 108-page text, which he later revised in 1837 and republished as *A Catechism of Scripture, Doctrine, and Practice for Families and Sabbath Schools, Designed Also for the Oral Instruction of Colored Persons.*[6] The following excerpts from this catechism provide an example of the format and also show how religion was used to promote subservience to the slave system.

Q. Is God present in every place?
A. Yes.

Q. What does he see and know?
A. All Things.

Q. Who is in duty bound to have justice done servants when they are wronged or abused or ill-treated by anyone?
A. The master.

Q. Is it right for the master to punish his servants cruelly?
A. No.

Q. What command has God given to servants, concerning obedience to their masters?
A. Servants obey in all things your masters according to the flesh, not in eye-service as men-pleasers, but in singleness of heart, fearing God.

Q. What are servants to count their masters worthy of?
A. All honor.

Q. How are they to do their service of their master?
A. With good will, doing service unto the Lord and not unto men.

Q. How are they to try to please their masters?
A. Please them well in all things, not answering again.

The Pedagogical Approach

The pedagogical approach, the second stage according to Rummery, chronologically followed the traditional (magisterial) approach and may have been a reaction to it. This approach sought to engage the learners as active participants. It individualized teaching and looked upon the teacher as a guide rather than an authority. Rummery observes that the Creed-commandments-sacraments sequence was kept, but teachers began to use formats other than just the question-and-answer one. There was also more use of biblical materials during this period, but the attention was more on Bible history than on the Bible itself.

The Catholic church has had a paradoxical history in regard to its use of the Bible. First, it was the protector and patron, so to speak, of the Sacred Scriptures, having received them as a precious legacy from pre-Christian (Old Testament) and apostolic times. Monks diligently copied manuscripts by hand, preserving them during the Middle Ages and the invasion of the barbarian hordes. This church can also be credited with having produced some of the best scripture scholars and biblical scholarship available. But this same church can also be rightly accused of keeping its own people in the dark and unfamiliar with the Bible. The following excerpt from the *Dogmatic Catechism*'s English translation in 1871 by Cardinal Manning presents the church's rationale for such a paradoxical position:

> Q. Would it not be well to make translations of the Bible into the vulgar tongues so that it might be put into the hands of all, even of the laity?
> A. The Church forbids that the Bible, literally translated from the vulgar tongue, should be given to be read by all persons indifferently. She even forbids absolution of sins to be given to those who choose to read it, or retain possession of it without permission. The proof that it cannot be a good thing to put the Bible into the hands of all persons is, that being full of mysteries, it would injure rather than profit the ignorant; and this is manifest from the zeal with which Protestants scatter abroad, everywhere and at great expense, an incredible number of vernacular translations of the Bible.[7]

Catholics, when compared to Protestants, still have a great unfamiliarity with the Bible; this is a result of the type of narrow and paternalistic thinking of the last century, as characterized by the above passage.

The Kerygmatic Approach

The third state, according to Rummery's analysis, employed the kerygmatic approach. The word *kerygmatic* is derived from the Greek word for "herald," *keryx*. Proclamation of the history of salvation with a Christocentric focus characterized this model. Since sharing the good news of Christ was such an essential aspect of this approach, it is not surprising that the use and study of the Bible grew in popularity. However, increased use of the Bible was not the only innovation that accompanied this approach. Rummery concedes that

> style and content changed too, especially when associated with the four sources of the kerygma, namely the Bible, the Liturgy, the teaching of Doctrines and the personal and community witness to the reality of what was being proclaimed.[8]

Whereas the previous two stages looked upon Sunday Mass attendance as an obligation, this approach perceived the liturgy in its social aspect as an encounter with God's Word. The good news is a *joyful* message brought by Christ.

Rummery makes a further distinction between the traditional (magisterial) and pedagogical approaches, when compared to the kerygmatic approach. The first two

> were characterized by what could be called a "pedagogy of object," i.e., they relied on concern with the handing on of "the faith," which was seen as unchanging. . . . On the other hand, the Kerygmatic approach allowed teachers to see themselves as the inner essential link between content and method in the approach. The Kerygmatic approach was more a "pedagogy of subject," i.e., it looked towards the recipients of the catechesis.[9]

The Anthropological Approach

The fourth stage is called the anthropological approach. Not surprisingly, its emphasis is on incarnational theology. Its anthropological focus leads it to deal with real life situations and incorporate them into the learning experience. Another characteristic of this approach is its tendency to study the Bible thematically rather than chronologically, as did other previous approaches. Symbols are important in anthropology. This fourth approach gives much attention to symbols in Sacred Scripture that lend themselves to thematic categorization and classification: bread, light, community, and so on. An attempt is also made to incorporate the students' particular life experiences into the learning experience. To make it more relevant sociologically and personally, current audiovisual and media resources are used to supplement what the text(s) themselves have to offer.

The Group-Centered Approach

The fifth and last stage, the group-centered approach, is, according to Rummery, a natural extension of the fourth stage. That stage dealt with the interpersonal dynamics of the individual. This is now expanded to a consideration of group dynamics and how learning takes place in non-directed groups as opposed to in formal educational settings. This approach acknowledges that (religious) learning can and does take place in "extra-class" and non-formal situations. Participants utilizing this approach relate to one another in a non-hierarchical way. Rather than a predetermined syllabus, the curriculum admits a reflection of life experiences of group members and their personal faith statements. Revelation is perceived as God speaking through the events of people's lives, and Christ is encountered in and through other persons. Rummery has certainly contributed to our understanding of the historical dynamics that have accompanied the development of catechetics. Present-day use of the term *catechesis* incorporates the dimensions of these latter stages and tries to combine the instructional focus on both children and adults by continued education and deepening of faith. *Catechesis,* therefore, means not only the pre-baptismal instruction given to those intending to adopt the faith, as it did for the early church, but, as Audinet insists, the term is also

> co-extensive with the teaching of the faith, from the first announcement of the kerygma to the higher forms of "scientific" theology. This definition underlines the unity between the various stages: the initial hearing of the Good News, or the preparation for baptism, and the more advanced teaching designed to nourish the Christian life.[10]

To understand fully what catechesis is, it must be borne in mind that the Word of God and the Christ-event, as it is revealed in that Word, determine the content of catechesis. The Word, as presented in the context of catechesis, calls a person to radical acceptance or nonacceptance, belief or disbelief, obedience or disobedience, of Christ and his way. In other words, the goal of catechesis is conversion. As Romney Moseley asserts, the faith that authentic conversion effects is not merely an "assent to the truth claims of doctrines and sacred text." Conversion, like faith, is "the activity of surrendering one's self totally to an ultimate and transcendent source of meaning and power. . . . In religious terms the heart is given completely to God."[11] Catechesis makes use of moral, dogmatic, doctrinal, and liturgical theology, scriptural exegesis, biblical theology, church history, hagiography, and a host of other sacred sciences, but its concern and intent does not stop at the content of these theological sciences:

> It goes beyond the technical aspects of these sciences to embrace the living and active initiative of God as he turns to man. The theological sciences provide catechesis with the matter and norms for judging its methods. But it is in itself the living word of God addressed to the man of today.[12]

THE IMPORTANCE OF CATECHESIS IN EVANGELIZATION AS STATED BY VATICAN II

THE RCIA AS CATECHETICAL METHOD

The church's realization of how important catechesis is in the process of evangelization may be seen by the attention given the subject by the Vatican II fathers in the several decrees they issued calling for the restoration of the catechumenate throughout the church. For example, the council's *Constitution on the Sacred Liturgy (Sacrosanctum Concilium)* declares:

> The catechumenate for adults, comprising several distinct steps, is to be restored and brought into use at the discretion of the local ordinary. By this means the time of the catechumenate, which is intended as a period of suitable instruction, may be sanctified by sacred rites to be celebrated at successive intervals of time (no. 64).

The Vatican's Congregation of Worship, after much study and consultation, produced a restored version of the ancient rite, which had been in disuse for so many centuries. The revised product, not finished until 1972, is called the Rite of Christian Initiation of Adults, or RCIA. It was not until 1974 that an English translation was available. This 151-page text and the change of mindset it calls for represent a challenge for many parishes and dioceses in this country. Yet many parishes and dioceses have taken serious steps for its implementation.

The RCIA process has four distinct stages: a pre-catechumenate period with no specific time limit; a formal catechumenate period, also having no determined length; a purification period, optimally scheduled during Lent preceding entry and acceptance into the church; and finally, a post-baptismal integration into the community during the Easter season wherein the newly baptized "neophytes" are to continue their growth in the faith and apostolate in a period called the "mystagogia." *Mystagogy* means "education in the mysteries." Reflections of the ancient rite of the early church can be seen in the restored rite by the use of such terms as "neophyte," "scrutiny," and "mystagogia." This rite involves the community of believers in the process of preparing those who are to be welcomed into the church, and it is therefore much more effective than the former method of private instruction given by the priest alone.

As Romney Moseley asserts, each stage of the RCIA should reflect "a progressive integration and intensification of the catechumen's relationship to God, Church, and the world."[13] The rites of enrollment, election, scrutinies, and the sacraments of initiation and reception should not become what Mark Searle calls "merely ecclesiastical graduations, marking the converts' progress through the catechumenal program."[14] Rather, authentic faith, an intimacy with the Lord, and a desire to help build the kingdom should be the outcomes of this period of serious formation.

The RCIA utilizes a number of ways to bring the candidates' faith to maturity. Clergy and catechists expose them to the official dogmas and precepts of the church. The candidates interact with parishioners formally and informally, providing them with opportunities to engage in dialogue about the faith and to witness how others live the faith. Participation in the liturgy and explanation of the rituals and symbols involved therein are also a great didactic means provided for the candidates.

The involvement of the community is of utmost importance to the success of the entire program, for, as Regis Duffy states:

The symbols and rituals of the RCIA assume their full meaning when a Christian community understands and celebrates them with a deepening sense of commitment. This ecclesial dimension is crucial because the catechumenal process is as necessary for the renewal of that community as it is for the preparation of its candidates.[15]

The RCIA, when successfully implemented, reportedly brings great optimism and growth to a parish's catechetical program. However, like all human endeavors, it has its drawbacks and shortcomings. One is the vagueness of some of the rituals in their speaking to present-day candidates. (The words *mystagogia* and *neophyte* are certainly mystifying in themselves.) Another deficiency—and it is closely related to the first—is the lack of cultural/ethnic adaptation in the rite itself. The best RCIA program in the world will not be able to overcome the difficulties inherent in liturgical ceremonies, texts, and symbols that do not speak to this or that particular people in their own cultural idiom. Cold "white" rites, anemic and sterile performance of rituals, and use of Euro-American symbols and worldview will render ineffective this and any other program that seeks to enlist and involve Blacks in the Catholic church. As one Black wag put it: "Convert me to what? God's frozen people?" The ecclesial dimension of the process mentioned earlier and the assistance given to the candidates by *interaction* with the community will perhaps offer the best starting point for cultural adaption of the RCIA. The Catholic church's worldview could then be mediated through the interpersonal relationships with Black parishioners and scholars.[16] This is a good practical basis for the Black cultural adaption the RCIA lacks in its present text form.

I also believe that there should be some wariness in accepting the RCIA as the only way for admitting adults into the church. As one of my priest friends said, "The RCIA makes it more difficult to be a catechumen than it is to be a Catholic!" There should not be just one program for acceptance in the church, but rather a diversity of programs. The RCIA could work very well for most parishes, but there should remain an openness to the Spirit and newly developing research as well. The RCIA optimally should involve the whole parish. But we should have individualized programs as well as group processes.

But even with this push for programmatic flexibility, we must still acknowledge and employ modern pedagogical principles which show that adult learning takes place more effectively when teaching/learning methods include working and learning in small groups; learning by doing; answering questions, concerns, and problems as soon as they arise; taking time to assimilate, reflect, discuss, share, explore, and dialogue rather than merely listening to lectures; using appropriate audiovisuals that complement discussions; and presenting the church's teachings in a way that is integrated with the process.

The RCIA is the Rite of Christian Initiation of Adults. There is also a great need for a rite for children. But whatever the age group, whatever the program used, the catechetical enterprise will have to take seriously the responsibility of Black cultural adaption if it hopes to be effective in the Black community.

BLACK INCULTURATION OF THE CATECHETICAL PROCESS

BLACK WORLDVIEW AND BLACK EPISTEMOLOGICAL FRAMEWORK AS A PRESUPPOSITION IN CATECHESIS

There are still those who question the need for a Black perspective on the catechetical process and its content. They believe that catechesis should be colorless; that the teaching principles employed therein are universally applicable across the ethnic spectrum. They maintain that any focused particularity that addresses specific ethnic histories, ways of knowing, ways of symbolizing, and sociopolitical considerations are strangely out of place in the catechetical arena.

Those who call for a "colorless" religious education program, that is, one that does not essentially and existentially incorporate into the learning experience the genius of the particular cultures of the students, participate in and promote the same sort of insidious racism (often unintentional) as expressed in the statement, "Oh, I've gotten to know you so well that I just don't see you as Black anymore." This statement and the aforementioned attitude deny the existence and significance of Blackness. The present sociological dynamics of ministry in the African American Catholic community makes it imperative to *affirm* Blackness. If the educator or catechists do not see Black students as Black *persons*, they will not undertake those very necessary steps to ensure that the communication process inherent in the educational endeavor addresses these particular students. Catechists will not utilize the richness of the historical context of this particular people and *their* "story" of how God has acted on *their* behalf. They will present inappropriate symbols and operate from a stance of ignorance of this particular people's social structure, language, and presuppositions.

One of the major corrective tasks that lies before catechesis in the United States is to eliminate its white bias, its middle-class bias, and its bias for emphasizing intellectual development over an integration of thinking, feeling, and experience. The catechists or pastoral ministers in the African American communities who refuse to incorporate Black cultural perspectives in catechesis and liturgy are doing a disservice to their Black charges, holding them back from realizing their true selves. As children of God, Blacks merely ask just to authentically be themselves in their relationship with God. As Toinette Eugene says, Black catechesis is more than "teaching little colored children what a friend we have in Jesus." This outstanding African American theologian goes on to identify one of the main problems of religious education of Black people within the Catholic church, particularly Black youth:

> There is neither reverence nor room for the very signs and symbols of Black liberation within the larger society and structure of the Church. . . . Black identity and advocacy must be introduced if the Spirit of the Church is to retain—or regain—vibrancy and vitality in the Black community.[17]

Toinette Eugene's observations find a resonant theme in an address given at the 1983 National Catholic Education Association Convention by the late Archbishop James Lyke, when he was auxiliary bishop of Cleveland. Insisting that in the Black community the power of the gospel is dissipated and blunted when it is fused with white cultural expression, he observed that "the catechist in the Black community all too often teaches the doctrines of the faith to the people in modes which do not communicate." Catechetical texts throughout the country are mostly written by whites for whites and do not include Black or other ethnic perspectives.

The National Conference of Catholic Bishops has theoretically acknowledged this problem. The bishops' 1979 document directed toward updating catechesis in this country, *The National Catechetical Directory*, in the chapter entitled "Catechesis of Cultural, Racial, and Ethnic Groups," states:

Ideally, the catechist will be a member of the particular racial, cultural, or ethnic group. Those who are not should understand and empathize with the group, besides having adequate catechetical formation. . . . Catechetical materials should affirm the identity and dignity of the members of the particular group, using findings of the behavioral sciences for this purpose.[18]

White Catholics and leaders need to heed the counsel of Black Catholic leaders and thinkers with regard to the theoretical and practical aspects of the African American inculturation of Catholicism. Blacks speak from the experience of their own worldview. Anthropologist Robert Redfield provides a definition for worldview. It is

the way a people characteristically look outward upon the universe. If "culture" suggests the way a people look to an anthropologist, "worldview" suggests how everything looks to a people. . . . It is the structure of things as man is aware of them. It is the way we see ourselves in relation to all else. Every worldview is a stage set. On that stage myself is an important character; in every worldview there is an "I" from which the view is taken.[19]

Worldview is an anthropological term closely related to the philosophical term *epistemology*. Epistemology concerns itself with the ways of knowing, that is, how information is perceived as it is filtered through the worldview of the subject. Epistemology is, more precisely, the philosophical discipline that studies the nature and source of knowing and the reliability of claims to knowledge. It is one of the foundational presuppositions of the educational process. Black epistemology, to paraphrase St. Paul, conditions Blacks to "see through a glass darkly"; they perceive reality Blackly, through Black eyes and Black minds. Granted, there are different levels of Black consciousness and perceptivity, but even those African Americans who have gained a relative degree of acceptance by the white world because of cultural reciprocity and adoption of a veneer of whiteness will experience the negative effects their Blackness evokes in this society, unless, of course, their skin color defies their visual identification as Blacks. Nevertheless, for the great majority of African Americans, their Black worldview and epistemological framework will receive reinforcement because this society will promptly and often remind them of their Blackness. Studies indicate that Black people are more conscious of themselves as Blacks than white people are conscious of themselves as whites.[20] Our epistemology and its accompanying worldview ground us in the perception of reality in terms of black and white. A great portion of our thoughts are in the context of a Black self in a white world. Catechists, particularly white catechists ministering to Black students, have to take this condition into consideration.

When Blacks identify certain needs and engage in dialogue about appropriate correctives, whites simply have to accept the fact that this is a Black-led dialogue, and that they, as whites, are learners. Initially it must be so. Indeed, for Blacks, the nature and source of their knowing and the reliability of their claims to knowledge are based on a unique experience, that of being Black. No white person can speak authoritatively about Black needs. So, when Black Catholicism insists on perceiving the Christ-event from a Black worldview, it has strong justification for doing so. Black Catholics wish to know how the whole of African American history participates in salvation history and the Christ-event.

THE CHRIST-EVENT AS UNIVERSAL AND PARTICULAR

THE FUSION OF SALVATION HISTORY AND AFRICAN AMERICAN HISTORY

The Christ-event has universal effect and implications. It encompasses all reality. It includes not only the life, death, and resurrection of Jesus, but also his effect as Cosmic Lord, Cultural Constant, and Personal Redeemer of each individual. Yes, the Christ-event encompasses the entire universe and every galaxy along with its past, present, and future, and possible creatures. It encompasses all earthly cultures and religions, whether they acknowledge him or not. It includes every person who has existed or who will ever exist in the future. In fact, every being, including time and history, is related to and accountable to Christ in an organic manner.

> Christ is the visible likeness of the invisible God. He is the first-born Son, superior to all created things. For by Him God created everything in heaven and on earth, the seen and the unseen things. . . . God created the whole universe through Him and for Him. He existed before all things, and in union with Him all things have their proper place. . . . Through the Son, then,

God decided to bring the whole universe back to Himself. God made peace through His Son's death on the cross, and so brought back to Himself all things, both on earth and in heaven (Col 1:15-20).

The Christ-event includes all that God has done and will do through Christ in both the eternal and temporal dimensions.

The nature and purpose of catechesis is to pass on the tradition of the Christ-event, the "story" of God's love as manifested in salvation history, and to do it in such a manner that students and seekers of truth see themselves as participants in that history and as objects of that divine love. Of course, in the process of application, accommodation, and adaption there must be an inviolable respect for the core content of revelation and the mystery, beauty, and integrity of the *anamnesis* ("remembering") of the Christ-event.

This is the responsibility of catechesis in general. But Black catechesis has the additional responsibility of showing the interconnectedness—in fact, the fusion—of salvation history with African American history. Each ethnic group, indeed each individual, must see how the universal salvation history applies to its own life in all the particularity that might entail.

The urgent need for this focused particularity of viewing salvation history in the socio-historical context of Black history is most evident in what is called American history, as it is taught in our schools. American history is predominantly a white, male, middleclass American history, and it ignores the history of Black America, Brown America, Red America, poor America, and women's America.

To teach a history, whether American, Black, or salvation history (understanding that the latter transcends all histories), is to propose a worldview and a value system. The latter has a tremendous effect on curriculum formation, since the curriculum, as Thomas Groome indicates, determines for catechesis which stories, myths, and symbols will be used to express past and present salvation history.

Another additional responsibility that Black Catholic catechesis has is its obligation to address Black liberation. Catechesis in the African American community cannot speak of God's love, Christ's redemption, and the Spirit's sanctifying action without also speaking about Black liberation. The particularity of application presupposes that one cannot speak about religion and the gospel abstractly in the Black community; they must also be presented in the light of and in the context of the existential situation of our Black oppressed condition here in America. The majority of African Americans instinctively know that the presentation of a meek and mild, gutless white Christ in our Black communities will not do. Whites are, for the most part, unaware that the Christ they propose is a "white Christ."

A Black worldview rejects the white American Christ. Historian Vincent Harding identifies this white Christ introduced to us by the white missionaries, and he maintains that our introduction to Christ as Blacks in America was ambivalent. We loved Christ, but we just could not accept the way he was presented by the missionaries and slave masters who called themselves Christians, yet perpetrated so many brutal acts upon us. Harding says that we first met this white Christ on slave ships.

> We heard his name sung in hymns of praise while we died in our thousands, chained in the stinking holds beneath the decks, locked in with terror and disease and sad memories of our families and homes. When we leaped from the ships to be seized by sharks, we saw his name carved on the ship's solid sides. When our women were raped in the cabins, they must have noticed the great and holy books on the shelves. Our introduction to this Christ was not propitious.[21]

Happily, ours is a unique perspective that allows us to abstract from this white Christ to make a distinction between "white-anity" and Christianity. Those who profess Christ do not always necessarily live Christ, so we have discovered.

Archbishop James Lyke and Dr. Nathan Jones (both now deceased) were among the earliest scholars to contribute to the sparse literature on Black Catholic catechesis. In their writings they underscored the need for a catechesis that addresses liberation. Nathan Jones stated with regard to Black liberation and catechesis:

> Religious education must equip persons to be change agents of attitudes and social structures. This will involve social analysis and critical thinking. . . . No longer can we tolerate any forms of Christian education (schools, CCD programs, adult Bible Study groups, catechumenates, prayer meetings or youth programs) which are disengaged from changing the condition of our people.[22]

Archbishop Lyke even predicted the failure of catechetical programs in the Black community that failed to incorporate the theme
of Black liberation. Using the term "liberation catechesis," he said
that this is "not a visionary system of ideals, but it is a practical plan
of response to a world of real needs." Expanding on this, he noted:

> Christian missionaries learned early that it is virtually impos-
> sible to preach the Gospel to a starving person. . . . So also is
> the case of those starving for justice. We do not doubt the good
> intentions of the catechist who comes into the Black commu-
> nity with a full arsenal of beautiful textbooks and following a
> pedagogy fashioned from that analytical perception which is so
> much a part of Euro-America, teaching a message of love which
> does not count the cost. We can predict the failure of such a
> catechist. Unfortunately, the love that the catechist will try to
> communicate is countered by the African American's world-
> view and lived experience. To speak of a love that does not
> mobilize against oppression is madness; to speak of a love that
> is not actively critical of a repressive milieu is inane, and to
> speak of love that does not give a positive direction to libera-
> tion is an insult.[23]

The incorporation of a pervading and multi-nuanced theme of Black
liberation will be one of the criteria for an authentic Black Catholic
catechesis.

However, it must be kept in mind that it is the worldview, in its
entirety, that must be considered when adapting catechetical programs to Black Catholic communities. The internalization of Black
insights, the appreciation of the "Black story," the prioritization of
Black people's goals from their sociological stance: all of these are
very important elements that must interact with the Catholic system
and worldview.

THE INTERPRETATION OF HOLISTIC SYSTEMS AS
METHODOLOGY FOR BLACK INCULTURATION
OF CATHOLIC CATECHESIS

Catholic worldview and Black cultural worldview must both be
seen as holistic systems in themselves. Individual elements in one
system must interact with essential elements in the other, but it must

be remembered that they do not do so in isolation: it is systems and worldviews that are in interaction.

Catholic catechesis, with its constitutive elements, must be in dynamic interaction with the *whole* system of Black culture and Black worldview. This is why merely putting Black faces in the catechetical text does not thereby make it a Black catechism. The whole system (culture/history/worldview) must be involved.

Christianization, for the most part, as it has been directed to Blacks in the African diaspora throughout the world, has not taken this holistic approach seriously. The few accommodations to the Afro-worldview that have been made have often consisted in merely artificially inserting a few select Afro practices and tokenisms into preset Christian rituals or catechetical programs. Black faces in catechisms and gospel choirs in otherwise unadapted eucharistic liturgies are examples of such superficiality. These artificial Afro-grafts on the white liturgical/catechetical body are to Black religious sensitivity what cacophony is to music.[24]

Third-world anthropologist Guerin Montilus, agreeing that Christianization indeed "should be perceived as a holistic act," goes on to describe the principle of holism and what it entails:

> In anthropology, holism is a principle stating that people must be understood in terms of their total being. Concretely, this principle means that spiritual life cannot be separate from the historical, the social, the political, the economic, or anything considered as part of the human reality.[25]

The *interpenetration* of holistic systems will allow a synthesis that will not only effect an organic and integral union of pertinent and appropriate individual elements within each system, but also an organic union of the two whole systems as well. It is similar to Max Black's example of the werewolf, which he used to describe what happens in a metaphor. The metaphoric process makes the human more wolfish and the wolf more human.[26] From a metaphoric point of view, the interaction of wolf and man creates a new synthesis.

Similarly, the evangelization (i.e., Christianization) of Afro-peoples should bring about cultural integration between the two systems (Catholic and Afro-worldviews); *but* the integration of the two systems that would effect a new synthesis has not occurred generally in Afro-Catholicism because there has been a failure to deal with the phenomenon holistically. Guerin Montilus declares that this is the reason many individuals in the Black world "become either schizophrenics, using two systems at the same time, or hysterical, that is emotionally vulnerable."[27] He uses Engelbert Mveng's analysis of the steps of the evangelization of Africa as an illustration of what happens when a holistic approach to evangelization is not used.[28] First, there is a break with the historical roots; second, isolation and abandonment follow; third, there is a complex of insecurity and dependency.[29] The reintegration that should follow does not do so. He describes the state of ennui felt by African Christians as a result of this cultural disintegration and lack of systematic synthesis:

> Tragedy then follows: material, social, emotional, cultural and religious deprivation generates a crisis, a loss of trust and confidence in oneself. All one has left is mimicry of the foreign priests, which allows the convert to survive, but without much enthusiasm for life.[30]

My "metaphoric model," in a calling for organic synthesis of holistic systems, offers a context for cultural reintegration. The two systems, in interacting together, will produce a new meaning as a result of their interaction. Holistic interpenetration of Afro and Catholic systems will generate *new* ecclesial concepts, ministries, liturgies, and catechesis. There will be less opportunity for the "cultural schizophrenia" spoken of by Mveng. This will make way for true inculturation of Catholicism, rather than Black *acculturation* to white Christianity. Dr. Montilus develops the idea of how truths appropriated by a people and their culture become a different entity:

> Truth is not static. Humankind must continually plunge more deeply into revelation. This is also the case with Catholic tradition. New truths emerge as the synthesis of well-founded truths and the facts of present experience. In this way, a community generates its own truths, for there is no community of faith which can be satisfied with simply repeating written formulations without discussing life, and confronting it for themselves.[31]

When I contend that Afro/African American and Catholic worldviews must interact with each other holistically, I mean that the elements of the Catholic faith—such as catechesis—must interact with those significant and pertinently related elements in the

Afro system. Thus, traditional Catholic catechesis must seriously make incorporative accommodations and adaptions to Black theology, Black spirituality, Black psychology, Black pedagogy, Black value systems, Black language, the Black aesthetic, Black art, and Black sociology, which accounts for diverse Black socio-economic classes, family structures, and living conditions.

This process does not consist just in simple accommodationism or surface adaptation. Eminent scholars like Aylward Shorter, Anscar Chapungco, and others provide a methodological context for understanding the inculturation process. *Acculturation,* for them, represents the superficial interaction of the two systems (of faith and culture). *Inculturation,* on the other hand, is the goal and desired result. Dr. Eva Marie Lumas, S.S.S., a leading African American catechetical scholar, expresses the distinctions very well, acknowledging that inculturation is an ongoing, reciprocal process between faith and culture.

> [The process] involves the radical imbuing of culture with the values of the gospel such that the culture becomes consciously oriented to the values contained in the teachings of Jesus Christ. At the same time, the faith is renewed and expanded.[32]

Faith and culture must take each other seriously in this dialogical and mutually informing process. Perhaps a definition of *culture* would be helpful here. That of Dr. Wade Nobles, a leading Afrocentrist scholar, should do:

> [Culture] is the vast structure of behaviors, ideas, attitudes, values, habits, beliefs, customs, language, rituals, ceremonies and practices peculiar to a particular group of people which provide them with a general design for living and patterns for interpreting reality.[33]

When we talk about African American culture, the current philosophical discussions of Afrocentricity provide a basis for understanding the state of Black American consciousness and the rootedness of the culture(s) of West Africa. There is a sense of Pan-Africanism involved also, for Black people throughout the African diaspora acknowledge not only their giftedness but also their common oppression. Afrocentric education that is grounded in the existential situation(s) and the history of Black people can provide important sources of pedagogy and content for catechetical methodology.

An Afrocentric catechesis must do several things. Again, Dr. Eva Marie Lumas articulates several of them. It must evangelize; affirm Blackness; synthesize the sacred and secular dimensions of Black life; call Blacks to conversion; liberate them from institutional and interpersonal relationships that restrict their spiritual, psychic, and physical freedom; and, of course, Afrocentric Catholic catechesis must cultivate a Black articulation of the Catholic faith.[34]

Let us now take a closer look at several of these "Black elements," as they must be in interaction with catechesis. We begin with Black theology.

BLACK THEOLOGY

First of all, a Black Catholic theology that is authentically Black and authentically Catholic must serve as the foundation for Black Catholic catechesis. It cannot merely be a Black ideology in Christian trappings. On the contrary, it must be a Black articulation of the Catholic experience, incorporating both faith and heritage. It must take into account the achievements and revelations of the past, but it must also include the pastoral dimensions of what is presently occurring in the sixteen hundred predominantly Black Catholic parishes throughout the country.

Black theology is part of the corpus of praxis theology and, as such, it "seeks to uncover the intrinsic relationship between powerful Christian symbols and the transformation of the social order."[35] Black theology is one of the liberation theologies that, according to Edward Braxton, "result from the cultural shifts, the turn to interiority, and the consciousness raising that these changes made inevitable."[36] Braxton further states:

> Because of its existential urgency such a theology will not be a fully worked-out conceptual system. It will tend to favor those elements of critical and dogmatic mediation which can effectively transform the larger culture. In the case of Black Theology, the biblical themes of Exodus, liberation, and election are particularly prominent.[37]

I believe, however, that Black Catholic theology does not and should not restrict itself merely to an Exodus/Liberation theme but must widen its scope to include an articulation of other themes such as realized eschatology, sacramental, systematic, moral and biblical theologies. Black Catholic American theology must retain both its universal dimension (as part of a global church in communion with Rome), and its particularized dimension (as locally rooted in North America and culturally rooted in Blackness).

Black Catholic theologian Toinette Eugene reminds us that the articulation of a Black Catholic theology is so new that it is being formulated right under our noses. "There is a sizable number of those," she writes, "who are Black and who do possess the competency and charisma to offer an interpretation of the Word by means of a Black Catholic orthopraxis."[38] An authentic and faithful catechesis is indeed developing from the Black experience, and it is being formulated by Black Catholics who rely on their own religious instincts to generate appropriate theories, methodologies, and practices. Black Catholic catechesis must be placed on a firm theological foundation. Eugene provides a useful description of what Black theology is:

> It is that theology which arises out of the need to articulate the significance of Black Christian presence in an often hostile and always oppressive white world. It is Black people reflecting on their Black experiences, and attempting to define the relevance of the Gospel of Christ for their lives.[39]

I think that one of the key contributions Eugene has made to Black theology is the manner in which she deals with the question of tradition. Catholicism is a faith very conscious of and bound by tradition. Dr. Eugene acknowledges this fact and suggests how tradition itself can be a freeing element for a church structure so bound by tradition, *if* the concept of tradition is broadened. Tradition should not be restricted just to the Roman Catholic perspective. She feels that it should be open to include the accumulated wisdoms of the churches of the Reformation. It should not just embrace European and American Catholic perspectives, but also what has happened among the Black Protestant Christian churches in this country:

> A Black articulation must make it clear that tradition refers first and foremost to the theological reflection of the Church upon the nature of *all* Christianity, from the time of the early Church until now. Tradition did not begin with the Council of

Trent. . . . In working within tradition, a Black articulation must
of necessity focus as much on the broader Christian tradition
of the Black Church in America as it does on that of white
Western Catholicism.[40]

Such an ecumenical perspective will encourage Catholic catechesis
to pay more attention to the catechetical approaches of other denominations—and thereby learn from their successes and failures.
Regarding some of those other denominations, James Lyke says that
most Baptist and Methodist catechesis still uses "far more Euro-
American conceptualizations than Afro-American," but their *approaches*
nonetheless compensate by incorporating social justice and Black self-
awareness themes in their programs.[41] Lyke claims, however, that Black
Anglicans and Black Lutheran churches have done little in accommo-
dating their catechetical programs to a Black motif.

The theological foundation upon which catechesis is based will
be made stronger as Black Catholic academic theologians in touch
with the pastoral dimensions of their own people dialogue with the
official magisterium of the church. Appropriate Black Catholic theological methodologies will evolve as these men and women reflect
on, systematize, and "dogmatize" our own unique perspectives.

BLACK SPIRITUALITY

Black spirituality is an important phenomenon that authentic Black
Catholic catechesis cannot ignore. By "Black spirituality" I mean
the underlying motif that characterizes Black people's relationship
with God. It is a spirituality of joy even in the midst of adversity.
Father Cyprian Davis, O.S.B., has identified certain distinguishing
qualities of Black spirituality.[42] He indicates that the prayer experience of whatever kind is nearly always *communal*. This, he says, is
the hallmark of Black spirituality. He observes that joy and human
warmth pervade Black worship and spill over into song and dance.
Dr. Davis insists that *emotion* is an important element in Black spirituality, and that prayer embraces body as well as soul. Black
spirituality is holistic, not dualistic, in its view of humankind.

Black spirituality is, Davis declares, a spirituality of the biblical
Word as it is living in our lives today:

The words of the Bible involve us today. Christ is on His cross
down the street. The Samaritan woman is at Jacob's Well on

the corner. Moses goes down to Pharaoh at the state capitol. The biblical word is concrete and sensible.[43]

Davis also maintains that in Black spirituality the transcendent remains transcendent, but it always breaks forth into the everyday. He sees the following as the major elements in Black spirituality:

> a sense that joy is the important spiritual good; a high value placed on emotional response; a communal and contemplative approach to prayer; a sense of God's power and presence everywhere; a fundamental rejection of any "body-is-evil" spirituality; an awareness of the social justice dimension of religion; and a sense that Blacks are as a people, a spiritual people—that we have a heritage to pass on.[44]

African American spirituality has several sources informing it. First, there are the Traditional African Religions and their respective characteristics as they exist in and of themselves in Africa. Their practices—such as ancestor veneration; God being both immanent and transcendent; and the conception of death as a transitional phase in existence rather than an absolute end of life—still find resonance in African American culture. Michael Dash, Jonathan Jackson, and Stephen Rason have done a masterful job of identifying other sources of African American spirituality.[45]

They include Protestant and Evangelical traditions, as Baptist and Methodist traditions claim a significant number of American Blacks; civil religion, as Blacks still celebrate the Fourth of July and other major American holidays and events; Roman Catholicism, especially its earliest influences as found in Maryland, Kentucky, and southern Louisiana. The Bible itself, particularly the stories that relate the condition of the oppressed Jews; and, of course, Islam. This last source's influence is a result not just of the fact that many of the enslaved Africans were themselves Muslims but of the present-day influence of the Nation of Islam (and its leader, Minister Louis Farrakhan) and orthodox Islam itself, which is attracting growing numbers of African Americans.

Popular Black folk religion provides examples of ways through which African American spirituality is expressed: (1) full sensory-engaging worship; (2) intimate prayer; (3) cathartic shouting; (4) triumphant singing; (5) politically relevant religious education; and (6) prophetic imaginative preaching.

BLACK AESTHETIC

Black catechesis must also employ principles that exist in the Black aesthetic or way of appreciating, experiencing, and utilizing the beautiful and the artful. Active audience participation can be seen as one readily recognizable trait anywhere in the African diaspora, whether applied to music, reading, theater, dance, or other art forms. The Black catechetical process requires similar adherence to this principle, wherein there are no spectators but only active participants. The Black aesthetic demands that the teaching/learning experience be a performance that includes *style*. This may indeed be a challenge to those who are unaccustomed to perceiving the educational/catechetical ministry in this light. Black homes often have a much higher noise level (stereos, television, more persons occupying less space), and there is more active visual stimuli in them than in many white homes. Thus the catechist will have to take into consideration the fact that more stimuli, aural and visual, will be required to satisfy this state of stimuli expectancy. Studies indicate that preschool Black children have a higher movement repertoire than do preschool white children. Asking them to "be still" while learning could stunt creative and active involvement in the learning process.

The Black aesthetic blurs the separation between the sacred and the secular, so catechists in the Black community are challenged to link occurrences within the social process with those of the divine will. The social and political processes are arenas wherein divine reality is creatively at work.

ART

Black catechesis will necessarily have to imbue itself with the literature, music, and art of African Americans if it is to be truly effective. Scholars have repeatedly stated that Black concepts about God, religion, life, sexuality, and death are found in Black music (spiritual and secular), art, and literature. Songs, poetry, literature, and art contain the rhythm and soul of a people. Therein are found a culture's symbols and meanings. Black art is functional. It not only entertains, it educates. Our Black stories, songs and symbols are functional; they contain codes of freedom; trials and aspirations of our people. *Our* God is also functional! God is not just abstract obligations. God loves and liberates. For Blacks, Christ is more immanent (Brother) than transcendent (Lord). "He woke me up this morning and guides me along the way."

Black art easily accommodates itself to a teaching function. The works of Houston Conwill serve as an example. Conwill's interest in African American healing traditions inspired him to do ritual installations during 1975 through 1978, one of which was *Juju Funk*. The focus of this installation consisted in a ceremonial space at the center of the room. Judith Wilson describes it:

> Initially, this area was defined by a length of red carpet, in which European-derived overtones of prestige, and ceremony, extravagant gestures of hospitality, combined with the artist's wish to evoke "the blood of the ancestors." At one end of the carpet stood a chair draped with side-stitched, embossed latex strips, while a latex-wrapped bucket sat on a dais at the opposite end. The chair served as a ceremonial throne for Conwill, who in the role of shaman/priest, presided over the ritual proceedings. The bucket, termed "gutbucket" by the artist, served as a multi-referential source of spiritual sustenance. It simultaneously alluded to: 1) ancestral courage ("guts"); 2) Afro-American survival tactics (not wasting any source of potential nourishment, Southern Blacks routinely collected the innards of slaughtered animals in gutbuckets); 3) Blues were played during the ritual performance, sustaining a musical legacy—the blues (with this genre's battery of African-derived instruments including the washtub bass, a.k.a. the "gutbucket," and its African-derived tonal qualities often described as a guttural or gutbucket sound).[46]

Notice how this art form instructs about heritage, survival techniques, examples of resourcefulness and music, all done holistically in a manner in which different elements complement and support one another. All forms of Black art can be used in the catechetical arena: sculpture, painting, song, dance, literature, and poetry. Black artists have excelled in these areas, and it is up to catechists to do their own research to "bring something ever new from the storehouse" of Black riches so that the teaching/learning process may have relevancy.

BLACK LANGUAGE

The Catholic bishops of this country addressed the question of language in the 1979 *National Catechetical Directory*:

The language of the particular group should be used in the catechesis of its members; not just its vocabulary, but its thought patterns, cultural idioms, customs and symbols. Catechetical materials should suit its characteristics and needs. Rather than simply translating or adapting materials prepared for others it is generally necessary to develop new materials.[47]

A small number of Black Catholic scholars and pastors have taken up this challenge to produce catechetical materials in an idiom more akin to the language and thought patterns of Black Americans. Some of these materials are highly professional in quality and consist not only in texts and photographs but also cassette tapes and filmstrips.

Black people have always had a great respect for words, both their content and their energy. The rich tradition includes a wide array of animal, haunt, oral preacher stories, conjure tales, master/slave anecdotes, exaggerations or lying tales, trickster yarns, homilies and proverbs, riddles, ballads, epics, hero tales and legends, games, sermons, blues, spirituals, slave and work songs, autobiographies and novels. The rhythm and rhyme of youngsters playing "the Dozens"; the Black preacher's magnificently colorful and stylistic language and phrases punctuated with guttural percussive aspirations; the double/hidden meanings used in the blues and spirituals—these are just a few of the many examples that illustrate the importance this culture attributes to the creative use of the language, verbal skills, and style which exist in the Black communities throughout this country. Euro-American culture(s) have more respect for the written word than it does for the spoken word. Generally speaking, the opposite is true in Black culture. Black language is not locked into the visual-written tradition of Euro-Americans. Differences between Euro and Afro language use are apparent in the dynamics that occur during verbal interaction. For example, in a Euro-American setting,

the speaker and listener maintain a separate psychological space. Speech is delivered in controlled, low-key, detached, and slow-paced tempo. The listener is expected to wait until the speaker finishes the message before a reply is given. Any animated cries . . . during the speaker's delivery would be considered out of order in proper Euro-American language circles.[48]

On the other hand, the language of Black folks,

whether it occurs on street corners, in beauty shops, barber shops, parties, love raps, play-grounds, or in political speeches and church sermons, is characterized by the interrelatedness of speaker and listener. The act of speaking is a dramatic pre sentation of one's personhood to those who share a background of similar acculturation. The listener acts as an echo chamber, repeating, cosigning, validating, and affirming the message of the speaker. . . . During this call-response dialogue, the speaker and listener are joined together in a common psycholinguistic space. Each participant has the opportunity to expand the message through amplification and repetition.[49]

I do not necessarily endorse the catechists' use of so-called "Black English"; this is a very delicate question, as court cases have shown. But catechists ought to know and study Black English so as to become used to it in order to understand and communicate with their students as efficiently as possible.

Do not accuse Black youths and adults of not being abstract enough. Their ability to deal with abstractions exists and has often been overlooked. Many white catechists do not see the eloquence that is actually there. In this regard, psychologist Joseph L. White states:

The metaphor in Black language is a teaching device. Speakers depend on the common background between themselves and their listeners to establish impact and associate meanings to the words. Presentational symbols in the form of visual imagery are substituted for abstract concepts to expand and clarify meanings from an African-American perspective.[50]

The ability to engage in abstract thinking is still there, it is merely done in a different manner.

It is also hoped that catechists will become aware that the phenomenon called "code-switching" will be of inestimable aid to them as they attempt to catechize persons across a wide spectrum of backgrounds. Code-switching has worked for preachers who must preach to both the educated doctor and the illiterate garbage collector who may be in their congregations. An example can be seen in this saying, which my grandfather used: "Do not calculate your juvenile poultry until the process of incubation has fully materialized," and without a pause for breath he would add, "Don't count your chickens before they hatch." Catechists will have to develop a flexibility that permits them to change modes and codes easily, repeating various forms of conceptualization and verbalization. Needless to say, they should never criticize the language-use of their students in such a way as to damage their self-esteem.

We live in a pluralistic society. "Proper English" as spoken by Euro-American society, however, is still the main language of commerce, and it is an important criterion for employability. Youngsters and oldsters speaking Black English could look upon that idiom as the language to be used in their primary group, but if they are to "make it" in America, they will have to become bi-lingual and learn standard English too.

This question of sensitivity to the use of Black English in catechesis must also address the regional peculiarities in Black language as it is spoken throughout this country. The Black language spoken in Lafayette, Louisiana, with its patois-laden idiomatic expressions and creole, is different from the Black English spoken in the urban ghettos of the North; and both differ from that which is spoken in Prichard, Alabama, and the Gullah areas of South Carolina and Georgia. Such regional particularities represent another challenge to those who produce Black catechetical materials. Nevertheless, the rewards in the harvest of souls will make all the effort worthwhile.

Black Catholic catechesis will have to listen attentively to and heed the research results emanating from Black psychology and pedagogy, and any other behavioral and social science that offers a valid perspective on the Black experience. This is what the metaphoric synthesis is all about: blending the story of Jesus with that of African Americans.

In conclusion, religious education is indeed the "handmaiden" of evangelization; it plays a very necessary and crucial part in the spreading of the gospel. The etymological origin of the word *education* is found in a Latin word meaning "to lead out"; presumably it implies a leading out from ignorance to knowledge. Some linguists maintain that the "lig" in the word "religion" comes from the same root as the "lig" in ligament; it means "to bind together." Religion therefore binds us to God and to our neighbor in a dynamic interconnected relationship. Catechesis leads us out of the darkness of ignorance into God's marvelous light, allowing God's Word to illumine the relationships we have with our God and with God's other children. Black catechesis sharpens this focus of illumination on the Black sheep of Christ's flock, making sure that *they* are fed and taught and given the opportunity to grow in freedom, knowledge, grace, faith, and God's abiding love.

NOTES

[1] Jacques Audinet, "Catechesis," *Encyclopedia of Theology: The Concise Sacramentum Mundi*, ed. Karl Rahner (New York: The Seabury Press, 1975), p. 173.

[2] Ibid.

[3] M. E. Jegen, "Catechesis II," *New Catholic Encyclopedia*, vol. 3 (New York: McGraw-Hill, 1976), p. 209.

[4] Ibid., p. 213.

[5] R. M. Rummery, *Catechesis and Religious Education in a Pluralistic Society* (Huntington, Ind.: Our Sunday Visitor, 1976), p. 6.

[6] See Erskine Clarke, *Wrestlin' Jacob: A Portrait of Religion in the Old South* (Atlanta: John Knox Press, 1979), p. 51.

[7] Rummery, *Catechesis and Religious Education in a Pluralistic Society*, cites this excerpt of the *Dogmatic Catechism*'s English translation in 1871, by Cardinal Manning, from Michael Donnellan, *What to Believe* (Dublin: Gill & Son/Logos Books, 1968), p. 21.

[8] Rummery, *Catechesis and Religious Education in a Pluralistic Society*, p. 11.

[9] Ibid., p. 18.

[10] Audinet, "Catechesis," p. 176.

[11] Romney Moseley, "Faith Development and Conversion in the Catechumenate," in Robert Duggan, ed., *Conversion and the Catechumenate* (Ramsey, N.J.: Paulist Press, 1984), p. 157.

[12] Audinet, "Catechesis," p. 176.

[13] Moseley, "Faith Development and Conversion," p. 157.

[14] Mark Searle, "Faith and Sacraments in the Conversion Process," in Duggan, *Conversion and the Catechumenate*, p. 64.

[15] Regis A. Duffy, O.F.M., "The Rites and Rituals of Commitment," in Duggan, *Conversion and the Catechumenate*, p. 84.

[16] See Moseley, "Faith Development and Conversion," p. 157.

[17] Toinette Eugene, "Training Religious Leaders for a New Generation," *Freeing the Spirit* 1:4 (Fall-Winter 1972), p. 54, and 2:1 (Spring 1973), pp. 52-55.

[18] United States Catholic Conference, *The National Catechetical Directory* (Washington, D.C.: United States Catholic Conference, 1979), no. 194.

[19] Robert Redfield, *The Primitive World and Its Transformations* (Ithaca, N.Y.: Cornell University Press, 1953), p. 86.

[20] See, for example, Kenneth and Mamie Clark, "What Do Blacks Think of Themselves?" *Ebony Magazine* 36:1 (November 1980), pp. 176-82.

[21] Vincent Harding, "Black Power and the American Christ," in *Black Theology: A Documentary History, 1966-1979*, ed. Gayraud S. Wilmore and James H. Cone (Maryknoll, N.Y.: Orbis Books, 1979), p. 36.

[22] Nathan Jones, Ph.D., "Making It Plain," in *Telling It Like It Is: A Black Catholic Perspective on Christian Education* (Oakland, Calif.: The National Black Sisters' Conference, 1983), p. 147.

[23] James Lyke, O.F.M., Ph.D., *A Black Perspective on the National Catechetical Directory, 1982,* p. 14. This is an unpublished essay written by Lyke and used as the springboard text to get discussion started at the Black Catholic Catechetical Symposium held November 1-4, 1982, in Santa Cruz, California.

[24] Of course, some of the examples of religious syncretism in Haiti, Jamaica, Cuba, and other Caribbean, Central and South American countries represent more substantial cultural accommodations to Afro cultures and are an exception to what has, until recently, happened in North America and the African continent, where the Afro-Catholic synthesis has been superficial. Also, one may rightly question the orthodoxy of many of the elements synthesized in Haiti and other countries in the former group.

[25] Guerin Montilus, "Culture and Faith: A Believing People," in *Telling It Like It Is*, p. 37.

[26] See Max Black, *Models and Metaphors: Studies in Language and Philosophy* (Ithaca, N.Y.: Cornell University Press, 1962), p. 44.

[27] Montilus, "Culture and Faith," p. 37.

[28] Ibid. Montilus cites Engelbert Mveng, "A la recherche d'un nouveau dialogue entre le christianisme, le génie culturel et les religions africaines actuelles" (Présence Africaine, No. 9, 4ᵉ trimstre 1975), pp. 4436-66.

[29] Montilus, "Culture and Faith," p. 37.

[30] Ibid., p. 38.

[31] Ibid., p. 41.

[32] See Sr. Eva Marie Lumas, S.S.S., "The Nature and Goals of Africentric Catholic Catechesis," in *God Bless Them . . . African American Catechetical Camp Meetin': A Gathering to Chart a New Course* (Washington, D.C.: United States Catholic Conference, 1995).

[33] As cited in Asa Hilliard, Lucretia Payton-Stewart, and Larry O. Williams, *Infusion of African American Content in the School Curriculum: The Proceedings of the First National Conference* (Morristown, N.J.: Aaron Press, 1989), p. 6.

[34] See Lumas, "The Nature and Goals of Africentric Catholic Catechesis."

[35] Edward K. Braxton, *The Wisdom Community* (New York: Paulist Press, 1980), p. 125.

[36] Ibid.

[37] Ibid.

[38] Toinette Eugene, "Developing Black Catholic Belief: Catechism as a Black Articulation of the Faith," *Theology: A Portrait in Black*, ed. Thaddeus Posey, O.F.M.Cap. (Washington, D.C.: The National Black Clergy Caucus, 1980), p. 143.

[39] Ibid., p. 149.

[40] Ibid., p. 156.

[41] Lyke, *A Black Perspective on the National Catechetical Directory*, p. 37.

[42] Cyprian Davis, O.S.B., Ph.D., made a series of presentations at the St. Charles Lwanga Institute in Techny, Illinois, in June 1984. A number of us Black Catholic scholars were invited there to address Black seminarians from around the country in order to supply what they were not receiving in their predominantly white educational environments. Fr. Davis addressed the topic of Black spirituality during this time.

[43] Ibid.

[44] Ibid.

[45] See *Hidden Wholeness: An African American Spirituality for Individuals and Communities* (Cleveland: United Church Press, 1997).

[46] Judith Wilson, "Creating a Necessary Space: The Art of Houston Conwill, 1975-1983," *The International Review of African American Art* 6:1, pp. 51-52.

[47] *The National Catechetical Directory*, no. 194.

[48] Joseph L. White, ed., *The Psychology of Blacks: An Afro-American Perspective* (Englewood Cliffs, N.J.: Prentice-Hall, 1984), p. 12.

[49] Ibid., p. 35.

[50] Ibid., p. 37.

10

The Oral African Tradition Versus the Ocular Western Tradition

The Spirit in Worship

CLARENCE RUFUS J. RIVERS

Author's Preface

Brothers and Sisters in Christ: Although some sayings may be hard for us to hear and bear, we have been told to be open to the liberating truth. And the truth is that worship in most of our churches, most of the time, is dull and uninspiring. Whereas the worshipping congregation should be a dramatic dance of life, instead it is all too often like the dry bones in the vision of Ezekiel, a static, stagnant sprawl of lifeless limbs, a tableau of death. We seem to be there merely physically, not really hearing anything that moves us, not saying anything that moves others. We appear deaf and dumb, unmoved and unmoving. And to the extent that we appear deaf and dumb and dead and lifeless, to that extent we are not witnesses for everlasting life, but witnesses for never-ending death. [1]

My maternal grandmother, Eugenia Houser-Echols-Tarver, of Selma, Alabama, used to express great admiration for the

Catholic church in Selma (and, by extension, for the Catholic church in general). She was in the habit of narrating a cornucopia of the church's good deeds, then topping off the subject by proclaiming "If there ever was a Christian, he was a Catholic!" But when confronted with the question why she had not become a Catholic, she explained, without missing a beat, that the church's worship "was too cold." She admired the "beauty of Catholic ritual" in spite of its being "odd."

This article of mine had its beginning as a humorous monologue/lecture, developed in my search for reasons why our worship was so lifeless, for the most part, even when I myself found it to be "beautiful but cold." In its last printed and published form, it is a part of the two-volume set *Soulful Worship* and *The Spirit in Worship.*[2] Only there is it in the appropriate context of my own search for vital, converting, transforming worship.

Were I rewriting the article, I would change nothing essential, but there are a few details that I would revise. For example, I might no longer use the word *structure* (near the end of the section "Puritanism and Discursiveness as Obstacles to Celebration") as a metaphor for some of the things I observed disapprovingly as attempts to revitalize worship in the decade following Vatican II. I now recognize the fact that lack of essential dramatic structure is one of the elements, perhaps *the* element that leaves traditional worship unmoved and unmoving—lifeless. Movement, from beginning to middle to end, is one of the elements that Aristotle recommends in his *Poetics.*

Such movement is achieved by subtle means that escape rigid defining, but could be handed on in an apprenticeship program in the art of public worship that we call liturgy. For this reason I have spent the better part of the last fifteen years looking for the means to establish a college of apprenticeship to graduate worship professionals who, beyond the knowledge of liturgiology, would acquire the skills of liturgical impresarios (for lack of a better word), knowing how to script, produce, and direct the drama of traditional worship, so that even my grandmother could be "warmed" and moved.

CLARENCE RUFUS J. RIVERS
APRIL 1998

∽

The Oral African Tradition
Versus the Ocular Western Tradition

PURITANISM AND DISCURSIVENESS
AS OBSTACLES TO CELEBRATION

Much of the church is virtually a prisoner of the Western cultural thrust. In fact, I would say that the single greatest obstacle standing in the way of effective, dramatic worship is Western culture itself, with its tendencies toward puritanism, discursiveness, and literal-mindedness. A people obsessed with and possessed by these tendencies will find it difficult to celebrate.

They will have a bias towards detachment and will therefore be suspicious of involving emotion and enjoyment. They will readily insist that worship is not for entertainment. And since worship is not for entertainment, it makes no difference—in their minds—whether the cultic ministers and the congregation itself perform so poorly that they have no dramatic impact. In fact, they will frequently think that poor performance, a performance that is not entertaining, is virtuous simply because it is poor.

For example, several years ago I was invited to present a program in music and worship at Loyola University in New Orleans. After the Sunday mass in the campus church, an elderly lady was heard to comment as she left: "Well, it was very entertaining, but now we'll have to go somewhere to fulfill our Sunday obligation." The fact that she had enjoyed the mass had taken away, in her mind, its value. On another occasion, I was invited to prepare the Sunday liturgy for the young ladies of a college in Maryland. Afterwards, when one young lady came by to say how much she enjoyed mass, the chaplain corrected her for using the word "enjoyed." When a gentleman wrote to the editor of our diocesan newspaper suggesting that an improvement in reading and preaching would get more people to mass, a reply appeared in a subsequent issue explaining that we should not go to church to be entertained; and that, if people realized what a wonderful thing mass really is, they would be willing to endure the torture of poor reading and preaching.

Even the argument frequently put forward against "traditional" choirs and "classical" choir music is that it is "entertainment." "We don't go to church to be entertained, do we?" Well, as I figure it, we must take one of two alternatives: we can go to be entertained or we can go to be bored! There are no other possibilities! A thing, a person, or an experience is either entertaining or is boring. Nothing else is possible. Of course we go to church to be entertained and also to contribute to the entertainment. The members of a Christian religious assembly are there not merely as sponges to absorb; they are also there as witnesses of their faith and must therefore be active in the entertainment. And if anything is to be done away with, it is not entertainment; it is mere objective passivity and detached noninvolvement.

In traditional black churches, even when the congregation is listening to a soloist or the choir singing, or the deacon praying, or the preacher preaching, they are emotionally involved participants and not passive detached observers. Because of this tendency to be involved, even an overload of solo performance is not a threat to active congregational participation in the black churches. And the idea that one might try to increase congregational participation by doing away with the choir would be an unthought of absurdity in the black churches. Also absurd would be the notion that worship is not to entertain or to be the occasion of enjoyment. I have never heard a black church minister exhort his congregation to turn out for some particular religious celebration when he did not promise: "We're going to have a good time!" Having a good time is so much a characteristic of the traditional black church that the phrase "to have church" has become, in the black community, synonymous with "to have a good time," to have an intensely moving and enjoyable experience. I remember very distinctly driving past a bar in New Orleans where a bunch of young men were "carrying on" so that someone yelled to them, "What are you doing?" And the reply came back, "We're having church!"

The Western tendency would probably be to consider this "good time" the result of a regrettable "emotionalism" in the black church, and would consider the atmosphere in the European and American churches to be the result of a more desirable "intellectual" approach. Involving emotion is somehow considered the enemy of thought and reason, perception and understanding. A few years ago, in preparation for its annual convention, the Federation of Diocesan Liturgical Commissions published a booklet which distinguished between music that has "an emphasis on beat" and music that has "a melodic emphasis." The first, it said, tends to elicit "physical, impulsive, even unconscious movement," whereas the latter would tend "to elicit a feeling of repose and to lead the listener inwardly into an attitude of interior reflection." Moreover, it said that "beat music" would tend to produce "a style of worship that has a horizontal or humanistic theological dimension" while melody music would tend to produce a "style of liturgy that has a vertical or spiritually elevating, theological dimension."

This is the same kind of nonsense which is liable to call music that doesn't move you "serious" music, implying that music which does move you is merely frivolous and "emotional" and not very "intellectual." A people possessed of these tendencies will more readily communicate to "enlighten the intellect" than to move the heart, and will therefore, in the context of liturgy, produce sermons, prayers and commentaries that are tediously prosaic, didactic, and explanatory. On Easter Sunday, they are most likely to monotonously drone: "Easter Sunday is the greatest feast of the church," rather than dramatically and dynamically proclaim: "I have risen, and I am still with you!" Our commentaries in worship are easily the equivalent of explaining a joke rather than telling one. Some thinkers of the Western tradition tend to see mythic and poetic expressions of faith as a necessary baby's pabulum for those members of the church with lesser intellectual capacity.

A people possessed by these Western tendencies will tend to think that there is a technological solution to liturgical problems, that is, they will look for that perfect liturgical structure. They will always have an eye out for "new" liturgies and "experimental" rites, and they are very prone to "gimmickry."

If the puritanism and discursiveness and literal-mindedness of Western culture are the problem, then perhaps some understanding of these tendencies will make it possible for people to begin to deal with them. To begin with, let me simply assert that the puritan tendency has no exclusive claim to religiousness, nor has discursiveness an exclusive claim to intellectuality. Emotion is also a way of knowing and relating to the world. Note what Léopold Sédar Senghor, the poet-philosopher President of Senegal, has to say:

Intellect is one, in the sense that it exists to apprehend an Other—objective reality, if you wish, the nature of which has its own laws. But its modes of knowing—its "thought forms"— vary with the psycho-physiology of each race.

The elan vital of the black African, his self-abandonment to the Other (his e-motion), is therefore animated by his reason— reason, note, that is not the reason of seeing of the European white, which is more reason of set categories into which the outside world is forced. African reason is more logos than ratio. For ratio is compasses, square and sextant, scale and yardstick, whereas logos, before its tempering at the hands of Aristotle, before becoming a diamond precision cutting tool, was the living Word, the most specifically human expression of the neuro-sensorial impression. It does not force the object, without touching-feeling it, into the hard and fast categories of logic. The black African logos, rather, in its ascent to the Verbum, removes the rust from reality to bring out its primordial color, its grain and texture, sound and odor. It permeates reality with its light rays to restore its transparency, by penetrating in its primitive humidity, its sur-reality, its outward appearance, to its underlying *sub*-stance. The classic European reason is analytic, and exploits; the black African reason is intuitive and shares the life of the Other.[3]

THE ORIGINS OF PURITANISM AND DISCURSIVENESS IN OCULARITY

The origins of Euroamerican puritanism are not in religion itself as we may have thought; in fact, it can be demonstrated that most traditional Western religions, if taken at their word, are sensual and incarnational and sacramental; they have formal statements against puritanical, Jansenistic, Manichaean and Victorian type heresies. The mystics of Western religion have frequently used sensual and even sexual imagery to express their outreach toward and their involvement with the divine. The visible, palpable world is affirmed as good. At least, this has been the theory in most Western religions; but in fact and in practice the heretical tendencies mentioned above still dominate most Western religions.

They dominate in Western religion because they dominate the whole of Western culture. Western religion simply reflects Western culture, and Western culture tends to be a puritan culture. In Western culture, whatever stimulates the senses pleasurably is suspect. Haven't you heard people say, "Oh, I enjoyed that so much it was a sin"? The average person has been so infected by the disease of puritanism that Madison Avenue is able to exploit our puritanism almost as much as it exploits our sexual drives. For instance, do you remember the mouthwash commercial that presumed that you believed that nothing pleasant tasting could possibly do you any good? All those other mouthwashes, it commented with disdain, were sweeter than soda pop. To be sure that a germ was killed, you had to practically gag on something! And do you remember the dog food commercial where this dog is gobbling up some kind of slop and the mother is explaining to the little boy how good it is for the dog. And the little boy replies: "Well, if it's so good for him, why does he like it so much?" Why did the little boy ask that? Because we, in this puritan ethos, teach our children that the things that are distasteful are the things that are good for you, and the things that you enjoy can't really be very good or useful. Have you ever heard a teacher say, "I'm not here to entertain; I am here to teach"? . . . just as if good teaching were bound to be a dull affair.

The origins of these "heretical" tendencies, as I said above, are not in religion itself. I personally came to what I think is an understanding of these tendencies when I read a book by the anthropologist Edmund Carpenter. In his book, *Oh, What a Blow That Phantom Gave Me!*, Carpenter talks about the senses and the different ways in which they perceive. And it was from his comments that I came to understand that Western culture is not, as it thinks, intellectual; it is ocular. Western culture is not essentially "of the intellect"; it is essentially "of the eye." It tends to comprehend the world through the bias of the sense of sight, a bias that is somehow connected with a book-oriented culture, a culture in which sight dominates and mutes the other senses.

This sight-biased cultural orientation has probably been subtly developing for centuries before the Greek and Roman civilizations, and especially so after Western society began to depend on reading and writing as the chief vehicle of its culture. But it was Plato and Aristotle who gave this bias the form of "philosophic truth." Plato told us that there is indeed a hierarchy of the senses, with sight at the top and touch at the bottom. Now, can't you see where that must lead? Sight—on high, lofty (therefore spiritual and ennobling) versus touch—low, on the bottom, in the basement, base (therefore debasingly, degradingly sensual).

Then, along came Aristotle and, in the very first sentence of his *Metaphysics,* he paves the way not only for a plague of Savonarolas and Tanqueries and others of that ascetic ilk, but also for Descartes and a whole pestilence of rationalists and voluntarists. There, in the very first sentence of his *Metaphysics,* Aristotle exhorts us: "Of all the senses, trust only the sense of sight."

Now, I ask you, if "seeing is believing," what will happen to the faith that "cometh by hearing"? But more to the point, if we trust sight but not touch, where will this leave us, if some things can be known only by touch?

Let's consider the nature of the eye and its manner of knowing, of sensing. When used in isolation, it perceives a flat, continuous world without interval, without interface, without rhythm, without a third dimension. Infants born without arms and legs do not see in depth, in three dimensions. It is by the sense of touch that we perceive the third dimension, that we perceive interfaces, and intervals, and dimensional spaces between things. These latter are the causes of "discontinuity," "suddenness" and "rhythms." The eye, however, is geared to perceive the continuing line, and it fosters a perception of a world in which one thing is connected with the other, whether in fact it is connected or not. It abhors suddenness and discontinuity (the very thing that touch delights in). That is why we blink when some object is brought too quickly before our eyes. And this is why a people whose view of music tends to be ocular and therefore linear tend to be very unsophisticated in matters of rhythm, because rhythm is created by breaking the continuity of a musical line.

While favoring continuity, lineality, and connectedness, abhorring suddenness, and being unable to perceive a third dimension, at the same time the eye focuses on only one thing at a time. It focuses on a particular and abstracts it from a total situation. From this there grows the "intellectual" (more precisely, ocular) ability to distinguish and to analyze—the ability to separate conceptually things that in reality are not separate. This mental faculty comes from the fact that the Western mind tends to view the world through the bias of the eye, a sense that focuses, pinpoints, abstracts, locating each object in a physical space against a two-dimensional background.

Because the eye abhors being touched and is irked by "suddenness," it tends to view reality in detachment, thus when one's culture is dominated by the bias of the eye, one will automatically tend towards being a detached, uninvolved observer. It is therefore an ocular people who are afraid of emotional involvement, not an intellectual people.

For, in fact, the eye has no exclusive claim to the act of perceiving. It is a way of perceiving, merely one way of perceiving. It is not a means of complete perception. The other senses perceive also; and when not muted by the bias of the eye, they will perceive realities that are imperceptible to the eye; and they will tend to produce a cultural thrust different from the Western one.

THE AURAL TRADITION: THE SOUND OF SOUL

Opposite to the ocular tradition of Western culture, there are the oral/aural traditions of other cultures. The Bible itself was produced out of and in an oral culture. But, on the other hand, much of the fundamentalist interpretation of the Bible is the result of an ocular culture that demands "literal truth" and "history" from a document whose originators had no such notions. And so to justify the Bible we send scholars to the Holy Land to dig up Noah's ark and the walls of Jericho, while our theologians make a great fuss over the clinical details of "virgin birth"; the originators of the Bible, however, would have had no such concerns.

A people whose tradition is oral do not have the hang-up of literal-mindedness. They tend to be "poetic" in their use of language. Black Americans, for example, strongly influenced by the African oral tradition, tend to be poetic rather than literal-minded in their use of language. I am convinced that one of the reasons that Representative Adam Clayton Powell was drummed out of Congress, while Senator Dodd was allowed to finish his term in peace, was that white people did not understand Adam's "rhetoric," his black use of language. This is also the reason why, in the beginning, before the unjust actions of the boxing commission won him sympathy, Muhammad Ali's "talk" rubbed people the wrong way.

Another example: the average suburban white preacher would not dare to use unexplained classical references and allusions in his sermons or to bandy about or, more exactly, play with the names of Barth and Bultmann in the pulpit; and yet I have heard black preachers in Harlem and Brooklyn doing just that. And they get away with it, because their congregations are sensitive to the "poetic" meaning that the preacher is delivering and do not therefore need a discursive and historical knowledge of the facts being presented. For instance, in his last talk, delivered to the garbage collectors of Memphis, Martin Luther King had no fear of talking over the heads of his hearers, because his hearers were more attuned to the poetry of what was being said than to the factual details. Dr. King intoned: "And I would see Plato, Aristotle, Socrates, Euripides, and Aristophanes assemble around the Parthenon." And his audience voiced obvious delight in hearing him play on the like-sounding syllables of the Greek names. They knew by inference that these were great men of history but they felt no need to know that Plato was a philosopher and Aristophanes was a playwright. A people brought up in an oral culture are not only not literal-minded, their whole approach to life is different. They have a different way of knowing and relating to the surrounding world, a way that is based on the way in which the other senses perceive when not dominated and muted by the sense of sight. Remember what President Senghor said above. He also said:

> Let us consider the e-motion, that ec-static reaching out of the black African, then. The subject goes out of the Ego to sympathize with, to identify that Ego with the Thou, to die to self to be born again in that Other. The Negro does not assimilate but is assimilated by the Other. He does not put an end to another life but fortifies his own life therewith, living a life of com-union—sym-biosis. He knows, has cognizance of—*cum-noscit*—the Other. Subject and Object meet in the dialectic of the very act of knowing; a lingering caress in the night, the intimacy of body fused with body, the act of love whence will be brought forth the fruit of mutual knowledge. "Je veux je tu me sentes," said a Senegalese voter to his member of parliament to show that he wanted him to know him and be able to distinguish him from the rest. In Wolof, the word for "to greet" is neyu. An old and distinguished man once told me that the word had the same root as noyi, "to breathe" so that neyu would mean "to breathe unto oneself"—to feel. "I think, therefore I am," said Descartes, a European par excellence. "I am, I dance the Other, I am," the black African might counter. Unlike Descartes, he does not need a form word, a grammatical tool, as my teacher Ferdinand Brunet used to tell me—a conjunction—to express the reality of his being, but an object-complement. The Negro needs not to think but to live the Other, to dance the Other. In black Africa, you dance because you feel. And to dance is a verb with precisely that object-complement; you never dance without dancing something or someone. Now, to dance is to uncover reality, to re-create, to fill one's being with vital force, to live a fuller life, to BE, which, after all, is the highest mode of knowing. The African mode of know-

ing, then, is at one and the same time an uncovering and a creation—re-creation—in both senses of that word.

Young Negro intellectuals who have read their Marx superficially and who are still encumbered with the inferiority complex instilled into them by the colonizer, have taxed me with reducing black African knowing to mere emotion and with denying that there were black African reason or mental processes. But they have read me superficially, as they superficially read the "scientific socialists" before me.

Now, take the European white in his attitude towards the outside world. The white is (or was, from the time of Aristotle until the "stupid" nineteenth century) objective intelligence. A being characterized first and foremost by will, armed for the fray, bird of prey, spectator and nothing more, his first act is to distinguish, to perform a separation upon, the Object. He keeps it at a distance. He immobilizes it, outside time—even, were it possible, outside space. He holds it in his stare. He kills it. With the precision instrument of his intellect, he ruthlessly dissects it into its component facts. Scientist, but urged on by practical considerations, the European white uses the Other, now reduced to lifelessness, for his practical ends. He makes the Other a means to those ends; he assimilates it in a centripetal movement. He eats that Other and in doing so, destroys it. "The whites are cannibals," a wise old man of my country said to me once; "they have no respect for life." And it is this *manducatio* that they call "humanizing nature," or more appropriately, "taming nature." The old man added (and he had seen and heard a great deal and long reflected on these things): "But these whites don't realize that you can't tame God, the source of all life and in whom all life participates." He concluded, "It is life that humanizes, not being killed. I have the feeling it will all come to a bad end. In their mad urge to destroy, the whites are going to bring trouble down on the heads of the lot of us." Naturally, I might add, the old man spoke in much more vivid language, which I retell inadequately.

The black African is enveloped, one might say, inside his black skin. He lives in primordial night. In the first place he does not make the white's distinction between himself and the Object, whether it be tree or stone, man or beast, a thing in nature or a social circumstance. He does not hold it at arm's length for scrutiny. He rather becomes receptive to the impres-

sion it emanates, and, like the blind man, takes hold of it, full
of life, with no attempt to hold it in a stare, without killing it.
He turns it round and about in his little hands, getting to know
it by the feel of it. The black African is a child of the third day
of creation, a pure sensory field. It is in his subjectivity, at the
tip of his antennae, just like an insect, that he discovers the
Other. Observe his action. He feels with every fiber of his being,
to his very entrails, reaching out in a centrifugal movement—
e-motion—to the Object guided by the waves emanating from
that Other.[4]

THE AURAL TRADITION, THE SOURCE OF LITURGY;
THE OCULAR TRADITION, THE SOURCE OF LITURGIOLOGY

The term oral/aural tradition may be misleading, for generally in
so-called oral/aural cultures all the senses are involved without the
dominance of the eye over the others. There is a natural tendency
for interpenetration and interplay creating a concert or orchestra-
tion in which the ear sees, the eye hears, and where one both smells
and tastes color, wherein all the senses, unmuted, engage in every
experience. Moreover, there is no hesitance to be involved with the
object perceived, since such hesitance results from the dominance of
the eye, whose way of knowing is in detachment.

A people whose roots are in a "literate" tradition will tend to listen to music. Their other senses are restrained by the tendency of
the eye toward uninvolved observation and detachment. Whereas a
people whose roots are in an oral tradition have no such restraints
and they will inevitably tend to merge with music, to become involved with it, to dance. And if not to actually dance, then at least to
give oneself over entirely to the sentiment of the song. I remember
how, for instance, my aunt used to respond to my singing when I
was a child. Almost always she was so much into the song that there
were tears in her eyes by the second verse. She was always sensitive
to the meaning of the song, even of what a child was singing as he
"played" around the house. This was a habit that was nurtured in
the traditional black church.

In the traditional black churches, even when a congregation is
listening to a solo singer or a choir, the people are so involved in the
performance that they are sensitive to and react to every nuance in
that performance. But in Western churches it is possible for a con-

gregation to be singing aloud themselves, and still to be singing in a detached manner as if they were not there and the performance had no meaning.

Now which situation would you say involved more understanding—the former "emotional" one in the black church, or the latter "intellectual" one in the Western church? The answer is obvious, especially if you are asking about understanding that leads to liturgical celebration as opposed to the understanding that leads to a lecture in liturgiology.

The West needs to understand that the kind of understanding that leads to liturgiology is not superior to or more intellectual than the understanding that leads to liturgy, any more than the understanding that produces drama criticism is more intellectual than the understanding that produces drama. Moreover, liturgiology will not produce liturgy, any more than drama criticism will produce plays! And the failure of Western civilization is that it has tended more and more toward producing drama criticism and less and less toward producing plays. At the 1975 meeting of the North American Academy of Liturgy, in one of the discussion groups, someone noted that at this meeting of some of the country's top liturgists (liturgiologists?), the quality of worship was poor; and the response came back that we had not assembled to have good liturgy but to talk about liturgy. The attitude indicated in the response is remarkable, but is altogether typically "Western." There is no necessity to be a part of, or involved in the object of one's understanding.

Reacting in quite the opposite manner, President Senghor writes: "At a football game, even as a spectator, I participate with my whole body. When I listen to a jazz tune or to a black African singing, I have to bridle myself (I'm a civilized man now, you see!) not to join in singing and dancing myself. I remember, for instance, Père Jeuland, when conducting the choir in Dakar Cathedral, used to often reproach us that we 'jazzed' the plainsong. 'When will you stop being Negroes?' he would exclaim. About that time Georges Hardy was writing: 'The most civilized Negro, even in white tie and tails, quivers to the beat of the tomtom.' And he was right!"

Although President Senghor does in fact read and write in a manner far superior to most people who are "literate," yet his psychic roots are in a tradition that is oral, not ocular, a tradition in which it is all right for touch and taste and smell and hearing to be on an equal plane with seeing; where sight is not allowed to debase the other senses nor to mute them, but rather interplays with them. In this tradition, where the detachment-demanding eye does not dominate, it is all right to be emotionally involved.

In this tradition, "spirituality" itself demands emotional, effective, dramatic, soulful performance in worship. In the African and the Afro-American tradition, the emotional is not the opposite of the spiritual. Quite to the contrary, a preacher who fails to move his congregation by an effective performance "does not have the Spirit with him," and a singer who performs without feeling is said to lack "soul." As in the original biblical concept of the spiritual, the spirit or the soul is the life principle, the source of life and liveliness, of dynamism and movement, of motion and emotion. That which is unmoved and unmoving is not spiritual; it is dead!

Again, the Westerner would probably think of the spiritual possession phenomenon in the black cults as a regrettable form of "emotionalism." But President Senghor responds: "For emotion, under the semblance, at first, of a fall from consciousness, is quite to the contrary, an accession to a higher state of knowing. It is a certain way of apprehending the world. It is the integrity of knowing since 'the Subject so moved and the Object moving are united in an indissoluble synthesis, in a dance, a love dance.'"

Before going further let's stop to clarify something. Let me state apodictically—l am not trying to say that Western culture is no good. I am definitely trying to say that it is not all good. I am specifically trying to say that the thrust of Western culture tends to be anti-artistic, antipoetic, anti-mythic, anti-emotional, which is the opposite side of being pro-discursive, pro-detachment, pro-technological, and is not therefore conducive to the creation of good celebrations, particularly religious celebrations.

Further, and very importantly, when I say that Euroamerican culture tends to be discursive—I do not mean to imply that all Europeans and Euroamericans operate exclusively on the discursive level, nor conversely that Africans and Afro-Americans and other oral peoples operate only on the poetic or mythic level. The existence of poetry and music and dance in the West attest to the former, and the very writings of black historians and philosophers like Fanon and Senghor and DuBois and Bennett and Harding attest to the discursive powers of blacks. I am talking about the main tendencies of cultures. Moreover, the human needs of any people are both poetic and discursive; to lack either to any large degree would be a serious human defect.

Therefore it cannot be concluded from the discursive tendency of Western culture that Westerners can be humanly satisfied only by

being discursive or that Africans can be satisfied only by being poetic. We can conclude, however, that Afro-Americans might learn
technology from Euroamericans, and that Euroamericans might well
turn to Africans and Afro-Americans and other "aural" cultures to
learn the art of celebration and even the art of education.

From peoples of "aural culture," the West can learn to use its
mythic, poetic and dramatic faculties to construct worship and to
develop a less technological theology. And this will be very necessary for Western religion, if it is not to lose its sense of transcendence.
For the human psyche does not reach beyond the here and now by
scientific analysis. Such would ultimately doom Western religion to
relating exclusively to the "status quo." Such effort would be like
searching for the soul under a microscope and would, of course, be
doomed to failure.

From peoples of "aural cultures," the West can also learn to become dramatically expressive and emotionally involved. These things
it seems to me, are at the heart of effective communication, or in
"theological" terms, are at the heart of being an effective witness of
faith. Objective detachment and analytical explanations are useful,
but are not the means of communicating faith.

NOTES

[1] Excerpt from unpublished sermon by Fr. Rivers cited in Donald M.
Clark, "Elders and Ancestors," in *Plenty Good Room*, Nov.-Dec. 1993), p.
8.

[2] Clarence Rufus J. Rivers, *Soulful Worship*, 2 vols. (Cincinnati:
Stimuli, 1974); *The Spirit in Worship* (Cincinnati: Stimuli, 1973).

[3] Léopold Sédar Senghor, "The Psychology of the African Negro," *Freeing the Spirit*, Vol. III, No. 3, 1974.

[4] Ibid.

11

Varietates Legitimae and an African-American Liturgical Tradition

D. REGINALD WHITT, O.P.

In the spring of 1994, a friend excitedly telephoned me to report that the issue of "an African-American Catholic rite" had become a dead letter. At the time that issue was the subject of a study on the part of the National Black Catholic Congress staff, unanimously commissioned by congress delegates in 1992. In anticipation of the commission, I had published a 1990 article questioning the propriety of seeking such a "rite" in the form of an African-American Catholic ecclesial community "separate but equal" vis-à-vis the Latin church.[1] Hence, my friend thought that I would be eager to know that the question was moot. His authority for so declaring was the "instruction on the Roman liturgy and inculturation," *Varietates Legitimae*, which the Congregation for Divine Worship and the Discipline of the Sacraments (hereafter CDW) had issued in January 1994.[2] According to my friend, this instruction, subtitled the "fourth instruction for the correct application of the conciliar constitution on the liturgy" and specifically addressed to implementing articles 37-40 of *Sacrosanctum Concilium* (which provide for liturgical inculturation), definitively declared that no "new rites" were ecclesiastically possible. Given the tenor of my 1990 article, he was certain that I would welcome this news. That was not my response, however, because of what is said in *Sacrosanctum Concilium*, article 4,

---

Originally published in *Worship* 71 (1997), pp. 504-37.

which I understood to constitute conciliar teaching to the effect that the Church's supreme authority anticipated the development of new rites which could be recognized as legitimate.[3] How, then, could CDW instruct to the contrary?

This essay will show, first of all, that *Varietates Legitimae* does not deny the possibility of new rites arising in the Church. Indeed, the instruction says nothing on the subject. In addition, nonetheless, *Varietates Legitimae* sheds some light on how new rites might arise due to liturgical inculturation. More importantly, the document shows the Holy See's great sensitivity to the needs of diverse communities of Latin Catholic faithful to worship in accord with their own cultures, even to the extent of doing so according to specially adapted liturgical books. Rather than rendering moot the question of an "African-American rite," and despite shortcomings to be discussed herein, *Varietates Legitimae* encourages the development of a distinct African-American mode of celebrating the Western Catholic liturgy.

RITUAL FAMILY, RITE AND CHURCH

As a preliminary matter, the terms "rite" and "liturgy" must be distinguished. "Rite," most unfortunately, gets used for all kinds of church-related things: it is used for an individual service, like "the marriage 'rite'"; or for a bundle of related services, as in the "'rites' of Christian initiation" (baptism, confirmation and Eucharist), or "the last 'rites'" (penance, anointing and Viaticum), or "the funeral 'rites'" (the wake, the requiem Mass and burial service). Then again, "rite" is also used to indicate the way a particular Latin Catholic community celebrates all or some of its services: the "Hispano-Mozarabic rite" of Toledo has a different way of celebrating Mass than does the "Ambrosian rite" of Milan—and both differ from the Mass of the "Roman rite." In addition, my own religious order, and the Carmelites and Carthusians once celebrated the Mass and Hours in different ways than most members of the Latin church. While most Latin Catholics were said to follow the "Roman rite," we worshipped according to the "Dominican rite," the "Carmelite rite," and the "Carthusian rite." And there is the additional practice of describing a church—a whole community of Catholic believers—as a "rite": so-called Catholics of the "Maronite rite," the "Malabar rite," the "Ukrainian rite," etc. When the 1992 National Black Catholic Congress commissioned a comprehensive study "to determine the desirability and feasibility of establishing an African-American Catholic Rite," everybody interviewed about it said that such a "rite" might entail anything from a revision of Roman liturgical books to the erection of an ecclesiastical community separate from the Latin church and directly under the pope. Canonically speaking, they were all wrong.

Not any of those things, individually or together, constitutes a rite in the law of the Catholic Church. Not the way you get married, nor the way you get buried; not the way you celebrate Mass, and certainly not your church. A Maronite Catholic belongs to the Maronite Catholic Church—not to the "Maronite rite"; a Latin Catholic belongs to the Latin Catholic Church—not to the "Latin rite," and certainly not to the "Roman rite." This does not mean that there is no such thing in the Church as a "rite." There most surely is such a thing, defined in the twenty-eighth canon of the 1991 Code of Canons of the Eastern Churches: "a rite is a liturgical, theological, spiritual and disciplinary patrimony distinguished by the culture and historical circumstances of peoples, and which is expressed in its own manner of living the faith by each church *sui iuris.*"[4]

A proper understanding of "rite" begins with understanding the term "church *sui iuris.*" It has been noted that Maronite, Malabar, Ukrainian and Latin Catholics belong to churches and not to "rites." Their churches—Maronite, Malabar, Ukrainian and Latin—are churches *sui iuris.* These are communities of the faithful that are joined together by a hierarchy according to the norm of law, which the Church's supreme authority recognizes as *sui iuris* (that is, self-governing).[5] There are twenty-one churches *sui iuris*; in the Catholic Church worldwide (in alphabetical order) these are the Albanian, Armenian, Belarussian, Bulgarian, Chaldean, Coptic, Ethiopian, Georgian, Greek, Italo-Albanian, Latin, Malabar, Malankar, Maronite, Melkite, Russian, Ruthenian, Slovak, Syrian, Ukrainian and Yugoslavian Catholic churches. And the people of each of these churches *sui iuris* have inherited a liturgical, theological, spiritual and disciplinary patrimony derived from one of six ancient patriarchate traditions. The Armenian Catholic Church has its own Armenian tradition. The Coptic and Ethiopian Catholic churches have the Alexandrine tradition, from the church of Egypt's ancient capital, Alexandria. The Chaldean Catholic Church of Iraq and the Malabar Catholic Church of India have the Chaldean tradition. The Malankar church of India and the Maronite and Syrian churches of greater Syria and Palestine have the Antiochene tradition, inherited from the church in which Christ's followers were first called "Christians." All the other Eastern Catholic churches *sui iuris* (everybody from the Albanians to the Yugoslavians) have a tradition that comes from the imperial church of Constantinople. There is only one Western Catholic church *sui iuris*, the Latin church whose tradition not surprisingly arises from the apostolic church of Rome.

From these six different and discrete traditions, the peoples belonging to each of the twenty-one churches *sui iuris* have developed distinct ways of celebrating the liturgy, special theological insights that they stress, spiritualities that speak to and from their different experiences, and laws and customary disciplines suited to the ways they live out the Catholic Christian life. In other words, the peoples of the different churches *sui iuris* have brought their own cultures and the changes they have experienced to bear on the traditions inherited from their patriarchates. They have inculturated those inherited traditions so that, for example, the Constantinopolitan tradition has been differentiated into thirteen recognized varieties! Those recognized patrimonial varieties, those inculturated and personalized liturgical, theological, spiritual and disciplinary religious heritages, are what the universal Church calls "rites." Their relationship to the respective churches *sui iuris* and patriarchate traditions can be charted as follows:

Tradition	Patrimony/Canonical Rite	Church *Sui Iuris*
Alexandrine	Coptic	Coptic Catholic Church
	Egyptian	Ethiopian Catholic Church
Antiochene	Malankar	Malankar Catholic Church
	Maronite	Maronite Catholic Church
Armenian	Armenian	Armenian Catholic Church
Chaldean	Chaldean	Chaldean Catholic Church
	Syro-Malabar	Malabar Catholic Church
Constantinopolitan	Albanian	Albanian Catholic Church
	[eleven other rites]	
	Byzantine-Yugoslavian	Yugoslavian Catholic Church
Roman	Latin	Latin Catholic Church

The Latin Catholic Church, drawing from the apostolic Roman tradition, has the Latin rite. In turn, the Latin rite has a disciplinary patrimony—the most recent expression of which is the 1983 Code of Canon Law, along with a body of other legislation from the pope himself and from the dicasteries of the Roman curia. Still, our current discipline derives from a canonical tradition reaching as far back as the first ecumenical council of Nicaea in 325, and through several local and ecumenical councils, and at least ten centuries of papal legislation. The Latin rite also has its own spiritual and theological patrimony. Among others, we have the spiritualities of the various religious orders and of spiritual writers and mystics such as St. Catherine of Siena, St. Ignatius Loyola, St. Teresa of Avila, St. Therese of Lisieux, Dorothy Day, G. K. Chesterton and Thomas Merton. We have the theological legacies of Latin Christians like Cyprian of Carthage, Augustine of Hippo, Thomas Aquinas, Bonaventure, Robert Bellarmine and Alphonsus Liguori.

The Latin rite also has a liturgical patrimony. In similarity to the different families of spirituality and schools of theology in the Latin rite, the liturgical patrimony of the Latin rite has three canonically recognized liturgical traditions, or "ritual families." We have the Ambrosian, the Hispano-Mozarabic and the Roman ritual families. It is unfortunate, but these ritual families are often also called "rites" even by the Holy See. That is why *Varietates Legitimae* continually speaks about the "Roman rite." To be canonically accurate, it is not the "Roman rite," but the Roman ritual family in the liturgical patrimony of the canonical Latin rite. What the Spaniards do in Toledo follows the Hispano-Mozarabic ritual family in the Latin rite's liturgical patrimony, and the Milanese follow the Ambrosian ritual family in the same liturgical patrimony of the Latin rite. When the black Catholic congress commissioned that study about establishing an "African-American rite," it could well be interpreted as meaning the development and recognition of an African-American ritual family, a black American worshipping tradition, in the liturgical patrimony of the canonical Latin rite.

From hereon, therefore, this essay will make the following terminological distinctions. The terms "Roman rite" and "Roman liturgy" will refer only to the chief ritual family in the Latin church, which is one of the three ritual families comprised in the liturgical component of the canonical Latin rite. And the term "'canonical rite," whether Latin, Albanian, Ethiopian or Maronite, will refer to the entire ethno-religious heritage of a Catholic people: a liturgical, theological, spiritual and disciplinary complex derived from a patriarchate's tradition that distinguishes a community of the faithful.

The black Catholic congress's commission to study an "African-American rite" ambiguously embraces the canonical notion of a liturgical, theological, spiritual and disciplinary patrimony drawn from the apostolic Roman tradition and distinguished by the culture and historical experiences of Americans of African ancestry. However, the commission addresses this notion rather awkwardly, because you cannot "establish" a canonical rite. You inherit your rite, as part of who you are as a Catholic Christian people, and all the Holy See does or does not do in its regard is *recognize* that, indeed, that is what you have because of who you are. *Varietates Legitimae* does not come close to dealing with that concept. *Varietates Legitimae* only deals with inculturation of the so-called "Roman rite"—that is, with the cultural adaptation of the Roman ritual family of the canonical Latin rite. The instruction says nothing that denies the possibility of new canonical rites arising, nor does it deny the potential emergence of new ritual families in the Latin rite. It simply refuses to encourage the latter prospect.

The story of *Varietates Legitimae* begins in 1963 with the very first document promulgated by the Second Vatican Council, the *Constitution on the Sacred Liturgy, Sacrosanctum Concilium*. Although bishops from the Eastern churches took part in drafting that constitution, the document was almost exclusively devoted to the liturgical patrimony of the Latin church. Indeed, it was primarily concerned with that patrimony's Roman ritual family, i.e., with the "Roman rite." Article 3 of *Sacrosanctum Concilium* tells us so: "[T]he principles which follow about fostering and reforming the liturgy . . . and practical norms [which] must be established [for that purpose] . . . can or ought to be applied first of all to the Roman rite as well as to all the other rites, although the practical norms that follow are to be understood to regard the Roman rite alone, unless it concern those things which from the very nature of the matter also affect the other rites."[6]

Before the bishops at the council approved this text, an amendment had changed earlier language which had said that the norms of the constitution applied "first of all to the Roman rite as well as the other rites, Eastern and Western."[7] The conciliar commission on the liturgy explained that, when the text referred to the "Roman rite," it referred to all the liturgical traditions that were embraced within the rite of the Latin church—the ritual varieties of the religious orders previously mentioned, as well as the Ambrosian and Mozarabic ritual families. A further objection was raised that this inclusive use of the term "Roman rite" to mean more than just the Roman liturgy was confusing. In response, the commission stated that it would keep the term "Roman rite," but it would only apply the term "in the strict sense," i.e., excluding *any* of "the other rites, either Latin or Eastern." "This formula, about which more than enough has been debated in the council and in the commission, was preserved by design. *For it concerns the Roman rite in the strict sense, as the text clearly explains, and not the other rites, either Latin or Eastern,* 'unless it concern those things which from the nature itself of the matter also affect the other rites.'"[8]

So, the principles and norms of *Sacrosanctum Concilium* do not apply to any liturgical traditions of an Eastern church or of the Latin church, except for the Roman ritual family, unless the subject matter being addressed obviously affects those other liturgical traditions.

Sacrosanctum Concilium regularly uses the word "rite" to mean a liturgical tradition within the patrimony of a true canonical rite. This observation is important because of what article 4 of the constitution said. That previously cited article said that the Church gives equal respect to "all the legitimately recognized rites"[9] in any of the twenty-one Catholic churches, which the conciliar liturgical commission explained meant not only the liturgical traditions in use in 1963, but "perhaps other rites to be recognized in the future."[10] An early schema of the constitution had declared that the Church accorded equal right and honor to "all the legitimately existing rites" ("omnes ritus legitime vigentes"); the phrase had been amended to speak of "all the legitimately recognized rites" ("omnes ritus legitime *agnitos*") to make it clear that honor and equality were extended not only to rites then in use, but also to other rites that might be recognized in the future.[11]

In other words, the Second Vatican Council opens the Church to the development and recognition of new ritual families within any of the six basic traditions of the universal Church. These new ritual families can appear within any of the twenty-one recognized canonical rites (like the Latin rite of the Latin church). And furthermore, if combined with new theological, spiritual or disciplinary cultures, these new liturgical traditions might be part of a *new* canonical rite. Now, since 1963, no new canonical rite has been recognized. Indeed, the concept was only defined for certain in the 1990 Eastern code. That code deals with all twenty-one of the Eastern churches *sui iuris*, with all their different canonical rites, and therefore had to define the term. Since the Latin church only has the one Latin rite, the 1983 Latin Code of Canon Law had no need to define what a rite is. And, as previously mentioned, *Varietates Legitimae* has little to do with such canonical rites, new or old, except that it speaks about one of the ritual families, the Roman, in the Latin canonical rite. In addition, since 1963, no new ritual family has been recognized as such. This is not to say that none may have appeared, but only that none has been recognized. *Sacrosanctum Concilium*, article 4 foresees their appearance and authorizes their recognition. *Varietates Legitimae* does have something to say about that.

RITUAL FAMILIES IN THE LATIN RITE

Varietates Legitimae comes to us from CDW, which has the authority to regulate and promote the liturgy in the Latin church. The Congregation for the Oriental Churches does this for the twenty-one Eastern churches.[12] CDW supervises the drafting and revision of liturgical texts, including the particularized calendars (special arrangements for feast days and such) and the special texts for the Mass and Hours of all the dioceses and religious institutions that are entitled to observe such distinctive feasts and liturgical texts. For example, CDW reviews the calendars and liturgical texts of all three of the recognized ritual families that have developed within the canonical Latin rite.[13]

One of these ritual families is the "Roman rite," which includes the liturgical variations developed within it (e.g., the special "Seraphic Missal" used in the Franciscan family and the proper liturgical books of other religious institutes). In addition, there are the two other Latin ritual families. CDW has confirmed the liturgical books of the Ambrosian and Hispano-Mozarabic liturgical traditions with the understanding that they represent ritual families distinct from the Roman.[14] CDW has described these liturgical families as arising from the ancient Roman tradition. They derived from the unique ancestral unity of Judaeo-Christian worship and display a basic creativity of texts and calendars. They adapted to diverse cultural contexts (in order to resolve theological questions, or due to enrichment from the cultures of the faithful, or due to changing from one language to another) until they reached a level of crystallization or codification. CDW says that these liturgical families provide unvaried conservation of one living liturgical tradition adapted to diverse cultures and expressed in different forms and formularies. Relying on article 4 of *Sacrosanctum Concilium,* CDW expressly lists the Roman, Ambrosian and Hispano-Mozarabic ritual families as legitimately recognized liturgical "rites" which enjoy "a special right of subsistence in the ecclesial lived experience . . . concretized in their conservation, in their growth and being adapted to modern needs."[15] The missals of these other Latin liturgical traditions are not called "Roman missals," but by their own proper names: the *Missale Hispano-Mozarabicum* and the *Missale Ambrosianum.*

Without limiting their number to already recognized traditions, CDW has spoken of the variety of liturgical families in the West as a manifestation of the Church's unity in diversity: "When the Apostolic See, in the modern ecclesial context proper to the Christian West, confirms the texts for a rite different from the Roman, it does nothing other than underline that the same and unique history of salvation is actualized with celebrative modalities different among themselves, but in the unity of a single Body which is the Church, precisely because the 'liturgical communion' underlines the fact that *sentire cum ecclesia* is joined with *agere in ecclesia,* with *orare cum et pro ecclesia,* and *credere per ecclesiam.*"[16]

So it would seem that CDW's authority to authorize dioceses to develop particular liturgical texts, and to review and confirm those texts, implicitly includes the authority to recognize the legitimacy of other Latin ritual families distinct from the "Roman rite." That might occur in the case of communities of non-Catholic Western Christians already possessing a distinct liturgical tradition, who enter full communion with the Latin church. This has actually been suggested concerning those previously belonging to the Anglican communion.[17] In fact, since 1984 CDW has permitted at least five Latin Catholic congregations of former Episcopalians in the United States to use the *Book of Divine Worship,* a slightly modified version of the 1979 American *Book of Common Prayer.* These congregations use the book to celebrate the Eucharist, morning and evening prayer, baptisms and funerals, in either modern or "Tudor" English. It is said that this practice is being allowed "to keep as much of their 'Anglican heritage' as possible."[18] A distinct Western ritual family might also be recognized in the case of African-American Christians, some of whom are Catholics, but whose ethno-religious worship may be actualized in ways sufficiently distinct as to exhaust the limits of the Roman liturgy. This recognition would not, however, constitute a *canonical* rite. That would entail further recognition by the Holy See of a Western theological, spiritual and disciplinary tradition distinguished by the culture and history of the African-American community.

In addition to the special liturgical texts and calendars of non-Roman liturgical families in the Latin rite, CDW reviews all the calendars and all the translations and adaptations of official "Roman rite" liturgical books. These are prepared by episcopal conferences around the world and submitted to CDW, which approves them when those documents are found to comply with the general liturgical norms or the norms for profound liturgical adaptation discussed below.

LITURGICAL INSTRUCTIONS

Sacrosanctum Concilium reserved ultimate regulation of the liturgy to the Holy See and individual diocesan bishops, but it also committed the process of liturgical reform within certain defined limits to national episcopal conferences,[19] and expressed the desire that these conferences establish liturgical commissions. Assisted by experts and directed by the episcopal conferences, these liturgical commissions would regulate pastoral liturgical action in the concerned countries, and promote necessary studies and experiments concerning liturgical adaptations which the conferences might propose to the Holy See.[20]

Articles 37-40 of the constitution provided the norms for adapting the Roman liturgy to the cultures and traditions of various peoples. *Sacrosanctum Concilium* declared that the Church had no desire to impose rigid uniformity in the liturgy, but instead wished to cultivate and encourage the spiritual gifts and customs of various peoples, and be sympathetic to whatever was not inseparably tied to error or superstition. These spiritual customs were to be preserved intact and, provided they were consistent with the authentic spirit of the liturgy, they could be incorporated into it (art. 37). When revising liturgical books, an episcopal conference was to provide for legitimate variations and adaptations for different peoples—especially but not exclusively in mission lands—*provided* the substantial unity of the Roman rite was preserved (art. 38). Hence, within the limits provided in the *editio typica* of a liturgical book, the episcopal conferences could specify adaptations for things like sacramental celebrations, liturgical language and sacred music, in accord with the constitution's fundamental norms (art. 39).

Without requiring preservation of the substantial unity of the "Roman rite,"[21] article 40 of *Sacrosanctum Concilium* provided a process for what it called "major accommodations" of the liturgy to the spiritual lives of different cultures. In those cases, episcopal conferences were attentively and prudently to consider what elements from the traditions and genius of the individual peoples might advantageously be admitted into Catholic worship. The adaptations that were judged useful or necessary would be proposed to the Holy See, for introduction after it gave its consent. The bishops were to consult experts in the fields concerning the adaptations in the course of formulating their proposals. And to ensure that such justifiable major adaptations might be made with necessary prudence, the Holy See would then give the episcopal conference faculties to permit and direct necessary preliminary experiments among certain suitable groups of the faithful and for a determined time.[22]

Because it has the job of regulating *and* promoting the liturgical life of the Latin church, CDW has supervised the implementation of *Sacrosanctum Concilium* over the past 30-some years. CDW prepared the *editiones typicae*, the standard Latin editions of the "Roman rite" liturgical books: the Roman Missal; the Liturgy of the Hours; the baptismal, marriage and funeral ritual books; and the Roman Pontifical. And CDW has issued "general instructions" along with these liturgical books, which govern how the books are to be used. But these books and general instructions took years to put together, while the Church's bishops and people needed help as soon as the council called for the liturgy to be reformed.

To provide that help, from 1964 to 1969 CDW was assisted by the Consilium for the Implementation of the Liturgical Constitution, whose authority included issuing a special instruction setting forth the liturgical responsibilities of episcopal conferences, and responding to their proposals and questions until the liturgical renewal had been completed. In 1964 the Consilium issued the first instruction on the correct implementation of *Sacrosanctum Concilium,* entitled *Inter Oecumenici,*[23] which encouraged the various episcopal conferences and their liturgical commissions to study, propose and regulate liturgical adaptations.[24]

In 1967, the Consilium explained the procedure to be followed in the introduction of profound cultural adaptations. A liturgical commission was to complete its preparatory studies and propose adaptations which the episcopal conference would then approve. The conference would then request the Holy See to authorize liturgical experimentation according to those proposals. The Holy See would determine the forms of experimentation to be undertaken, and then the experiments would be carried out by certain suitable groups for a limited time under the control of the diocesan bishop.[25] Hence, where *Sacrosanctum Concilium* envisioned episcopal conferences taking the initiative to study, plan, request and direct liturgical adaptations according to the traditions and genius of individual peoples in their territories, CDW, the Consilium and *Inter Oecumenici* provided the juridical structures and methodology for those bishops to do so.

In 1967, the Consilium also issued a short second instruction on the liturgy, entitled *Tres abhinc annos.*[26] For the most part, that second instruction only contained specific rubrical changes: how often and when a celebrant was to genuflect and kiss the altar; how many prayers could be said at a single Mass; matters of liturgical choreography.

In 1970, after the promulgation of the *editio typica* of the Roman Missal and Lectionary, and the issuance of the general instruction on how they were to be used, CDW issued a third instruction, entitled *Liturgicae instaurationes.*[27] This was a cautionary document, indicating that the many textual options and rubrical flexibility in the official liturgical books permitted adaptation to local conditions and cultures and, therefore, that there was "no need for purely personal improvisations, which can only trivialize the liturgy."[28] Hence, the third instruction encouraged diocesan bishops to engage actively in governing, guiding, encouraging and sometimes reproving pastoral liturgical activities, because the link between the liturgy and the faith was too close for the distortion of one not to warp the other. Bishops were to use their diocesan liturgical commissions to obtain complete information about the religious and social conditions of their faithful, assessing their spiritual needs and the ways most likely to help them liturgically. The bishops were to use all the options provided in the new liturgical books, and actually evaluate which options favored true reform and which ones obstructed it.

Nobody was to go beyond the simplifying limits of the liturgical books: if priests took anything away, they ran the danger of stripping worship of its sacred symbolism and proper beauty: "the liturgical reform bears absolutely no relation to what is called 'secularizing the world,'" and making liturgy effective did not lie in experimenting with services and changing them again and again, or in stripping them bare. Effective worship lay solely in entering more deeply into the Word of God and the mystery being celebrated. This alone made the Church's services authentic, "not what some priest decides, indulging his own preferences," because the various liturgical traditions and the services conducted within them "are in fact the property of the whole Church."[29] The third instruction reminded bishops, clergy and the faithful that nobody has the right to hijack the liturgy and bend it to his or her or their own quirks: it is the property of the whole Church.

So, there are two sides to the Catholic liturgy, no matter what tradition one follows. On the one hand, as the third instruction emphasized, the liturgy belongs to the whole Church. Each individual service and the distinct ritual families to which they belong, the canonical rites of which those families form parts, and indeed the six ancient traditions of the patriarchates—they all belong to the whole people of God and are not to be modified blithely or at will. On the other hand, because Christ comes to his people where they are, and the Gospel is preached in their context, Catholics hear the one Word and celebrate the one true faith in different ways. And as different peoples embrace the faith, they embrace it according to their different cultures. Therefore, twenty-four years after *Liturgical instaurationes*, CDW directly addressed liturgical inculturation in its fourth instruction, *Varietates Legitimae*.

VARIETATES LEGITIMAE

Specifically implementing articles 37-40 of *Sacrosanctum Concilium* concerning the adaptation of the Roman liturgy to different cultures, *Varietates Legitimae* follows up the first generation of postconciliar efforts by providing precise principles and the definitive canonical procedure for what is now called liturgical "inculturation." *Varietates Legitimae* defines inculturation as the incarnation of the Gospel in autonomous cultures and the simultaneous introduction of those cultures into the Church's life. Hence, inculturation signifies "an intimate transformation of the authentic cultural values by their integration into Christianity and the implantation of Christianity into different human cultures."[30] Acknowledging that the theological principles concerning faith and inculturation have yet to be examined in depth, the instruction is intended to assist bishops and episcopal conferences in making adaptations in the liturgical books anticipated pursuant to articles 37-39 of *Sacrosanctum Concilium*. In addition,

Varietates Legitimae has been issued to help episcopal conferences bring about the more profound and difficult adaptations foreseen in article 40 of that constitution where pastoral need requires.[31]

Thus understood, liturgical inculturation constitutes one aspect of inculturating the Gospel and calls for integrating the permanent values of a given people's culture into the ways in which they live the faith. Liturgical inculturation is to be an intrinsic part of a unified pastoral strategy which takes account of the human situation. Since liturgical inculturation is produced by a progressive maturity in the faith of a people, *Varietates Legitimae* considers the inculturation process to be a patient and complex undertaking which requires methodical research and ongoing discernment.[32]

The instruction notes that pastoral situations differ because some countries did not have Christian traditions and have only been exposed to the Roman liturgy in modern times, whereas others have long-standing Western Christian traditions that are culturally expressed in the "Roman rite." It is also necessary in some historically Christian countries to confront increased indifference or disinterest toward religion by finding the most suitable means of reaching hearts and minds. Moreover, in some Christian countries, particular problems are raised because more than one culture coexist.[33] Hence, how much liturgical inculturation is necessary depends upon the distinct situations in which the Church is found. Where a population has different cultures, satisfactory solutions require a precise evaluation of the circumstances.[34] *Varietates Legitimae*, article 49 notes that several cultures coexist in a number of countries and sometimes influence each other so much as gradually to form a new culture. At other times, however, one coexisting culture seeks to affirm its own identity or even opposes the other in order to stress its own existence. Episcopal conferences must carefully examine each case individually and respect the riches of each culture and those who defend them. Moreover, these conferences may neither ignore nor neglect a minority culture with which they are not familiar.[35]

Recalling the message of CDW's third instruction, *Varietates Legitimae* states that the Church's faith is liturgically expressed in a symbolic and communitarian form, which is why we have laws for organized worship, the preparation of texts and the celebration of liturgical ceremonies (which it inappropriately calls "rites").[36] Liturgical legislation secures the orthodoxy of worship, not only by avoiding errors, but also by passing on the faith in its integrity so that the Church's rule of prayer (*lex orandi*) might correspond to her rule of faith (*lex credendi*). The Holy See is responsible for such legislation along with the episcopal conferences and diocesan bishops of the territories concerned, according to the prescriptions of law.[37]

Episcopal conferences are to prepare for inculturation by consulting with experts in the assessment of local cultural values and in the Roman liturgical tradition.[38] They are to examine the preliminary historical, anthropological, exegetical and theological studies of these experts in the light of the pastoral experience of the local clergy, especially the native clergy. Conferences might also seek the valuable advice of "wise people" (*sapientum*) of the place whose human wisdom is enriched by the Gospel.[39]

The instruction emphatically provides that the inculturation process is to maintain the substantial unity of the Roman liturgical rite.[40] With unmistakable clarity article 36 says that this unity "is currently expressed in the typical editions of liturgical books, published by authority of the supreme pontiff and in the liturgical books approved by the episcopal conferences for their areas and confirmed by the Apostolic See. *The work of inculturation does not foresee the creation of new families of rites*; inculturation responds to the needs of a particular culture and leads to adaptations *which still remain part of the Roman rite.*"[41]

Varietates Legitimae, therefore, understands both the level of inculturation provided in *Sacrosanctum Concilium*, articles 37-39 and the profound liturgical inculturation envisaged in article 40 as liturgical developments remaining within the Roman liturgical tradition.[42] Neither form of inculturation is directed to developing new ritual or liturgical families like the Ambrosian or Hispano-Mozarabic traditions.

MINOR INCULTURATIONS

Varietates Legitimae describes the first level of inculturation foreseen in articles 37-39 of *Sacrosanctum Concilium* as principally concerned with the liturgical books. Translators must be attentive to the special characteristics of Latin liturgical language, and also to the demands of oral communication and the literary qualities of the living language of the people.[43] The Latin *editiones typicae* of the liturgical books indicate the adaptations permissible in the celebration of the sacraments. For example, the general instruction of the Roman Missal allows each episcopal conference to develop norms for the celebration of the Eucharist suited to the traditions and character of peoples, regions and different communities.[44] However, while it allows for legitimate differences and adaptations in conformity with *Sacrosanctum Concilium*, the Roman Missal must remain the sign and instrument of unity. In another document, CDW explained how this is so: "[T]he elements which constitute the substantial unity of the Roman Missal are found invariably in it: the General Instruction with the general calendar, the same Order of Mass readings, the same Order of Mass with the four Eucharistic Prayers, together with the lesser euchology. The particularities existing by concession of the Apostolic See in the *editiones typicae* of the Roman Missal for the diverse episcopal conferences do not alter this substantial unity, nor do they constitute a novelty in the liturgical history of the Roman rite, but rather tend to enrich the prayer of the Church."[45]

Varietates Legitimae, article 62 provides the detailed procedure to be followed in making these adaptations. An episcopal conference is to prepare its own edition of the liturgical books, decide about the translations and which legally envisioned adaptations to introduce. The acts of the conference, including the final vote, are to be signed by the conference president and secretary and sent to CDW with two copies of the approved text. These must be accompanied by brief and precise explanations of each proposed adaptation indicating any parts taken from already approved liturgical books and those that are newly composed. Once CDW has given its approving *recognitio*, the episcopal conference promulgates the decree indicating the time when the approved text goes into effect.[46]

PROFOUND INCULTURATION

Articles 63-65 address more radical instances of liturgical inculturation pursuant to article 40 of *Sacrosanctum Concilium* which go beyond the sort envisioned by the general instructions and *praenotanda* of the liturgical books. This effort presupposes that an episcopal conference has actually exhausted all the possibilities offered by the liturgical books. Having evaluated and even revised those adaptations, the conference must believe that more far-reaching innovations are required. *Varietates Legitimae* states that this level of inculturation may be useful or necessary for any of the liturgical books or practices discussed previously without requiring profound adaptations in others. Moreover, these more radical adaptations do not aim at a transformation of the Roman ritual tradition, "but rather obtain their own place within it."[47] When one or more diocesan bishops detect continuing problems regarding the liturgical participation of their faithful, the instruction provides that they can lay out their difficulties to the episcopal conference and examine with it the advantage of introducing more profound adaptations, "if the good of souls so requires."[48] The conference will then examine what liturgical celebrations need modification in light of the traditions and mentality of the people, by having its own or a regional liturgical commission study the different cultural elements involved and their eventual inclusion in the liturgy. This commission is to obtain appropriate expert advice, even consulting non-Christian persons about the religious or cultural significance of such elements. [49]

Radical liturgical inculturation requires a period of experimentation. Before any such trials, however, the conference sends its proposal to CDW, describing the planned innovations, the reasons supporting them, the criteria used and a plan for experimentation along with the minutes of the conference's discussion and vote.[50] Once the conference and CDW jointly examine the proposal, if the case so warrants, CDW will grant the conference a faculty to conduct the experiment.

The episcopal conference supervises the experimentation process, usually assisted by its own liturgical commission.[51] At the close of the trial period, the conference must decide whether the experimentation has achieved the proposal's goals or whether certain elements need revision, and send its conclusions to CDW along with a report on the experiments. Having examined that documentation, CDW will be able to issue a decree of approval, perhaps with its own observations, so that the variations or changes may be introduced within the country.[52] *Varietates Legitimae* declares that CDW is ready to receive and examine such proposals, with due regard for the good of the concerned local churches and the common good of the whole Church, and to assist the inculturation process where it seems useful or necessary. And it will do so in accord with the instruction's principles, in a spirit of confident collaboration and mutual responsibility.[52]

COMMENTARY

Varietates Legitimae is noteworthy for what it does and does not say concerning inculturation, about other Latin ritual families, and about canonical rites.

1. *Inculturation Enhances and Does Not Breach Roman Liturgical Unity*

First of all, *Varietates Legitimae* declares that the substantial unity of the Roman liturgy must be observed, no matter how profound the degree of liturgical inculturation in Latin church communities. Articles 36 and 52 emphasize that the "Roman rite" is the norm, as it is expressed in the *editiones typicae* of the liturgical books. Hence, the particular minor variations which episcopal conferences introduce into their liturgical books, taking advantage of the options provided in the general instructions and *praenotanda* of the *editiones typicae* do not depart from that ritual unity. On the other hand, *Varietates Legitimae* also states that innovations in pursuit of more profound inculturation do not aim in the slightest at (*minime tendunt*) transforming the Roman liturgical heritage, but obtain their own place within it; that is, they enlarge or broaden the Roman ritual family.[54] In so doing, adaptations of the Roman liturgy pursuant to article 40 of *Sacrosanctum Concilium* might be said to enlarge the variety of "other Latin rites" in that group of liturgical traditions deemed to exist within the limits of the Roman ritual family.[55] No matter how radically one might legitimately adapt the Roman Missal, *Varietates Legitimae* claims that the result will still fall within the Roman ritual family: it will not be a new ritual family, equal to the Roman, Ambrosian or Hispano-Mozarabic.

This interpretation of *Sacrosanctum Concilium,* article 40 differs from that of other liturgical scholars who participated in drafting that article. Luykx and McManus, for example, have emphasized the constitution's silence about maintaining "substantial unity with the Roman rite" in cases of profound liturgical inculturation,[56] implying (or at least inferring) that radical adaptations might lead to new Latin ritual families. As the authoritative interpretation of the liturgical constitution, *Varietates Legitimae* increases the distance between inculturation of the Roman liturgy and the emergence of any non-Roman Western worshipping tradition.[57]

This more cautious approach was applied to the one profound adaptation of the Roman liturgy that is universally held to constitute a major inculturation. The liturgical inculturation proper to the Catholic people of Zaire may constitute a phenomenon just short of a new Latin ritual heritage on a par with the Ambrosian or Mozarabic traditions.[58] The Zairois inculturation was accomplished before *Varietates Legitimae,* under the original norms of *Sacrosanctum Concilium,* article 40. Those earlier norms envisioned a pattern of research on the part of an episcopal conference, using the work of experts, as to what elements of a people's tradition and culture should be brought into divine worship. Then, upon the conference's request, the Holy See would permit a period of trial use and experimentation, followed finally by an act of the Holy See approving this major adaptation of the Roman liturgy. The Holy See approved "The Roman Missal for the Dioceses of Zaire"[59]—whose very name indicates that this complex of services remains within the Roman ritual family—in 1988, nearly twenty years after study and planning for it commenced in 1969.[60]

The eucharistic liturgy in the Zairois missal features distinct aspects of middle-belt African culture: at the beginning of Mass the saints and the people's ancestors are invoked because they are in communion with God, and they are invited to be present at the contemporary celebration; in addition to the customary Roman liturgical ministers, there is an announcer—who is neither a religious nor a cleric—whose function is to announce the coming celebration and arouse the community's mood of celebration; the penitential rite follows the homily, and is then followed by a rite of peace which might be manifested by a communal washing of hands; there is rhythmic movement and a recessional dance, and new variety of images, allusions and distinctive words used in a particular Eucharistic prayer, which employs call and response. This eucharistic order is a system of complex liturgical acts designed for an entire nation with a fairly unified culture. It is the norm for how the Catholics of Zaire celebrate the Eucharist, legitimately provided by a particular set of liturgical books, radically different from the *Ordo Missae* characteristic of the Roman liturgy's unity.[61] Nonetheless, the decree approving the Zairois missal describes those liturgical books as "introducing a new ritual structure *having observed the unity of the Roman rite*"![62] What that decree implied about profound liturgical inculturations, *Varietates Legitimae* establishes as a general rule: even drastic modifications of the Roman liturgy do not normally entail a departure from the Roman ritual family.

2. Liturgical Inculturation May Inexorably Promote Development of Additional Latin Ritual Families

Second, *Varietates Legitimae*, article 5 states that the process of liturgical inculturation is a part of a far larger enterprise, of a unified pastoral strategy of Gospel inculturation "able to offer these cultures the knowledge of the hidden mystery and help them to bring forth *original expressions of Christian life, celebration and thought from their own living tradition*."[63] Hence, liturgical inculturation may be said to be intrinsically related to inculturating the entire Roman patriarchate's tradition, enfleshing the Latin rite's theological, spiritual, and disciplinary patrimony along with its liturgy in the culture and historical identity of a distinct people. At the same time, that Christian people and their way of living the faith are to be introduced into the life of the Latin church.

In this connection, *Varietates Legitimae* also recognizes that the phenomenon of different cultures coexisting within a given population may require different versions of liturgical books expressing the distinct cultural geniuses of the peoples. The degree of inculturation required depends on the situations of the peoples, so that each coexisting cultural community may worship God in the Church according to its own spiritual qualities. Episcopal conferences must respect the riches of *each* culture, and are not permitted to disregard or slight less familiar ones. Rather, they are required to engage in precise evaluations to reach pastorally satisfactory solutions. Hence, to engage in fruitful worship, one community may need liturgical books either differently or more profoundly adapted than those used by another cultural group in the same country. Article 64 of *Varietates Legitimae* even authorizes individual diocesan bishops to bring the liturgical concerns of minority communities to the attention of the episcopal conference and initiate the conference's study of such matters.

There is one pertinent pastoral situation that the instruction fails to address: communities of the faithful whose religious culture is Christian but has not customarily been expressed within the Roman liturgy, for example, that of African-Americans. However, the above mentioned principles and norms indicate that such situations are not to be ignored. It is appropriate at this point to assess *Varietates Legitimae* in light of the phenomenon of African-American Christianity, which is an autonomous non-Catholic Western faith. For example, the initial question asked about developing the Zairois order of Mass focused on the role of the priest celebrant: "How does a Chief act or what does he do when he presides at the town meeting?"[64] When addressed to African-Americans such a question would involve something far less exotic or secular, e.g.: "What is the role of the preacher in a Black Church service or what does he do when he prays or sings?"[65] A different sort of inculturation seems necessary when a people has developed and continues to celebrate Christian faith on a different Western cultural and historical axis. If one assumes that black Catholics share in this ethno-religious patrimony, the inculturation process may be less one of enfleshing the Gospel (which has already occurred) by introducing the tradition of the Roman patriarchate (which, in fact, has also been accomplished) than of admitting the orthodox elements of that different Christian patrimony to enliven the community's expression of Catholic faith within that patriarchate's tradition.

Preliminary cultural, exegetical and theological studies would be required, as well as consultation with black Catholic clergy and others with pertinent pastoral experience. Advice might be sought from "wise people" in non-Catholic African-American communities. The NCCD might conclude that specially adapted liturgical books are necessary to promote fuller participation in the liturgy. The conference might even determine that profound innovations are needed, such as the introduction of elements from other approved texts,[66] or even practices or ritual language from non-Catholic African-American Christian services. Moreover, since *Varietates Legitimae* declares the Church's interest in appealing to persons disinterested in religion, the NCCB might determine that a liturgy reflecting the Black Church tradition would provide the most fitting means of conducting a "new evangelization" among unchurched African-Americans.

The question in this and other instances of inculturating orthodox religious values from non-Catholic Christian traditions is to what extent such a Latin Catholic liturgy would have a place within the "Roman rite." Although *Varietates Legitimae* states that the inculturation process is not geared toward the creation of new ritual families, the instruction neither denies nor precludes that possibility. The clear intention of the document is to preserve the substantial unity of the Roman liturgical tradition, but it equally intends to provide for cultural diversity in Catholic worship.[67] The Holy See has expressed its willingness to adapt the structure of the Roman liturgy to different cultures, and even to enlarge the context of the Roman ritual family to enrich the Latin church with the gifts of her newer faithful when cases so require. It explicitly resists the notion that liturgical inculturation may generate new Latin ritual families.

But the flexible limits of the Roman liturgy expressed in the instruction may not always be sufficiently pliable. CDW has previously noted that the universality of orthodox liturgical faith is enmeshed in the particularity of different liturgical traditions, formulated through successive inculturation in the past.[68] *Sacrosanctum*

Concilium, article 4 and the provisions of *Varietates Legitimae* indicate that the demands of evangelization continue to expose the currently formulated Roman liturgical books to new cultural contexts which legitimately require adaptations that may sometimes be substantial. Like the ancient metropolises from which the current diverse liturgical families developed, new Latin Christian cultural matrices may begin to express themselves "in the best of ways according to the law of the progressive and organic formulation of the deposit of faith."[69] *Varietates Legitimae* raises the question to what extent the liturgy of the Roman ritual family will be able to contain them all. In other words, despite the cautious declarations of *Varietates Legitimae*, liturgical inculturation may inexorably involve the development of new Latin ritual families, or even new Western canonical rites.

3. Inculturation Also Raises Questions about New Western Rites

Varietates Legitimae does not refer to "rite" in the full canonical sense, but only to its liturgical component. And even though the instruction does not favor the creation of new ritual families, the faithful worshipping according to new traditions that have their own place within the Roman ritual family, or even to those in substantial unity with the "Roman rite," may nonetheless develop a distinct canonical rite, distinguished by their inculturated theological and spiritual heritage. An inculturated Roman liturgical tradition is only one element of the ethno-religious heritage that may differentiate another Western Catholic rite. Such is the case among Eastern Catholics, most of whose different canonical rites share common liturgical traditions arising from four of the five Eastern patriarchal sources. For example, all of the rites arising from the Constantinopolitan tradition celebrate the so-called Byzantine liturgy. Only the Armenian and Latin churches *sui iuris* celebrate liturgies following traditions uniquely their own.

In treating different levels of liturgical inculturation, however, *Varietates Legitimae* suggests a process according to which a full canonical rite might gain recognition. As previously noted, any amount of liturgical adaptation reflects not only the cultic genius of a community but also its corresponding ethno-religious heritage. More extensive adaptations of the Roman liturgical books should indicate the more noteworthy ethno-religious distinctiveness of the faithful for whom the books are provided. Therefore, liturgical inculturation is not only part of the development of a new ritual family in the

West, but is the most evident and significant indicator of the history, culture, theology and spirituality of a Catholic community which constitutes a rite.[70]

Hence, the development of inculturated liturgical books may indicate the first stage in the recognition not only of a new Latin ritual family, but of another Western rite. This would be less the case when the liturgical books are adapted within the framework of the general instructions and *praenotanda* as provided in *Varietates Legitimae,* articles 53-62. It would be more evident where profound adaptations are made in accordance with articles 63-70 of the instruction.[71] If thoroughly conducted, the preliminary studies required for such liturgical changes should simultaneously indicate the theological, spiritual, historical and cultural values and characteristics that distinguish the particular community. In proposing adaptations, the concerned episcopal conference might also recommend that the Holy See consider recognizing a distinct rite for that community.[72]

This might not, however, always be the case. There may be communities of the faithful with distinct ethno-religious heritages that nonetheless do not require major innovations in the Roman liturgical books, but whose Catholic theological and spiritual patrimony remains sufficiently distinct to justify recognition as a distinct rite in the Latin church. In such instances, *Varietates Legitimae* has little to contribute directly. However, on the basis of any studies the episcopal conference may have made pursuant to that instruction, or even in their absence, the faithful themselves can petition the Holy See to investigate the possibility of recognizing their rite.[73] In such a case, the concerned episcopal conference would likely be asked to make the initial analysis and propose appropriate action.[74]

AFRICAN-AMERICAN CATHOLIC LITURGY

In light of this review of *Varietates Legitimae,* my friend's enthusiastic declaration was both inaccurate and hasty. The instruction does not preclude the emergence of new rites in the Church, but is only concerned with the process of inculturating the Roman liturgy of the Latin rite. *Varietates Legitimae* seeks to discourage the use of such liturgical inculturation to promote the emergence of new, non-Roman, ritual families in the Latin rite, but it does not contradict the recognition that such phenomena may nonetheless result, as taught by *Sacrosanctum Concilium,* article 4.

Hence, *Varietates Legitimae* does not put an end to study and discussion of an African-American Catholic "rite"—nor to any of the options which that customarily multivalent term might entail: Roman liturgical books adapted, whether minimally or profoundly, to incorporate the permanent and praiseworthy values of African-American Christianity into the worship of black Latin Catholics; or a particular Latin church jurisdiction specifically addressed to the pastoral care of African-Americans; or even a distinct African-American canonical rite that would find expression in a new Western church *sui iuris*.

It is noteworthy that, in January 1995, the National Black Catholic Congress staff published the results of an opinion survey it conducted as the first step in its study of an "African-American rite."[75] Nearly three-fourths of the survey's respondents opposed creation of a separate and distinct African-American "branch of the Church," i.e., a black Catholic church *sui iuris*. However, nearly two-thirds strongly supported an increased African-American cultural emphasis in the liturgy.[76] Such affirmative support for liturgical inculturation among African-American Catholics increases the value of *Varietates Legitimae* to the pursuit of an authentic African-American Catholic Roman liturgy. At the least, it implies the continuing need to develop adaptations in the Roman liturgical books that are attuned to the culture and religious traditions—the ethno-religious heritage—of African-Americans.[77]

Depending on the degree of variance between that African-American ethno-religious heritage and the religious ethos of the non-black Latin Catholic majority displayed in the liturgical books currently approved for use in the United States, the manifest need for liturgical services specifically attuned to a unique African-American Christian vision might even entail profound adaptation of the *editiones typicae*. According to *Varietates Legitimae*, these books would enhance the breadth of the Roman ritual family's varied multicultural scope. Like the Zairois missal, such books and services would be in substantial unity with the "Roman rite." Indeed, despite the survey respondents' apparent distaste for the notion of an African-American Catholic church *sui iuris*, a distinct African-American ethno-religious patrimony derived from the tradition of the Roman patriarchate might be intrinsically connected to the emergence of a canonical rite, or to something similar to one.

All of these matters, of course, require preliminary expert studies on the historical, anthropological, exegetical and theological significance of African-American culture and religion in light of pastoral experience. Fortunately, the episcopal conference of the United States, the NCCB, has conducted such studies and produced two statements in their wake: *In Spirit and Truth: Black Catholic Reflections on the Order of Mass* (1988), and *Plenty Good Room: The Spirit and Truth of African American Catholic Worship* (1991). These findings should now be precisely assessed in the light of *Varietates Legitimae*, other pertinent legislation and magisterial documents, and current circumstances, including the results of the Congress's opinion survey. Rather than cast doubt on its salience, *Varietates Legitimae* has breathed additional vigor into the issue of an "African-American Catholic rite."

NOTES

[1] See D. R. Whitt, "Not Rite Now: An African-American Church?," *Church* 6 (Spring 1990) 5-10, 34.

[2] See Cong. for Divine Worship and the Discipline of the Sacraments, instr. on the Roman liturgy and inculturation, *Varietates Legitimae*, 25 January 1994, *Acta Apostolicae Sedis* [AAS] 87 (1995) 288-314; *Notitiae* 30 (1994) 80-115; trans. and reprinted *Origins* 23 (1994) 745-56. Concerning "inculturation," see the discussion accompanying notes 30-39, *infra*.

[3] See the discussion of *Sacrosanctum Concilium*, art. 4, accompanying notes 6-11, *infra*.

[4] *Codex Canonum Ecclesiarum Orientalium, Fontium annotatione auctus* [hereafter, CCEO], auctoritate Ioannis Pauli PP. II promulgatus (Roma: Libreria Editrice Vaticana 1995) c. 28, section 1. This text is based on *Lumen gentium*, art. 23, *AAS* 57 (1965) 27, *Orientalium Ecclesiarum*, arts. 1-5, ibid., 76-78, and on Pope Paul VI's inaugural discourse on the work of the Eastern code commission, which had accented the patrimony inherited from the ancient traditions and its evolution in each one of the Eastern churches. See Paul VI, alloc. *Dum hic praesentes*, 18 March 1974, *AAS* 66 (1974) 243-49.

[5] See CCEO c. 27: "Coetus fidelium hierarchia ad normam iuris iunctus, quem uti sui iuris expresse vel tacite agnoscit suprema Ecclesiae Auctoritas, vocatur in hoc Codice Ecclesia sui iuris."

[6] *Sacrosanctum Concilium*, art. 3, *AAS* 56 (1964) 98.

[7] "[A]d alios ritus, orientales et occidentales." *Modi a Patribus Conciliaribus proposit a Commissione Conciliari de Sacra Liturgia examinati*: I Prooemium, cap. I, *De principis generalibus ad Sacram Liturgiam instaurandum atque fovendam* (Urbs Vaticana: Typis Polyglottis Vaticanis 1963) 11. The change was made in response to the objection that the original phrase was confusing and would lead to doubts about

what liturgical principles would apply to Eastern Catholics. See ibid., 10; Anthony Gregory Vuccino, titular archbishop of Apro, *Animadversiones*, n.d., in *Acta Synodalia Sacrosancti, Oecumenici Concilii Vaticani II*, Appendix, 366; *Textus in Schematum propositus*, 1-Schema Constitutionis de Sacra Liturgia, line 16 (Cong. Gen. 21, 17 November 1962), in *Acta Synodalia* I, pars 3, 115.

[8] *Modi*, 11, quoting I-Schema Constitutionis de sacra Liturgia, art. 3, in *Acta Synodalia* I, pars 3, 115 (emphasis added). See, e. g., S.C. Rites (Consilium), instr. *Inter Oecumenici*, art. 9, 26 September 1964, *AAS* 56 (1964) 879; trans. *Documents on the Liturgy, 1963-1979, Conciliar, Papal, and Curial Texts* [hereafter cited DOL, with document and paragraph numbers] (Collegeville: The Liturgical Press 1982) no. 23 para. 301.

[9] See *Sacrosanctum Concilium*, art. 4, *AAS* 56 (1964) 98.

[10] See 3-*Relatio*, in *Acta Synodalia* I, pars 3, 121. See also Annibale Bugnini, C.M., *La riforma liturgica, 1948-1975* (Roma: Centro Liturgico Vincenziano-Edizioni Liturgiche 1983) 44, trans. Matthew J. O'Connell, *The Reform of the Liturgy, 1948-1975* (Collegeville: The Liturgical Press 1990) 33; Frederick R. McManus, "The Possibility of New Rites in the Church," *Jurist* 50 (1990) 456; Cipriano Vagaggini, "General Norms for the Reform and Fostering of the Liturgy," in *The Commentary on the Constitution and Instruction on the Sacred Liturgy*, ed. Annibale Bugnini, C.M., and Charles Braga, C.M., trans. Vincent P. Mallon (New York: Benziger Bros. 1965) 58. The council approved the amendment by 2,191 votes to 10. See *Acta Synodalia* I, pars 3, 158.

[11] *Textus in Schemate propositus* and *Textus a Commissione emendatus*, I-Schema Constitutionis de Sacra Liturgia, line 24, in *Acta Synodalia* I, pars 3, 115 (emphasis in original).

[12] See John Paul II, ap. const. *Pastor Bonus*, arts. 48-49, 58, 28 June 1988, *AAS* 80 (1988) 873, 875. See, e.g., Cong. for the Oriental Churches, *Istruzione per l'applicazione delle prescrizioni liturgiche del Codice dei Canoni delle Chiese Orientali* (Roma: Libreria Editrice Vaticana 1996).

[13] See Cong. for Divine Worship and the Discipline of the Sacraments, "Riti nella Chiesa," *Notitiae* 28 (1992) 367-68.

[14] Both decrees of confirmation recognize the reformed *Missale Hispano-Mozarabicum* and *Missale Ambrosianum* as complying with *Sacrosanctum Concilium*, art. 50, that particular liturgical rites be restored to their patrimonial patterns. See Cong. for Divine Worship, decr. *Hispaniae Dioecesium*, 17 July 1988, reprinted in *Notitiae* 24 (1988) 672; idem, decr. *Mediolanensis*, 30 November 1974, reprinted in *Notitiae* 11 (1975) 45.

[15] "Riti nella Chiesa," 365, citing *Sacrosanctum Concilium*, art. 4.

[16] "Riti nella Chiesa," 368 (emphasis in original).

[17] See, e.g., Aidan Nichols, *The Panther and the Hind: A Theological History of Anglicanism* (Edinburgh: T &T Clark 1993) 178-80; idem, "The

'Bridge' Church," *Catholic World Report* 3 (January 1993) 25-27; William Oddie, "Only Rome," ibid., 28-29. Cf. McManus, 440.

[18] "Vatican approves Anglican liturgy," *The Tablet* (London) 239 (23 February 1985) 198.

[19] See *Sacrosanctum Concilium*, art. 22 , sections 1-2, *AAS* 56 (1964) 106.

[20] See ibid., art. 44, *AAS* 56 (1964) 112. For the same reasons, every diocese was also to have a liturgical commission. See ibid., art. 45, *AAS* 56 (1964) 112-13.

[21] See McManus, 452; Boniface Luykx, "Norms for Adapting the Liturgy to the Genius and Traditions of Various Peoples," in Bugnini and Braga, 105.

[22] See *Sacrosanctum Concilium*, art. 40, *AAS* 56 (1964) 111.

[23] S.C. Rites (Consilium), instr. *Inter Oecumenici*, 26 September 1964, *AAS* 56 (1964) 877-900; trans. DOL no. 23.

[24] See *Inter Oecumenici*, art. 23, *AAS* 56 (1964) 882; DOL no. 23 para. 315. Three varieties of assembly were identified: national conferences of bishops (see Paul VI, m.p. *Sacram liturgiam*, art. X, 25 January 1964, *AAS* 56 (1964) 143; DOL no. 20, para. 288); an international assembly of bishops and other local ordinaries which had already been lawfully constituted; and an assembly yet to be constituted with the permission of the Holy See, consisting of bishops, and perhaps other local ordinaries, from several nations sharing the same language and culture. The instruction also provided for the expeditious establishment of territorial liturgical commissions, and declared that a bishops' assembly might assign the implementation of studies and liturgical experiments pursuant to *Sacrosanctum Concilium*, art. 40, to its liturgical commission. See *Inter Oecumenici*, arts. 44-45 (a), *AAS* 56 (1964) 886-87; DOL no. 23, para. 337. Article 47 of *Inter Oecumenici* provided for diocesan liturgical commissions, but did not suggest that these had any competence to study or experiment with major cultural adaptations of the liturgy.

[25] See Consilium, letter *Dans sa récente*, 21 June 1967; trans. DOL no. 41 para. 482, citing *Sacrosanctum Concilium* 40 section 2.

[26] See S.C. Rites (Consilium), instr. *Tres abhinc annos*, 4 May 1967, *AAS* 59 (1967) 442-48; trans. DOL no. 38. The instruction's title referred to the three years since *Inter Oecumenici* had been issued.

[27] S.C. Divine Worship, instr. *Liturgicae instaurationes*, 5 September 1970 *AAS* 62 (1970) 692-704; trans. DOL no. 52.

[28] The Holy See was aware of two improvisational trends in this regard. On the one hand, there were those (in particular it would seem priests) who, trying to hold onto old liturgical practices, resisted making the changes mandated by the new books. On the other hand, there were others (also for the most part priests) who, alleging pastoral needs, were resorting to personal innovations, hasty and ill-advised measures, and to

"new creations and additions or to simplification of rites." And frequently these practices conflicted with the most basic liturgical norms and upset the consciences of the faithful and, therefore, obstructed the cause of genuine liturgical renewal.

²⁹ *Liturgicae instaurationes*, art. 1, *AAS* 62 (1970) 695; DOL no. 52 para. 512. This caution was directed not only to how services were conducted, but also to the texts that were read to the people. The books of the Bible have a primacy due to their unique dignity: in those books God speaks to his people; in his own Word, Christ continues to proclaim his Gospel. Hence, it was never allowed to substitute Bible texts with readings from other sacred or profane authors, ancient or modern; nor should anyone *sua sponte* undertake to make changes, substitutions, deletions or additions to the biblical text. Further, the purpose of the homily was to explain the Word of God to the faithful, and it was the priest's job to apply that Word to the mentality of the times, not to engage in dialogues with the congregation; and the liturgies of Word and Eucharist were to be celebrated in the same place, in a single act of worship.

Concerning liturgical music, the third instruction said that the Church barred no style of sacred music from her worship, but emphasized the point that the music must possess sacredness, fit the spirit of the service and not obstruct the congregation's ability to worship. In other words, choirs or cantors were not to give performances, and the music was not to overpower everything else going on.

³⁰ See *Varietates Legitimae*, art. 4, *AAS* 87 (1995) 289-90; *Notitiae* 30 (1994) 82-83; *Origins* 23 (1994) 747. The instruction explains the change in terminology from "cultural adaptation" to "inculturation" as follows: the missionary expression "adaptation" (*aptatio*) might imply transitory and merely external modifications of the liturgy; "inculturation" (*inculturatio*) better expresses a double movement: the penetration of the Gospel into a given sociocultural milieu, which gives inner fruitfulness to the spiritual qualities and gifts proper to each people, strengthens those qualities, perfects them and restores them in Christ; and the Church's assimilation of such values when they are compatible with the Gospel, which deepens understanding of Christ's message and gives it more effective expression in the liturgy and other aspects of the life of the community of believers. "By inculturation, the church makes the Gospel incarnate in different cultures and at the same time introduces peoples, together with their cultures, into her own community." Ibid., quoting John Paul II, enc. letter *Redemptoris missio*, 7 December 1990, art. 52, *AAS* 83 (1991) 300.

³¹ See *Varietates Legitimae*, art. 3, *AAS* 87 (1995) 289; *Notitiae* 30 (1994) 81; *Origins* 23 (1994) 747.

³² See ibid., art. 5, *AAS* 87 (1995) 290-91; *Notitiae* 30 (1994) 83-84; *Origins* 23 (1994) 747.

³³ See ibid., arts. 6-8. *AAS* 87 (1995) 291-92; *Notitiae* 30 (1994) 84-85; *Origins* 23 (1994) 747-48.

³⁴ See ibid., art. 29, *AAS* 87 (1995) 307; *Notitiae* 30 (1994) 96; *Origins* 23 (1994), 750-51.

³⁵ The conferences are also to weigh the risks of a Christian community becoming inward looking, as well as the use of inculturation for political ends. See ibid., art. 49, *AAS* 87 (1995) 307; *Notitiae* 30 (1994) 104; *Origins* 23 (1994) 753.

³⁶ See, e.g., ibid., arts. 27, 30, *AAS* 87 (1995) 299, 300; *Notitiae* 30 (1994) 94, 96.

³⁷ See ibid., arts. 27, 37, *AAS* 87 (1995) 299, 302-3; *Notitiae* 30 (1994) 94-95, 99-100; *Origins* 23 (1994) 750, 751-52. Wherefore, the instruction cites the rule of *Sacrosanctum Concilium*, art. 22 section 3: except for occasions when the liturgical books published after the constitution leave a choice to the pastoral sensitivity of the celebrant or the one presiding, no one, not even a priest, is allowed *sua sponte* to add, remove or change anything in the liturgy. See c. 846 section 1. Inculturation is not to be left to the personal initiative of celebrants or the collective initiative of an assembly, "to avoid breaking up of the local church into little 'churches' or 'chapels' closed in upon themselves" (ad vitandam frequentem divisionem Ecclesiae localis in sic dictis "ecclesiolis," quae quodammodo in seipsis clausae manent). *Origins* 23 (1994) 752, translating *Varietates Legitimae*, art. 37 n. 82, *AAS* 87 (1995) 302-3; *Notitiae* 30 (1994) 100.

³⁸ See *Varietates Legitimae*, art. 30, *AAS* 87 (1995) 300; *Notitiae* 30 (1994) 96.

³⁹ See ibid.; *Origins* 23 (1994) 751.

⁴⁰ See ibid., art. 36, *AAS* 87 (1995) 302; *Notitiae* 30 (1994) 99 (emphasis in original): "Inculturationis processus perficiendus est Ritus romani *unitate substantiali* servata," citing *Sacrosanctum Concilium*, arts. 37-40.

⁴¹ *Origins* 23 (1994) 751 (emphasis added), translating *Varietates Legitimae*, art. 36, *AAS* 87 (1995) 302; *Notitiae* 30 (1994) 99. A more direct translation of the Latin words "novas familias rituales," of course, is "new ritual families"—a significant term for CDW—rather than "new families of rites." The second rendition at the least creates a novel term and, consequently, makes a rather important statement misleadingly ambiguous.

The quoted text cites the 26 January 1991 allocution given by Pope John Paul II to those participating in CDW's plenary session: "This is not to suggest to the particular churches that they have a new task to undertake following the application of liturgical reform, that is to say, adaptation or inculturation. Nor is it intended to mean inculturation as the creation of alternative rites. . . . It is a question of collaborating so that the Roman rite, maintaining its own identity, may incorporate suitable adaptations." Ibid., n. 77, quoting *AAS* 83 (1991) 940.

[42] See also *Varietates Legitimae*, art. 52, *AAS* 87 (1995) 307; *Notitiae* 30 (1994) 106. Arts. 53-61 of the instruction concern adaptations provided by the liturgical books pursuant to *Sacrosanctum Concilium*, arts. 37-39; arts. 63-64 deal with those envisioned by art. 40 of the constitution.

[43] See *Varietates Legitimae*, art. 53, *AAS* 87 (1995) 308; *Notitiae* 30 (1994) 106-7; *Origins* 23 (1994) 753.

[44] See ibid., art. 54, *AAS* 87 (1995) 308-9; *Notitiae* 30 (1994) 107; *Origins* 23 (1994) 753. The instruction mentions the gestures and postures of the faithful, the ways in which the altar and the book of the Gospels are venerated, the texts of the opening chants, the song at the preparation of the gifts and the communion song, the rite of peace . . . the material and form of sacred vessels, liturgical vestments. See ibid. In addition, episcopal conferences, and in some instances diocesan bishops, may introduce adaptations according to the *editiones typicae* of each book concerning the other sacraments and sacramentals. See ibid., arts. 55-59, *AAS* 87 (1995) 309-10; *Notitiae* 30 (1994) 108-10; *Origins* 23 (1994) 753-54. Moreover, each particular church and religious family may add its own proper celebrations to the calendar of the universal Church, after approval by the Holy See. See ibid., art. 60, *AAS* 87 (1995) 311; *Notitiae* 30 (1994) 111; *Origins* 23 (1994) 754.

[45] Cong. for Divine Worship and the Discipline of the Sacraments, "Il Messale Romano nella tradizione liturgica del Rito Romano," *Notitiae* 26 (1990) 519-20.

[46] See *Varietates Legitimae*, art. 62, *AAS* 87 (1995) 311; *Notitiae* 30 (1994)111; *Origins* 23 (1994) 754; See also cc. 455 section 2, 838 section 3.

[47] See ibid., art. 63, *AAS* 87 (1995) 311-12; *Notitiae* 30 (1994) 112: "Huiusmodi quoque aptationes minime tendunt ad Ritum romanum transformandum, sed potius intra ipsum suum obtinent locum."

[48] See ibid., art. 64, *AAS* 87 (1995) 312; *Notitiae* 30 (1994) 112; *Origins* 23 (1994) 754.

[49] Should the case warrant it, this preliminary investigation also may be conducted in collaboration with the episcopal conferences of neighboring countries or those with the same culture as the faithful concerned. See ibid., art. 65, *AAS* 87 (1995) 312; *Notitiae* 30 (1994) 113; *Origins* 23 (1994) 754.

[50] See ibid., art. 66, *AAS* 87 (1995) 313; *Notitiae* 30 (1994) 113; *Origins* 23 (1994) 754. The plan for preliminary experimentation must include the times and places for trial liturgical celebrations, and an indication of which groups will take part.

[51] See ibid., arts. 66-67, *AAS* 87 (1995) 313; *Notitiae* 30 (1994) 113-14; *Origins* 23 (1994) 754. The instruction admonishes the conferences

not to permit experimentation to exceed the fixed limitations of time and place. Moreover, the conference must ensure that pastors and faithful be informed of the limited and provisional nature of the trials, and not give them the kind of publicity that would affect liturgical practice elsewhere in the country. See ibid., art. 67, *AAS* 87 (1995) 313; *Notitiae* 30 (1994) 114; *Origins* 23 (14 April 1994) 754-55.

[52] See ibid., arts. 67-68, *AAS* 87 (1995) 313-14; *Notitiae* 30 (1994) 113-14; *Origins* 23 (1994) 755.

[53] See ibid., art. 64, *AAS* (1995) 312; *Notitiae* 30 (1994) 112; *Origins* 23 (1994) 754.

[54] This might be an alternative solution for introducing elements of the *Book of Common Prayer* into the worship of the Latin church. McManus points out that "the churches of the Anglican communion . . . have already created their own revised and reformed liturgies that are in close harmony with the fundamental principles of the constitution on the liturgy." McManus, 457. A profoundly adapted Roman Missal incorporating the elements of Anglican liturgies might reflect that heritage within the context of the Roman liturgical tradition.

[55] See the discussion, *supra*, concerning the "rites" of Western religious orders deemed to exist within the embrace of the "Roman rite," yet so distinguished from it as not to be directly subject to the provisions of *Sacrosanctum Concilium*, art. 3. For example, the *Missel Romain pour les Diocèses du Zaïre* presents a Mass distinguished markedly from that of the *editio typica* of the Roman Missal in several ways: "an invocation of ancestors, both by way of veneration and by way of calling righteous persons of the past to be present at the celebration; the role of announcer or herald, only in part like that of deacon; a communal washing of hands as a sign of peace; rhythmic movement and recessional dance; use of language, imagery, and allusions in a distinctive anaphora. . . . All this is described summarily and most inadequately in order to suggest, first, that within the tenor of *Sacrosanctum Concilium* 40 and with considerable dependence upon the Roman *Ordo Missae*, a new eucharistic rite can be developed; second, that this demands both immense study and, on the part of the bishops especially, persistence in dealing with the Roman curial office." McManus, 455.

[56] See McManus, 452: "Here the conciliar text . . . makes no mention of maintaining intact the elusive 'substantial unity of the Roman rite.'" See also Luykx, 105.

[57] CDW's interpretation of *Sacrosanctum Concilium*, art. 40, is not, however, without theoretical and pragmatic foundation. There seems to be no bright line to distinguish a major inculturation from a minor one, except perhaps the depth of variation, departure and replacement of substantive components at the Roman liturgy. McManus himself concedes that "there is no easy way to distinguish objectively the difference between the lesser adaptations . . . and those judged to be more profound.

... Concretely and canonically, at the present moment and *in full conformity with the letter of Sacrosanctum Concilium* 38-40, the difference between minor and major adaptations is between what the Roman See enumerates as minor in the official service books and everything else." McManus, 452 (emphasis added). According to *Varietates Legitimae* a major variation will not leave the limits of the Roman ritual family, no matter its severity.

[58] See generally Praenotanda *Missale Hispano-Mozarabicum*, reprinted in *Notitiae* 24 (1988) 673-727; *Missale Ambrosianum*, 472-558. Cf. "*Le Missel Romain pour les Diocèses du Zaïre*," *Notitiae* 24 (1998) 454-72, described *supra* note 55 and *infra*.

[59] *Le Missel Romain pour les Diocèses du Zaïre*." See *Notitiae* 24 (1988) 454-72.

[60] See generally Chris Nwaka Egbulem, *The "Rite Zaïrois" in the Context of Liturgical Inculturation in Middle-Belt Africa since the Second Vatican Council* (Washington, D.C.: The Catholic University of America 1990). See also idem, *The Power of Africentric Celebrations: Inspirations from the Zairean Liturgy* (New York: Crossroad Pub. Co. 1996).

[61] It is also worth noting the anecdotal evidence that, while one can participate in the Mass according to this missal in Kinshasa, folks in other parts of Zaire have supplied *their* own cultural adaptations even to that missal!

[62] " ... novam rituum structuram ... introducendam, servata tamen substantiali ritus Romani unitate." *Zairensium Dioecesium*, in *Notitiae* 24 (1988) 457 (emphasis added). Concerning the proposal, experimentation, development and approval of the Zairois missal, see Egbulem, *The "Rite Zaïrois."* Except for the Anglican-influenced *Book of Divine Worship*, this writer is not aware of any other approved liturgical inculturation of equal significance to the Zairois. See also McManus, 454.

[63] *Varietates Legitimae*, art. 5 n.15, *Notitiae* 30 (1994) 83 (emphasis added), quoting John Paul II, ap. exhort. *Catechesi tradendae*, 16 October 1979, art. 53, *AAS* 71 (1979) 1320.

[64] Egbulem, *The "Rite Zaïrois,"* 18 (quoting Boniface Luykx, *Culte Chrétien en Afrique après Vatican II* [Immensée: Nouvelle Revue de Science Missionaire 1974] 94).

[65] See NCCB Secretariats for the Liturgy and for Black Catholics, *Plenty Good Room: The Spirit and Truth of African-American Catholic Worship*, art. 72 (Washington, D.C.: USCC Office for Publishing and Promotion Services 1991).

[66] For example, the invocation of ancestors from the Zairois missal. *Varietates Legitimae*, arts. 37 and 62 provide that, although episcopal conferences may not freely adopt adaptations conceded to one region, they may seek to add them to their own liturgical books. It is not clear whether matters introduced as part of a profound adaptation may be

adopted under the procedure for implementing *Sacrosanctum Concilium*, arts. 37-39.

[67] See Cong. for Divine Worship and the Discipline of the Sacraments, "Commentarium alla Quarta Istruzione per una corretta applicazione della Costituzione Conciliare sulla Sacra Liturgia," in *Notitiae* 30 (1994) 163: "The Roman rite is open to enrichment, not by being changed and becoming an irreconcilable melange, but by responding to cultural needs seen in pastoral before cultural terms, which require in given places and among certain peoples a transformation better to obtain the very goals sought in every rite as a manifestation of Christian liturgy."

[68] See "Riti nella Chiesa," 367.

[69] Ibid., 368.

[70] See McManus, 439.

[71] McManus has written that the policy favoring progressive liturgical inculturation "suggests that all the riches of a new liturgical rite might well be achieved through the several stages, steps and levels" provided by *Sacrosanctum Concilium*, up to and including "all manner of particular churches . . . not unlike the venerable patriarchal churches and their descendants and derivatives. To use the current terminology, this is to envision autonomous or *sui iuris* churches within what is now called the Latin Church." Ibid., 457-58.

[72] Given the complex issues involved, the recognition of a new Latin canonical rite would likely be treated by an interdicasterial commission representing the curial offices with authority in the areas concerned. See *Pastor Bonus*, art. 11, *AAS* 80 (1988) 865. For example, in cooperation with the Congregation for the Doctrine of the Faith and the Congregation for Bishops, CDW could authorize an experiment, entailing not only the use of new liturgical books, but also having a special pastoral jurisdiction in view, perhaps governed by a vicar or prefect apostolic who might supervise the experiment on behalf of the conference and the Holy See. Following a set period of successful experimentation and a favorable recommendation by the concerned dicasteries, the pope could recognize and name the new Latin *ritus*, define the faithful to whom it belongs, approve their liturgical books and erect one or more personal particular churches for them under canon 372 section 2 of the 1983 code.

Like the Eastern particular churches erected in Latin territories under canon 372 section 2, these dioceses would be territorial circumscriptions characterized by personal jurisdiction exercised only over the faithful in their territories belonging to the distinctive ethno-religious community. As particular churches of a different rite within the Latin church *sui iuris*, these Latin particular churches would remain affiliated to the Roman patriarch and subject to the common law of the 1983 code, unless the acts recognizing the rite or erecting the particular churches stated otherwise. Even if a church *sui iuris* subject to the Latin patriarch were erected for the new Western rite, the Roman Pontiff would continue to exercise patriarchal authority over it. See John D. Faris, *Eastern Catholic Churches: Constitution and Governance according to the Code of Canons of the Eastern Churches* (New York: Saint Maron Publications, 1992), 144-45.

[73] See *Pastor Bonus*, art. 13, *AAS* 80 (1988) 863. Of course, the faithful for whom special liturgical books are approved could also submit such a petition.

[74] See *Poster Bonus*, art. 26, section 1, *AAS* 80 (1988) 866. Upon a favorable finding by the conference, a period of experimentation like that described above might follow, along with the eventual recognition of the rite and erection of particular churches for its faithful, should their number and pastoral circumstances recommend it. Moreover, even if the ethno-religious patrimony of a distinct community of Latin Catholics were incapable of recognition as a rite other than the Latin rite, such a determination would not preclude the erection of a personal particular church for them. Bound together like the members of ethnic parishes on the basis of a distinct ethno-religious culture and identity, a community of the faithful for which the *editiones typicae* are specifically adapted or for which profoundly adapted Roman liturgical books are devised could be entrusted to the care of a proper bishop on the second basis provided by canon 372 section 2, i.e., a ground similar to rite. See canons 372 section 2 and 518.

[75] See *Report to the Board of Trustees, National Black Catholic Congress: A Study of Opinions of African American Catholics* (Baltimore: The National Black Catholic Congress 1995).

[76] The survey failed to pose any question concerning the erection of a special pastoral jurisdiction for African-Americans within the Latin church *sui iuris*. The Holy See has proposed such a pastoral provision several times, beginning with the Second Plenary Council of Baltimore, but each time the United States hierarchy has rejected it. See generally Cyprian Davis, *The History of Black Catholics in the United States* (New York: Crossroad Pub. Co. 1991) 116-237. The significance of this proposal, and of its omission from the survey, deserves further study.

[77] That such inculturation is necessary is not a novel proposition. See, e.g., the results of an informal survey taken by the late Archbishop of Atlanta, James P. Lyke, "Liturgical Expression in the Black Community," *Worship* 57 (1983) 14-26.

Conclusion

Speaking the Truth

Black Catholics in the United States

<u>CYPRIAN DAVIS, O.S.B.</u>

Over a dozen years ago James Cone published an essay on the Roman Catholic Church in the United States.[1] Originally a talk given at the College of the Notre Dame in Baltimore in 1988, it was a critique of the Catholic church in the United States from the viewpoint of an African American Protestant theologian and one of the foremost proponents of Black theology. Doctor Cone did not mince words. He remarked the willingness of Catholic liberals to espouse the cause of the poor in Latin America but to ignore totally the situation of American Blacks. As students of liberation theology and its theologians, they knew almost nothing about Black theologians and were unaware of African American history and culture.

As he pointed out, "There is one thing that most whites have in common; they act as if whites know everything, and they are therefore seldom open to learning anything from Black history and culture."[2] For Cone, "The Catholic Church is not what it claims to be: it is not a truly *universal* church, seeking to be accountable to the whole of humanity. It is a white *European* church, almost exclusively defined by issues and problems arising from that history and culture."[3]

Convinced that Catholicism was monolithic in theology, in culture, and in thought, Cone believed that it was almost impossible for a non-European, much less a Black, to do any creative theology. In his opinion any Blacks who were serious about their Catholic faith had to cut off all connection with their cultural roots. Somewhat

281

condescendingly he noted that Black Catholics were tolerated by the Catholic church, which "sometimes encourages their liturgical participation. . . . Blacks are especially useful as singers, dancers, and preachers at the Mass and in other liturgical settings."[4]

Another important Black theologian, J. Deotis Roberts, wrote in the same vein some five years after Cone's essay.[5] Roberts's article was written at the time when George Stallings, a Black priest of the Washington archdiocese, had demanded that his archbishop, Cardinal James Hickey, recognize a semi-autonomous parish known as the Imani Temple. Stallings wanted to establish an Afro-American rite that would be autonomous in liturgical practice and quasi-independent like Eastern Rite Catholics. Failing to get Hickey's permission, George Stallings would sever all ties with the Holy See in 1990.

Writing on the eve of Stallings's defection, Roberts was very much impressed by the stand that Stallings had taken. Roberts noted that "black Catholics have long sensed a powerlessness in a powerful church" and wanted a Black rite to express their "spirituality and culture in worship."[6] Roberts reiterated Cone when he wrote that "many devout black Catholics have decided that they cannot be black and Catholic, and . . . are returning to their roots."[7] Roberts too criticized the lack of Black Catholic theologians and what he considered to be the lack of leadership on the part of the Black Catholic bishops in the country.[8]

The judgments of both James Cone and J. Deotis Roberts, though harsh, contained much with which many Roman Catholics, white and Black, would agree. Most Black Catholics would also agree that neither Cone nor Roberts seems to understand the deep commitment in faith that has made Black Catholics remain rooted in the Catholic church. The writings of the African American Catholic scholars gathered in this volume in one way or another answer many of the objections of Cone and Roberts.

Within the last two decades Black Catholics have brought to American Catholicism a new complexion and a new insight. Their contribution has been in three major areas: Catholic theology, Catholic spirituality, and Catholic culture. These areas are not discrete elements but rather major components in any historical study of Catholicism. Beginning with the Sixth Black Catholic Congress in Washington, D.C., in 1987, the African American Catholic community renewed its links with the congress movement initiated by Daniel Rudd at the end of the last century. With more than fifteen hundred delegates from one hundred ten dioceses, the congress was both a celebration and a renewal. The congress displayed the strength of Black Catholicism and its contribution to Catholic life and culture and Catholic spirituality. The two subsequent congresses, the Seventh Black Catholic Congress held in New Orleans in 1987 with some twenty-seven hundred participants and the Eighth Black Catholic Congress in Baltimore in 1997 with over three thousand participants, dealt with Black Catholic identity, culture, and evangelization. The American bishops, white and Black, were part of these sessions. At these congresses the bishops and the clergy experienced a type of interaction and communication with the African American laity that would not have existed some thirty or forty years before.

The climax of the Eighth Black Catholic Congress in 1997 was the dedication of the Mother of Africa Chapel in the National Shrine of the Immaculate Conception in Washington, D.C. Many of the Catholic national and ethnic groups of the United States are represented by a chapel celebrating their culture and history in the national shrine. Black Catholics now have a chapel that honors their African heritage with the statue of Mary and Christ on the cross and a bas-relief on the walls that narrates the Middle Passage and the movement of the African American community from slavery to freedom in the United States. (The bas-relief appears on the cover of this book.)

The intellectual and cultural directions of the national Black Catholic congresses were the result of listening sessions with the laity and of meetings with Black Catholic scholars. As Shawn Copeland pointed out in her article, in 1978 some thirty or more Black Catholic scholars and thinkers addressed the issues of Black Catholic theology and Black Catholic spirituality at the Motherhouse of the Oblate Sisters of Providence just outside of Baltimore.[9] Two years later some of the same participants began a summer institute, the Institute of Black Catholic Studies, at Xavier University in New Orleans. Both the symposium and the institute continue today as a seed bed for Black theology within the Catholic tradition. This is the aspect that many, like Cone and Roberts, may fail to understand. The Catholic theologian, Black or white, works within a tradition, a tradition, in fact, which has more of North Africa, Egypt, Syria, and the Mediterranean than the European model that Cone criticizes. It is within this tradition that the authors in this collection have presented their works. In fact, they have done more. They have demonstrated that Catholic theology today must include issues raised by Black theologians. The same writers have shown that American Catholicism can no longer ignore the rich field of Black Catholic history.[10]

Perhaps in the area of spirituality a new awareness of the Black contribution is evident. In December 1996 the Holy See declared former slave Pierre Toussaint (1766-1853) a venerable. Born in Haiti, he was brought to New York by his French slave-owners in 1787. Eventually freed, he became a successful hairdresser who used his money, his energy, and his humor to aid the suffering, rescue the abandoned, and give material aid to the needy. A wonderfully kind and charitable man, he was considered a saint even during his lifetime.[11]

A people's saints are an indication of their religious culture and spirituality. The saints are part of popular piety, and popular piety has played a large role in the devotional life of African American Catholics. A renewed interest in Black saints has prompted the call for the beatification of Henriette DeLille, the foundress of the Holy Family Sisters; and Elizabeth Lange, the foundress of the Oblate Sisters of Providence.[12] In more recent times there has been a call to introduce the cause of Sister Thea Bowman, F.S.P.A., who died of cancer in 1990. She was a woman of deep spirituality and many talents. She was one of the founding members of the Institute of Black Catholic Studies.[13]

The most widely known contribution of Black Catholics to the American Catholic church has been in the area of Catholic culture. The music of Clarence Rivers, Eddie Bonnemere, Grayson Brown, Mary Lou Williams, Leon Roberts, Rawn Harbor, and many others has profoundly changed liturgical music. On the other hand, African American Catholic musicians have also added to the scope and breadth of African American sacred music.

Far too often Black Catholics found themselves singing the songs of Zion in a foreign land. With hesitation and with effort did we take down our harps to sing a new song. And then we realized that it was no longer a foreign land and no longer a strange song. The former things had passed away.

> You changed my mourning into dancing;
> You took off my sackcloth and clothed me
>   with gladness,
> That my soul might sing praise to you without
>   ceasing;
> O Lord, my God, forever will I give you
>   thanks.
>
> —Psalm 30:12-13

NOTES

[1] James Cone, " A Theological Challenge to the American Catholic Church," *Speaking the Truth: Ecumenism, Liberation, and Black Theology* (Grand Rapids, Mich.: William B. Eerdmans Publishing Co., 1986), pp. 50-60.

[2] Ibid., p. 53.

[3] Ibid., p. 57.

[4] Ibid., pp. 53, 57.

[5] J. Deotis Roberts, "The Status of Black Catholics," *Journal of Religious Thought* 48 (1991): 73-78.

[6] Ibid., p. 75.

[7] Ibid., p. 78.

[8] Ibid., pp. 76-77.

[9] See Thaddeus Posey, O.F.M. Cap., ed., *Theology: A Portrait in Black. Black Catholic Theological Symposium, October 12-15, 1978* (Pittsburgh: The Capuchin Press, 1980).

[10] It is ironic that one of the best-selling studies of the Roman Catholic church in the United States is a contemporary history of the church by a journalist, Charles R. Morris, *American Catholic: The Saints and Sinners Who Built America's Most Powerful Church* (New York: Random House, 1997). In this rather lengthy anecdotal history, Black Catholics are scarcely mentioned. When they are, they are quickly dismissed. James Cone is still right.

[11] Cyprian Davis, *The History of Black Catholics in the United States* (New York: Crossroad, 1990), pp. 91-94.

[12] For more on the lives of these two women, see Audrey Marie Detiege, *Henriette DeLille, Free Woman of Color* (New Orleans: Sisters of the Holy Family, 1976); Maria Mercedes Lannon, *Response to Love, The Story of Mother Mary Elizabeth Lange* (Washington, D.C.: Josephite Pastoral Center, 1992).

[13] See "Bowman, Thea," *New Catholic Encyclopedia*, vol. 19 (Supplement 1989-95). Pope John Paul II has beatified five Africans in the last decade: Blessed Victoria Rasoamanarivo (†1854), Blessed Isidore Bakanja (†1909), Blessed Josephine Bakhita (†1947), Blessed Anwarite Nengapeta (†1964), and Blessed Cyprian Iwene Tansi (†1964). The lives of Black saints have played a large role in African American spirituality.